Defensive Security Handbook

Best Practices for Securing Infrastructure

Lee Brotherston and Amanda Berlin

Beijing · Boston · Farnham · Sebastopol · Tokyo

Defensive Security Handbook

by Lee Brotherston and Amanda Berlin

Copyright © 2017 Lee Brotherston and Amanda Berlin. All rights reserved.

Printed in the United States of America.

Published by O'Reilly Media, Inc., 1005 Gravenstein Highway North, Sebastopol, CA 95472.

O'Reilly books may be purchased for educational, business, or sales promotional use. Online editions are also available for most titles (*http://oreilly.com/safari*). For more information, contact our corporate/institutional sales department: 800-998-9938 or *corporate@oreilly.com*.

Editors: Courtney Allen and Virginia Wilson	**Indexer:** Ellen Troutman-Zaig
Production Editor: Melanie Yarbrough	**Interior Designer:** David Futato
Copyeditor: Kim Cofer	**Cover Designer:** Karen Montgomery
Proofreader: Eliahu Sussman	**Illustrator:** Rebecca Demarest

April 2017:   First Edition

Revision History for the First Edition

2017-03-31:   First Release

See *http://oreilly.com/catalog/errata.csp?isbn=9781491960387* for release details.

978-1-491-96038-7

[LSI]

Table of Contents

Foreword

Spend any time in the information security world, and it will become quickly evident that most of the press and accolades go to those folks working on the offensive side of security. From finding new vulnerabilities, creating exploits, breaking into systems, bug bounties, the occasional cable TV show, and capture the flag contests, the red teams get all the glory. But there is more—much more—to the security world than just offense.

Being on the defensive side, the blue team, can seem a lonely, unappreciated battle. But doing defense is a vital, noble, and worthwhile pursuit. We defenders matter, greatly, to the future of our organizations and the jobs and livelihoods of our coworkers. When the bad guys win, people lose their jobs, organizations are distracted from their core goals, and the bad guys are often enriched to continue their nefarious pursuits. And, like something out of a cyberpunk novel, with the trend of the Internet of Things, soon actually lives may be at threat when the bad guys are successful.

So many of us got our start in the security world as tool engineers, running perhaps a firewall or IDS platform for our employer. Though those skills are highly valued, moving beyond them to a more holistic view of defensive security can sometimes be a challenge without the right resources to bring a bigger picture view. As we continue to experience a shortage of valuable information security defensive talent, we will need more folks than ever to continue to learn and grow into the defensive security role; and to do it well, they need a holistic view of the security landscape.

Another challenge we often face is that a great deal of the narrative around defenses, technology, threats, and thought leadership in the defensive security world comes from the vendors themselves, and their snazzy demos and marketing presentations. Though a lot can be learned from vendors in the space, as they are laser focused on the problems organizations are trying to solve, they also have a sometimes narrow view of the world. IT Security Vendors will often define the problem set as the problem they can solve with their technology, not necessarily the problem an organization actually has. Countering that view with a holistic view of defensive security is vital to helping organizations become as secure as they can be.

This is why I am so honored to write the forward for the *Defensive Security Handbook*. The world of security is changing rapidly, and we need more folks on the defensive side, learning from the best practices and the hard-won lessons of those who came before. This book does a great job of laying out key principles and skills, and giving a broad overview of the complex and growing landscape of the defensive security side of the world. Amanda Berlin and Lee Brotherston have laid out an overview of the multifaceted world of defensive security. Certainly, whole books have been written on tiny segments of the topics covered, but this handbook does a marvelous job of giving a defensive security professional an overview of the myriad of skill sets necessary to be successful. This handbook is a great primer for those new to the world of information security defense, those who want to expand their skills into more areas, and even those who have many years in the industry and are looking to make sure they are covering all their bases.

I think you'll find this a valuable resource to keep nearby and reference throughout your career. Best of luck on your path, and remember to keep fighting the good fight. Even when it may seem lonely and tough, remember what you are doing matters, and there are many out there who can and will help. Amanda and Lee have done a great job sharing their experience; now it's up to us to learn from their experience.

— Andrew Kalat
Cohost of the Defensive
Security Podcast
February 2017

Introduction

Over the last decade, technology adoption has exploded worldwide and corporations have struggled to keep pace. Usability and revenue creation have been the key motivating factors, often ignoring the proactive design and security required for long-term stability. With the increase of breaking news hacks, record-breaking data leaks, and ransomware attacks, it is our job to not only scrape by with default installs but to secure our data and assets to the best of our abilities. There will always be cases where you will walk into an environment that is a metaphorical train wreck with so many fires that you don't even know where to start. This book will give you what you need to create a solid and secure design for the majority of situations that you may encounter.

Modern attacks can occur for many different motivations and are perpetrated by people ranging from organized crime groups seeking to monetize breaches, through to hacktivists seeking to enact retribution on the organizations they deem to be immoral or counter to public interest. Whatever the motivation and whomever the attacker, a large number of attacks are organized and carried out by skilled individuals, often with funding.

This change in landscape has led to many organizations engaging in a game of InfoSec catch-up, often realizing that their information security program has either not received the executive backing that it required or simply never existed in the first place. These organizations are seeking to correct this and begin along the path to initiating or maturing their information security efforts. There is, however, a problem.

Information security is an industry that is currently undergoing a period of negative unemployment; that is, that there are more open positions than there are candidates to fill those positions. Hiring people is hard, and hiring good people is harder. For those seeking employment, this is can be an advantageous situation; however, it is a high risk for employers seeking to hire someone into an information security position as they would be instilling a certain amount of trust with possible high dollar assets to a new hire.

For this reason, many companies that are only now embarking on their information security program have taken the route to promote someone from another role such as a system administrator or architect to an information security practitioner role. Another common practice is hiring a more junior information security professional into a role than would normally be the case, and expect the newly appointed employee to learn on the job. This situation is precisely what this book is intended to address.

A large number of issues encountered by companies with an immature information security program can be remedied, or at least vastly reduced, with some basic security hygiene. The knee-jerk reaction to the task of inheriting a new and immature security department can be to buy as many devices with pretty blinky LEDs as possible, in the hope that they will remedy issues. Some people would rather pay another company to set up an outsourcing agreement, which can be leveraged in order to assist. Both of these options require money. Many organizations that are new to information security do not have the budget to undertake either of these solutions to the problem—using the tools that are already in the environment may well be all you have.

Our Goal

Our goal is to not only make this a standard that can be applied to most enterprise networks, but also be a little entertaining to read along the way. There are already deep-dive standards out there from a variety of government and private organizations that can drone on and on about the validity of one security measure or the next. We want this to be an informative dialog backed by real-life experiences in the industry. There will be good policy, best practices, code snippets, screenshots, walkthroughs, and snark all mixed in together. We want to reach out to the masses—the net admins who can't get approval to hire help; directors who want to know they aren't the only ones fighting the battles that we see day in and day out; and the people who are getting their hands dirty in the trenches and aren't even close to being ready to start down the path of reading whitepapers and RFCs.

Who This Book Is For

This book is designed to serve as a Security 101 handbook that is applicable to as many environments as possible, in order to drive maximum improvement in your security posture for the minimum financial spend. Types of positions that will be able to take away knowledge and actionable data from this include upper-level CIOs, directors, security analysts, systems administrators, and other technological roles.

Navigating the Book

We have deliberately written this so that you do not have to adopt an all-or-nothing approach. Each of the chapters can serve as a standalone body of knowledge for a particular area of interest, meaning that you can pick and choose which subjects work for you and your organization, and ignore any that you feel may not apply. The aim is not to achieve compliance with a particular framework or compliance regime, but to improve on the current situation in sensible, pragmatic, manageable chunks.

We have purposefully ordered this book to begin with the fundamentals of starting or redesigning an information security program. It will take you from the skeleton steps of program creation on a wild rollercoaster ride into the depths of more technical topics.

Many people fail to realize that a large amount of work and implementation can be performed in an enterprise before any major capital is spent. A common problem faced in information security is not being able to get buy in from C-level executives. A step in the right direction in getting a security budget would be to prove that you have completed due diligence in your work. A large portion of this book includes steps, tools, processes, and ideas to secure an environment with little-to-no capital.

After the skeleton steps of planning out the new and shiny security program, we move on to creating a base set of policies, standards, and procedures. Doing so early in the stages of your security program will give you a good starting point for growth and maturation. Using policies as a method to communicate expectations allows you to align people across your organization with regard to what is expected of them and their role.

We included user education early on in the book as it is never too early to start teaching employees what to watch out for (and using them as a key role in detection). However, depending on the current strength of your defenses, it should not be a major focus until a strong foundation has been formed. Attackers aren't going to bother with human interaction if they can just connect remotely without one.

The book then moves on to planning and dealing with breaches, disasters, compliance, and physical security, all of which combine the management and organizational side of information security with the physical tools and infrastructure needed to complete them. Being prepared in the case of any type of physical or technical emergency can mean the difference between a smooth and steady recovery or a complete company failure—and anything in between.

A good, solid ground-up design is just the beginning. Now that we've covered part of the design of the overall program, we start to get into more technical categories and security architecture, beginning with the two main categories of operating systems. Both Microsoft and Unix have their pros and cons, but in regards to Microsoft, some of what will be covered is installing the Enhanced Mitigation Experience Toolkit (EMET), Group Policy best practices, and Microsoft SQL security. For Unix, we will cover third-party updates and server/OS hardening, including disabling services, file permissions, host-based firewalls, disk partitions, and other access controls. Endpoint management also falls into this category. A common struggle that we see in corporations includes bring your own device (BYOD) practices and mobile device management (MDM). We will also go into managing and implementing endpoint encryption.

Two other important verticals that are often ignored (or not given as much love as they should be) are networking infrastructure and password management. While going over networking infrastructure, we will cover port security, disabling insecure technologies, device firmware, egress filtering, and more. We will cover segmentation, including implementing VLANs with ACLs to ensure the network isn't flat, delegation of permissions, and Network Access Controls. We will then look into vulnerability scanning and remediation. While most enterprise vulnerability scanners are not free, we talk about them in this chapter to prove their worth by using them for a free trial period (to work toward the purchase of the entire product) or getting the most out of a full version already in the organization.

Many organizations have their own development team; however, traditional training for developers typically focuses on performance optimization, scalability, and interoperability. Secure coding practices have only been included in software development training in relatively recent years. We discuss techniques that can be used to enhance the current situation and reduce the risk often associated with in-house development.

Purple teaming, which is the combination of both offensive (red team) and defensive (blue team) security, can be difficult to implement depending on staffing and corporate policies. It is a relatively new concept that has gained a significant amount of attention over the last couple of years. Chapter 18 covers some basic penetration testing concepts, as well as social engineering and open source intelligence.

Finally, some of the most time-intensive security practices and devices are covered as we go through IDS, IPS, SOC, logging, and monitoring. We have found that many organizations feel as though these technologies are a one-time install or setup procedure and you can walk away feeling protected. It is well worth the time, effort, and investment to have a continually in-progress configuration because your internal environment is always changing, as are the threats you should be concerned about. We won't be making any specific vendor recommendations, but rather have opted to discuss overall solutions and concepts that should stand the test of time a lot better than a specific vendor recommendation for the current toolset.

Oh, and the Extra Mile...that's the junk drawer where you will find our bits and pieces of configuration ideas and advice that didn't really have a home anywhere else.

Now that we have said all that, let's see what we can do about improving some things.

Conventions Used in This Book

The following typographical conventions are used in this book:

Italic
> Indicates new terms, URLs, email addresses, filenames, and file extensions.

`Constant width`
> Used for program listings, as well as within paragraphs to refer to program elements such as variable or function names, databases, data types, environment variables, statements, and keywords.

`Constant width bold`
> Shows commands or other text that should be typed literally by the user.

`Constant width italic`
> Shows text that should be replaced with user-supplied values or by values determined by context.

This element signifies a tip or suggestion.

This element signifies a general note.

This element indicates a warning or caution.

O'Reilly Safari

Safari (formerly Safari Books Online) is a membership-based training and reference platform for enterprise, government, educators, and individuals.

Members have access to thousands of books, training videos, Learning Paths, interactive tutorials, and curated playlists from over 250 publishers, including O'Reilly Media, Harvard Business Review, Prentice Hall Professional, Addison-Wesley Professional, Microsoft Press, Sams, Que, Peachpit Press, Adobe, Focal Press, Cisco Press, John Wiley & Sons, Syngress, Morgan Kaufmann, IBM Redbooks, Packt, Adobe Press, FT Press, Apress, Manning, New Riders, McGraw-Hill, Jones & Bartlett, and Course Technology, among others.

For more information, please visit *http://oreilly.com/safari*.

How to Contact Us

Please address comments and questions concerning this book to the publisher:

O'Reilly Media, Inc.
1005 Gravenstein Highway North
Sebastopol, CA 95472
800-998-9938 (in the United States or Canada)
707-829-0515 (international or local)
707-829-0104 (fax)

We have a web page for this book, where we list errata, examples, and any additional information. You can access this page at *http://oreil.ly/2mPWM6p*.

To comment or ask technical questions about this book, send email to *bookquestions@oreilly.com*.

For more information about our books, courses, conferences, and news, see our website at *http://www.oreilly.com*.

Find us on Facebook: *http://facebook.com/oreilly*

Follow us on Twitter: *http://twitter.com/oreillymedia*

Watch us on YouTube: *http://www.youtube.com/oreillymedia*

Acknowledgments

Amanda

I have so many people to thank; the plus of writing your own book is being able to keep going and going and going and...you get the idea. First and foremost I want to give special recognition to my three wonderful boys, Michael, James, and Wyatt. They have started to grow into such independent and amazing little men and without their support and understanding of my long hours over these last couple of years, I wouldn't be where I am today. My mom for her continued support and encouragement, and for cleaning my house when I travel.

My coauthor Lee has been absolutely amazing. We've both pulled some crazy long hours to get this done. Reviewing each other's work and bouncing ideas off of each other makes for a good friendship and working partner. I couldn't have hoped for a better match. Courtney and the rest of the team at O'Reilly for walking us through this process and answering our stupid questions on a regular basis. They made writing this book a way better experience than I would have ever thought. To Virginia at O'Reilly for doing an incredible final edit. The incredibly intelligent and insightful help from our technical editors, Chris Blow, Mark Boltz-Robinson, Alex Hamerstone, and Steven Maske. Gal Shpantzer for his valuable insight.

I want to thank the coworkers I've had over the years and all of the times you've been there for me, mistakes and all. The people who I consider my mentors; some I've had my entire career, others since starting down the path to information security: Rob Fuller, Bill Gardner, Wolfgang Goerlich, Dave Kennedy, Denao Ruttino, Jayson Street. A special thanks to @_sn0ww for the help with content on physical security and social engineering, and Alan Burchill for his Group Policy knowledge and content. The information security community has helped me to continue to evolve daily while struggling with imposter syndrome and self doubt on a daily basis. You've been there for me when I needed you, to lean on, learn from, teach, and relax. While there are too many of you to list, I've cherished our in-depth conversations over drinks, hangouts, Facebook, Twitter, basements, and every other platform there is out there. Finally I would like to thank my arms for always being at my side, my legs for supporting me, my hips for not lying, and my fingers for always being able to count on them. Thanks for believing in me.

Lee

First of all, I have to thank Amanda for being fantastic to work with throughout the entire process, for all the hard work that she has put into this book, always being a true professional, becoming a good friend, and putting up with my sometimes "fun" calendar.

Courtney Allen for believing in us, endlessly kicking butt on our behalf, getting this whole project started in the first place, providing endless sage advice, and becoming a good friend to both Amanda and myself in the process.

Our technical editors, Chris Blow, Mark Boltz-Robinson, Alex Hamerstone, and Steven Maske, for their feedback and advice.

Virginia Wilson for all of her work to make this happen, invaluable feedback, and huge amounts of reading.

O'Reilly Media for their help and support.

My wife Kirsty, and our children Noah, Amy, and Dylan for being so supportive of everything that I do, having incredible patience, and affording me the time to work on this. Thank you. I love you, x x x.

Ben Hughes, for whom "blame" is perhaps a better word...I jest...sort of :)

There are also a number of other people who make up the exciting Venn Diagram of InfoSec community, colleagues, and friends whom I want to thank for helping me out with this project in terms of emotional support, mentoring, advice, caffeine, and alcohol. To avoid committing some kind of InfoSec name-ordering faux pas, I am going to list these in alphabetical order:

James Arlen, Frederic Dorré, Bill Gambardella, Nick Johnston, Alex Muentz, Brendan O'Connor, Allan Stojanovic, Wade W. Wilson, everyone at DFIRWL, and the 487 other people that I have inevitably failed to mention.

CHAPTER 1

Creating a Security Program

Creating or improving upon a security program can be a daunting task. With so many facets to consider, the more initial thought and planning that is put into the creation of this program, the easier it will be to manage in the long run. In this chapter, we will cover the skeleton of a security program and initial administrative steps.

Do not fall into the habit of performing tasks, going through routines, or completing configuration with the mindset of, "This is how we've always done it." That type of thinking will only hinder progress and decrease security posture as time goes on.

> Humans are allergic to change. They love to say, "We've always done it this way." I try to fight that. That's why I have a clock on my wall that runs counter-clockwise."
>
> *Grace Hopper, "The Wit and Wisdom of Grace Hopper" (1987)*

We recommend that when creating the program, you follow this chapter in order. While we attempted to group the remaining chapters accordingly, they can be followed as best fits a company.

Lay the Groundwork

It is not necessary to reinvent the wheel in order to lay out the initial groundwork for an information security program. There are a few standards that can be of great use that we will cover in Chapter 8. The National Institute of Standards & Technology (NIST) has a risk-based cybersecurity framework that covers many aspects of a program. The NIST Framework Core consists of five concurrent and continuous functions—Identify, Protect, Detect, Respond, and Recover. When considered together, these functions provide a high-level, strategic view of the lifecycle of an organization's management of cybersecurity risk (*http://bit.ly/2mPhsY1*). Not only will a framework be a possible asset, so will compliance standards. Although poorly implemented compliance standards can hinder the overall security of an organization, they can also prove to be a great starting point for a new program. We will cover compliance standards in more depth in Chapter 8. While resources like these can be a phenomenal value add, you must always keep in mind that every organization is different, and some aspects covered may not be relevant (there are continuous recurring reminders of this throughout the book).

Establish Teams

As with many other departments, there are virtues in having the correct staff on the correct teams in regards to security. Open cross-team communication should be a primary goal, as without it the security posture is severely weakened. A good security team consists of the following:

Executive team
> A chief information office (CIO) or chief information security office (CISO) will provide the leverage and authority needed for businesswide decisions and changes. An executive team will also be able to provide a long-term vision, communicate corporate risks, establish objectives, provide funding, and suggest milestones.

Risk team
> Many organizations already have a risk assessment team, and this may be a subset of that team. In the majority of organizations, security is not going to be the number-one priority. This team will calculate risks surrounding many other areas of the business, from sales to marketing and financials. Security may not be something they are extremely familiar with. In this case they can either be taught security basics case by case, or a security risk analyst could be added to the team. A risk framework such as the Operationally Critical Threat, Asset, and Vulnerability Evaluation (OCTAVE) Framework can assist with this.

Security team
> The security team will perform tasks to assess and strengthen the environment. The majority of this book is focused toward this and the executive team. They are responsible for daily security operations, including managing assets, assessing threats and vulnerabilities, monitoring the environment for attacks and threats, managing risks, and providing training. In a large enough environment, this team can be broken up into a variety of subteams such as networking, operation, application, and offensive security.

Auditing team
> It is always a good idea to have a system of checks and balances. This is not only to look for gaps in the security processes and controls, but also to ensure the correct tasks and milestones are being covered.

Baseline Security Posture

The unknowns in any environment are going to be scary. How will you know what level of success the program has had without knowing where it started? At the beginning of any new security program or any deep dive into an existing one, a baseline and discovery phase should be one of the first and foremost tasks at hand for all teams. Throughout this book we will cover asset management several times in different ways. The baseline of the security of the organization is just another step in that management. Items that should be gathered include:

- Policies and procedures
- Endpoints—desktops and servers, including implementation date and software version
- Licensing and software renewal, as well as SSL certificates
- Internet footprint—domains, mail servers, dmz devices
- Networking devices—routers, switches, APs, IDS/IPS, and Network Traffic
- Logging and monitoring
- Ingress/egress points—ISP contacts, account numbers, and IP addresses
- External vendors, with or without remote access, and primary contacts

Assess Threats and Risks

Assessing threats and risks will be incredibly different for each and every organization. Each internal and external footprint is unique when combined with the individual infrastructure involved. Assessing these includes both a high-level overview, as well as in-depth knowledge of assets. Without the knowledge of the threats and risks your organization faces, it is more difficult to custom fit technologies and recommendations to provide a suitable defense. Risk management is often split into four steps: identify, assess, mitigate, and monitor.

Identify

Organizations should be concerned with a large amount of threats and risks that will cross industry verticals. Focusing on industry trends and specific threats will allow the security program to be customized and prioritized to become more efficient. Many organizations have put very little thought into what threats and risks they face on a day-to-day basis, and will continue to do so until they fall victim to them. Invaluable resources in this case are available through Information Sharing and Analysis Centers (ISACs), which are brought together by the National Council of ISACs (*http://www.nationalisacs.org*) to share sector-specific Information Security. "ISACs collect, analyze and disseminate actionable threat information to their members and provide members with tools to mitigate risks and enhance resiliency."[1]

Not only should industry-specific threats be identified, but also overall trending threats such as malware, ransomware, phishing, and remote exploits. Two very important places to make note of are the OWASP top 10 and the CIS 20 (previously known as SANS Top 20) Critical Security Controls. Every organization can make use of both these and the standards outlined by the Cloud Security Alliance. The majority of the items on these lists will be covered in more depth in this book, but keeping up-to-date with them year to year should be a key part of any strategic plan.

Assess

After the potential risks have been identified, assess these risks to determine if they apply to the particular environment. Tasks such as internal and external vulnerability scans, firewall rule audits, and asset management and discovery will lend a larger picture to the type of overall risk exposure.

Mitigate

Mitigation of risks is the meat and bones of why we're all here; it's also the purpose of the majority of this book. Options include avoiding, remediating, transferring, or accepting the risk. Some examples:

Risk avoidance
Dave decides that storing Social Security numbers for customers is an unneeded process and discontinues the practice.

Risk remediation
Alex starts turning off open ports, implementing stricter firewall rules, and patching endpoints.

Transferring of risk
Ian outsources credit card processing to a third-party as opposed to storing data on site.

Accepting risk
Kate knows that a certain endpoint has no access to other endpoints and runs a third-party application. This application has a low-risk vulnerability that is required for it to function. While nothing at that point can be changed or remediated with that vulnerability, the risk is low enough to accept.

---

1 *https://www.nationalisacs.org/about-isacs*

You should only accept risk as a last resort. If a risk ever makes it to this point, request full documentation from third-party vendors and the executive team, as well as documentation of processes that have been attempted prior to making this decision. Add at least an annual review of any accepted risks to ensure they are revisited accordingly.

Monitor

Keep track of the risk over time with scheduled quarterly or yearly meetings. Throughout the year, many changes will have taken place that affect the amount and type of risk that you should consider. As a part of any change monitoring or change control, determine if the change is affecting risk in any way.

Prioritize

Once threats and risks have been identified and assessed, they must also be prioritized from highest to lowest risk percentage for remediation, with a concentration on ongoing protection. This doesn't always have to be an expensive venture, however. A large amount of defensive mitigations can be performed at little or no cost to an organization. This enables many opportunities to start a security program without having a budget to do so. Performing the due diligence required to get the program off the ground for free should speak volumes to an executive team.

Do not always take vendor or third-party advice for prioritization. Every environment is different and should be treated as such. Prioritize tasks based on the bigger picture when all of the information has been collected.

This book wasn't written to be a sequential list of security tasks to complete. Prioritization can differ greatly from environment to environment. Just remember, if the environment is already on fire and under attack, don't start by creating policies or reversing malware. As a fire marshall, you shouldn't be worried about looking for the arsonist and point of origin when you haven't even put out the fire yet.

Create Milestones

Milestones will take you from where you are to where you want to be. They will be a general progression on the road to a secure environment. This is heading a little into project manager (PM) duties, but in many cases companies do not have dedicated PMs. Milestones can be broken up loosely into four lengths or tiers:

Tier 1: Quick wins

The earliest milestones to meet should be quick wins that can be accomplished in hours or days—high vulnerabilities such as one-off unused endpoints that can be eliminated, legacy devices that can be moved to a more secure network, and third-party patches all could fall under this category. We will mention many free solutions as the sales process can take a significant time to complete.

Tier 2: This year

Higher vulnerabilities that may need to go through a change management process, create a change in process, or be communicated to a significant amount of people might not end up in Tier 1. Major routing changes, user education implementation, and decommissioning shared accounts, services, and devices are all improvements that also require little-to-no-budget to accomplish.

Tier 3: Next year

Vulnerabilities and changes that require a significant amount of planning or that rely on other fixes to be applied first fall into this tier. Domain upgrades, server and major infrastructure device replacements, monitoring, and authentication changes are all good examples.

Tier 4: Long-term

Many times a milestone may take several years to accomplish, due to the length of a project, lack of budget, contract renewals, or difficulty of change. This could include items such as a network restructure, primary software replacement, or new datacenter builds.

It is helpful to tie milestones to critical controls and risks that have already been identified. Although starting with the higher risks and vulnerabilities is a good idea, they may not be easy fixes. In many cases, not only will these items take a significant amount of time and design, but they may require budget that is not available. All aspects need to be taken into account when creating each tier.

Use Cases, Tabletops, and Drills

Use cases are important for showcasing situations that may put critical infrastructure, sensitive data, or other assets at risk. Brainstorm with data owners and leaders to plan ahead for malicious attacks. It is best to come up with around three different use cases to focus on in the beginning and plan on building security mitigations and monitoring around them. Items such as ransomware, DDoS (Distributed Denial of Service), disgruntled employee, insider threat, and data exfiltration are all good examples of possible use cases. After several use cases have been chosen they can be broken down, analyzed, and correlated to each step of Lockheed Martin's Intrusion Kill Chain (*http://lmt.co/2miXqrZ*).

The Intrusion Kill Chain, sometimes called the Cyber Kill Chain, is "a model for actionable intelligence when defenders align enterprise defensive capabilities to the specific processes an adversary undertakes to target that enterprise." It is composed of seven steps as described in the Lockheed Martin whitepaper (*http://lmt.co/2miXqrZ*):

1. Reconnaissance: research, identification, and selection of targets, often represented as crawling internet websites such as conference proceedings and mailing lists for email addresses, social relationships, or information on specific technologies.

2. Weaponization: coupling a remote access trojan with an exploit into a deliverable payload, typically by means of an automated tool (weaponizer). Increasingly, client application data files such as Adobe Portable Document Format (PDF) or Microsoft Office documents serve as the weaponized deliverable.

3. Delivery: transmission of the weapon to the targeted environment. The three most prevalent delivery vectors for weaponized payload are email attachments, websites, and USB removable media.

4. Exploitation: After the weapon is delivered to victim host, exploitation triggers intruders' code. Most often, exploitation targets an application or operating system vulnerability, but it could also more simply exploit the users themselves or leverage an operating system feature that auto-executes code.

5. Installation: installation of a remote access trojan or backdoor on the victim system allows the adversary to maintain persistence inside the environment.

6. Command and Control (C2): Typically, compromised hosts must beacon outbound to an internet controller server to establish a C2 channel. APT malware especially requires manual interaction rather than conduct activity automatically. Once the C2 channel establishes, intruders have "hands on the keyboard" access inside the target environment.

7. Actions on Objectives: only now, after progressing through the first six phases, can intruders take actions to achieve their original objectives. Typically, this objective is data exfiltration, which involves collecting, encrypting and extracting information from the victim environment; violations of data integrity or availability are potential objectives as well. Alternatively, the intruders may only desire access to the initial victim box for use as a hop point to compromise additional systems and move laterally inside the network.

This whitepaper has a good amount of information that can be used for creating use cases as well.

Table 1-1 is an example of a step-by-step kill chain use case we've created for a ransomware attack.

Table 1-1. Ransomware use case

Kill chain step	Malicious action	Defensive mitigation	Potential monitoring
Reconnaissance	Attacker obtains email addresses, technologies used, and creates an organizational profile based on that information.	Create policies around sharing internal information on sites such as LinkedIn or using corporate email addresses for nonbusiness use. After a major breach has been seen on the news run a password reset. Even though they shouldn't, employees will reuse passwords for other services and sites.	Have corporate emails been seen in breaches elsewhere? How many emails are found with OSINT?
Weaponization	Attacker creates a malicious exploit to send to the victim, or uses a current exploit.	Knowledge and awareness of threats currently being used by attackers will allow for better constructed and tuned mitigation steps.	n/a
Delivery	A user receives a phishing email.	Assess which attachment types are needed in the organization. File types such as *.js* can be extremely harmful and are rarely exchanged from external sources. Implement mailing blacklists and greylists such as Spamhaus and dnsbl to block known malicious mail servers.	Instill the idea of "trust but verify" to your users. Implement Ad-Blocking Filetypes of a certain size known to be malicious and associated with ransomware. (Flag *.scr* files over 22 MB and *.js* over 15 MB.)
Exploitation	Endpoint downloads a JavaScript file or Word document with malicious macro.	Disable macros and malicious filetypes via group policy. Ensure any endpoint protection is up-to-date and installed.	Monitor proxy logs for unexpected file retrievals (e.g., JavaScript is the first file fetched from that host, host is on a threat intel list, etc.) Use proxies or IDS (if cleartext) to monitor for known deobfuscation strings.
Installation	The payload is executed on the end user's device. (Lucky, Cerber, and CryptoWall use the built-in Windows Cypto API to handle the encryption.)	Keep backups (that are not permanently attached) so that encrypted files can be restored easily. Depending on OS, you can use "filesystem firewalls" such as as Little Flocker (*https://www.littleflocker.com*) to permit access to files on per-process basis. That means that you can permit read access to MS Word, but not IE, for example. There are experimental techniques that can be used to block crypto-based ransomware (e.g., Decryptonite (*http://bit.ly/2miUj3w*))	High increase in Windows Crypto API over short amount of time. Excessive numbers in a domain or low % of meaningful strings in domain.
Command & Control (C&C)	The ransomware contacts a C&C server on the internet to transmit the decryption key.	Implement sinkhole DNS and autoblock outbound connections to known malicious IP addresses.	Connection to known C&C servers.

Kill chain step	Malicious action	Defensive mitigation	Potential monitoring
Actions & Objectives	The malware starts encrypting the files on the hard disk, mapped network drives, and USB devices. Once completed, a splash screen, desktop image, website, or text file appear with instructions for the ransom.	Implement Honey Directories—the ransomware goes into C:\$$ it sees another $$ directory, when it goes into C:\$$\$$ it sees another $$ directory, and so on.	Advanced file auditing can be enabled for alerting on an extreme increase in filesystem changes.

Many different defensive mitigations can be added at each step of the kill chain for an overall decrease in risk at each layer.

Following the creation and implementation of security controls around use cases, the testing of tabletop exercises and drills can serve as a proof of concept. A *tabletop exercise* is a meeting of key stakeholders and staff who walk step by step through the mitigation of some type of disaster, malfunction, attack, or other emergency in a low stress situation. A drill is when staff carries out as many of the processes, procedures, and mitigations that would be performed during one of the emergencies as possible.

While drills are limited in scope, they can be very useful to test specific controls for gaps and possible improvements. A disaster recovery plan can be carried out to some length, backups can be tested with the restoration of files, and services can be failed over to secondary cluster members.

Tabletop exercises are composed of several key groups or members.

- During a tabletop exercise there should be a moderator or facilitator who will deliver the scenario to be played out. This moderator can answer "what if" questions about the imaginary emergency, as well as lead discussion, pull in additional resources, and control the pace of the exercise. Inform the participants that it is perfectly acceptable to not have answers to questions during this exercise. The entire purpose of tabletops is to find the weaknesses in current processes to mitigate them prior to an actual incident.

- A member of the exercise should also evaluate the overall performance of the exercise, as well as create an after-action report. This evaluator should take meticulous notes and follow along any runbook to ensure accuracy. While the evaluator will be the main notetaker, other groups and individuals may have specific knowledge and understanding of situations. In this case, having each member provide the evaluator with her own notes at the conclusion of the tabletop is a good step.

- Participants make up the majority of this exercise. Included should be groups such as finance, HR, legal, security (both physical and information), management, marketing, and any other key department that may be required. Participants should be willing to engage in the conversation, challenge themselves and others politely, and work within the parameters of the exercise.

What to include in the tabletop:

- A handout to participants with the scenario and room for notes.
- Current runbook of how security situations are handled.
- Any policy and procedure manuals.
- List of tools and external services.

Post-exercise actions and questions:

- What went well?
- What could have gone better?
- Are any services or processes missing that would have improved resolution time or accuracy?
- Are any steps unneeded or irrelevant?
- Identify and document issues for corrective action.
- Change the plan appropriately for next time.

Tabletop Template

The Federal Emergency Management Agency (FEMA) has a collection of scenarios, presentations, and tabletops that can be used as templates (*http://bit.ly/2lHuOVP*).

Expanding Your Team and Skillsets

Finding a dedicated, passionate, and intelligent team can be one of the most difficult aspects of any professional's life.

What can you and your team do to expand knowledge and skillsets?

- Encourage staff to either set up a home lab or provide a lab for them. Labs can be used for testing out real-world scenarios, as well as practicing skills and learning new ones. Labs can be created at a relatively low cost by buying secondhand equipment. The best way to learn for the majority of people is hands-on, and with a lab there is no risk introduced into a production environment.
- Compete in or create Capture the Flag competitions (CTFs). CTFs are challenging, and they can provide cross training and team building, as well as increase communication skills. Most information security conferences have CTFs (*https://*

ctftime.org). If you are looking to expand a team, CTFs are a wonderful place to find new talent. Not only will participants be showing their level of knowledge, but also communication skills, how well they work with others in a team, and their willingness to help and teach others.

- Find or create a project. Automate something in the enterprise, find a need and fill it. It doesn't matter what the skillset, there will be a project out there that needs help. Documentation is needed on 99% or more of the open source projects out there.

- Attend, organize, volunteer, speak, sponsor, or train at an industry conference or local meetup. There are hundreds of them across the US and they almost always need volunteers. Just attending a conference has its benefits, but truly immersing yourself will push you further to learn and experience more. Many careers have been started by having a simple conversation about a passion over lunch or a beer. Networking is a game changer in our industry, but it's not the silver bullet for everyone. You can network all you want, but unless you are a desirable candidate it won't matter. Having a willingness and desire to learn, listen, collaborate, and the ability to think for yourself are all ideal traits in such a fast-paced industry.

- Participate in mentoring. Whether as a mentor or mentee, structured or unstructured, mentoring can be a valuable learning process both on and off the job.

Conclusion

Creating an information security program is no easy task. Many programs are broken or nonexistent, adding to the overall lack of security in the enterprise environment today. Use this book as a guide to work through the different areas and to suit them to a custom-tailored plan. Organizational skills, a good knowledgeable, hard-working team, strong leadership, and an understanding of the specific environment will all be crucial to an effective program.

CHAPTER 2

Asset Management and Documentation

As a whole, asset management is not an information security function. However, there are definitely components to it that assist in strengthening the overall security posture. It is one of the most difficult verticals to cover. Without proper asset management, an environment cannot be protected to its full potential. It is impossible to protect assets that are unknown. In larger networks, it is next to impossible to completely be aware of each and every device that is connected or every piece of software the users may have installed. However, with the correct security controls in place, it becomes much easier.

The majority of this chapter will cover how best to find assets, tie all of the information together, and document it for ease of use and troubleshooting. Above all else, the two most important things to remember about asset management are to ensure there is one source of truth, and that it is a process, not a project.

Additionally, each asset or group of assets must be assigned an owner and/or a custodian. An asset owner serves as a point of contact for the assigned asset, whereas a custodian has responsibility for the stored information. The assets are then categorized into different levels of importance based on the value of the information contained in them and the cost to the company if an asset is compromised.

Information Classification

The need for information classification has risen as the amount of data on digital storage has grown. Attackers use confidential data for their profit by selling it on the black market, to expose or cripple a specific organization, to commit fraud, or to aid in identity theft. While many industry compliance standards such as HIPAA and PCI DSS attempt to dictate the type of information that should be specifically guarded and segregated, that may not be the only data that is classified as confidential in an organization. There may also be contracts and other legal measures that must be consulted for classification and protection of certain data. Steps to correctly classify data can be described as follows:

1. Identify data sources to be protected. Completion of this step should produce a high-level description of data sources, where they reside, existing protection measures, data owners and custodians, and the type of resource. Obtaining this information can be difficult, but can be an added part of the documentation process as data owners and custodians are assigned and documented.

2. Identify information classes. Information class labels should convey the protection goals being addressed. Classification labels like Critical and Sensitive have different meanings to different people, so it is important that high-level class descriptions and associated protection measures are meaningful and well-defined to the individuals who will be classifying the information, as well as those who will be protecting it.

3. Map protections to set information classification levels. Security controls such as differing levels and methods of authentication, air-gapped networks, firewalls/ACLs, and encryption are some of the protections involved in this mapping.

4. Classify and protect information. All information that has been identified in step 1 should now be classified as dictated in step 2, and protected as in step 3.

5. Repeat as a necessary part of a yearly audit. Data footprints are ever expanding. As new software is installed or upgraded with add-ons data grows or changes in scope. A yearly audit of the current data footprint in the enterprise will be required to ensure data continues to be protected as documented.

Asset Management Implementation Steps

The asset management process can be separated out into four distinct steps: defining the lifecycle, information gathering, change tracking, and monitoring and reporting. Assets can be added to the environment at an alarming rate via scripted virtual machine roll outs or business acquisitions, refreshed to new hardware or software versions, or removed altogether. There are several enterprise-level tools that assist in identifying data on systems. A solution should be implemented that will track an asset from as early as possible until its eventual decommissioning.[1]

---

1 "Information Classification—Who, Why, and How" (*http://bit.ly/2lHI4tC*), SANS Institute InfoSec Reading Room.

Defining the Lifecycle

There are many lifecycle stages in between delivery and decommissioning: an asset may be moved; the person it's assigned to may no longer be employed; it may require repair or replacement; or it may go inactive while its assigned user is on leave of absence. Define lifecycle events and document them. Each department or person involved in each step should understand when and how assets are tracked at every point of their lifecycles. This assists with ensuring that any unplanned deviation from documented processes is caught. Following is a map of a very basic asset management lifecycle:

Procure

> This is the procurement step of the lifecycle where assets are initially added to be tracked. At this point, the initial device information, such as serial number, PO, asset owner, criticality, and model name and number, can be added to the tracking system.

Deploy

> When an asset is deployed by a sys admin, net admin, helpdesk member, or other employee, the location of the device can now be updated and any automated population can be tested. Remember: prior to deploying assets, they should be scanned for viruses and vulnerabilities or built with a custom secure image (if applicable) before being attached to the network.

Manage

> The management lifecycle step can contain many subsections depending on the level of documentation and tracking that is decided upon. Items can be moved to storage, upgraded, replaced, or returned, or *may* change users, locations, or departments.

Decommission

> Decommissioning assets is one of the most important steps of the lifecycle due to the inherent security risks regarding the disposal of potentially confidential data. When deciding on disposal options, different classifications of data can be tied to varying levels. There are many different ways to destroy data, and these have varying levels of security and cost. Options include:
>
> - Staging for disposal
>   - A single pass wipe: drives can be reused and provide a residual value return.
>   - Multiple wipes: increases the level of security; this still protects the residual value but adds cost.

— Degaussing: removes the ability to resell the drive and has no visual indicator that it has worked, but is a cheaper alternative to shredding and is often more practical.

— Full disk encryption: drives can be reused; this increases the level of security.

• Physical disposal

— Crushing/drilling/pinning: these are other low-cost options, all of which show physical evidence that they have been completed and deter ordinary criminals. These methods destroy the value of the unit and the data is still present on the platters despite them not being able to spin up.

— Shredding: the most secure form of data destruction and typically used for the highest levels of secure data, but it is expensive and destroys the ability for resale.

— Removed as asset from inventory

Information Gathering

Information gathering contains the most hurdles and has a huge amount of complexity from environment to environment. As stated previously, obtaining a good software package coupled with well thought-out processes will lead to gathering as much information as possible on network-connected assets. For initial collection, there are several methods to go about obtaining this information:

Address Resolution Protocol (ARP) cache
> Pulling the ARP cache from routers and switches will provide a list of IP and MAC addresses connected to the network.

Dynamic Host Configuration Protocol (DHCP)
> DHCP will contain all IP address reservations and possibly hostnames.

Nmap
> Running `nmap` against the entire range of networks can provide an amazing amount of information as it is a very comprehensive scanning tool. A simple scan to get started is this:

```
nmap -v -Pn -O 192.168.0.0/16 -oG output.txt
```

This command provides a verbose output (`-v`, or `-vv` for even more verbosity), and assumes all hosts are online, skipping discovery (`-Pn`) with operating system detection (`-O`) on 192.168.0.0 through 192.168.255.255, and outputs the results in a grepable format (`-oG`) to *output.txt*. Other options can be found on the Nmap website (*http://www.nmap.org*).

PowerShell

PowerShell is a very versatile and powerful tool in Windows environments. Starting with Windows 2008R2, the Active Directory Module was introduced. Prior to this, `dsquery`, `adsi`, and `ldap` commands were used to obtain information from AD. `Get-ADUser -filter *` can be used to return an entire list of users within an AD domain. There are many filters that can be added to return subsets of this list as well. To retrieve all domain computer accounts, run `Get-ADComputer -Filter 'ObjectClass -eq "Computer"' | Select -Expand DNSHostName`.

Simple Network Management Protocol (SNMP)

SNMP can provide a great amount of information on networked devices. By default, most SNMP version 2 read and write strings (the passwords used to query devices) are set to "public" and "private." SNMP settings should be changed to custom strings, and if possible switched to SNMP version 3, which supports username and password authentication. Many software packages, such as NetDisco, which we will cover later in this chapter, use SNMP to gather data.

Vulnerability management software

Data from a vulnerability scanner can be added into the asset management system. This assists in tracking risks and adding to the overall amount of useful information about assets.

Windows Management Interface (WMI)

WMI can be used to pull almost all important information from a Microsoft Windows device. Specific information can be gathered on components such as the CPU, memory, and disk, as well as system information such as OS, processes, and services. The command `WMIC` can be performed on a system locally, or the WMI API can be used with most programming languages—for example, remotely connecting with PowerShell uses the `Get-WmiObject` cmdlet.

Change Tracking

Keeping track of changes in hardware, software, and performance is a necessary step to having an up-to-date inventory. Certain modifications can significantly change the security risk for a device.

For example, Steven runs a section of the company that has just spun up a new service line. He has been working with marketing and they give him the okay to buy a domain and spin up a Wordpress site. Before configuring the site for the public, he installs Wordpress on his own machine and begins to install add-ons. First off, Wordpress itself has had a history of vulnerabilities, but add-ons can be written by anyone and can introduce vulnerabilities from privilege escalation to XSS. An endpoint change-tracking client could trigger an alert on the addition of unapproved or unlicensed software.

Mark decides he's had enough with this company and quits. Before leaving, he removes an expensive piece of software from his laptop to keep the license key for his own personal use. When his equipment is repurposed, his replacement will more than likely need to use that same software. The asset management software should have the list of software that was present, as well as any corresponding licensing keys.

Monitoring and Reporting

Monitoring and reporting on assets provides notifications of upcoming software licensing renewals and hardware warranty expirations. Trends can be discovered with the right amount of information, taking guesswork out of creating yearly budgets and equipment procurement plans. This information can also be used to assist in any equipment refresh processes.

A helpful security measure to implement is the monitoring and alerting of any unapproved devices. In a perfect world, an alert would fire when a device MAC shows up that isn't located in the asset management tracking program; however, in most cases outside of a lab or small network that would be close to impossible.

Alerts may also be created for lack of certain software or system settings if, for example, an endpoint has no antivirus or management software installed, isn't encrypted, or has unauthorized software. More than likely this will be done with some sort of endpoint monitoring software, but can also be accomplished in a more manual route with software such as Open Audit. Microsoft SCCM has the ability to report on installed software as well.

Asset Management Guidelines

In addition to the steps involved in implementing asset management, there is also a solid set of guidelines to keep in mind during the implementation process.

Automation

To accomplish these steps effectively, attempt to automate as many of them as possible. If any person along the chain of custody of an asset finds he is repeating a manual process, the question, "Can this be automated?" should be asked. The process should pull authoritative information from trustworthy locations on as many assets as possible. DNS can pull in hostnames and IP addresses; DHCP can tie MAC addresses to those IP addresses; and a vulnerability scanner may find entire networks that were previously unknown. Adding barcodes early on in the lifecycle can greatly assist with automation as well. Everything that can be automated leads to a more efficient process.

One Source of Truth

As there are many different ways to gather information about devices, such as DNS, DHCP, wireless connections, MAC address tables, software licenses, nmap scans, etc., it is important to select a software that will easily integrate with the technologies already present. Having conflicting information in several different locations like spreadsheets and SharePoint is not conducive to a complete picture regarding current assets. When choosing a software or method, it should be well communicated that it alone is the one source of truth regarding assets, and any deviation should be dealt with.

Organize a Company-Wide Team

Assets will enter the company from a variety of different areas. The purchasing department is the obvious first choice; third-party vendors may bring their own equipment; or there may be a BYOD (bring your own device) policy, which is a whole other can of worms. Types of departments that would benefit from being on an asset-management team include purchasing, receiving, helpdesk, communications, maintenance, and system administrators.

As with most other processes and procedures, it is close to impossible to plan for every possibility. Plan for the unplanned. If a member of the helpdesk team or another group that has access to the asset management software happens upon a device that has not been documented, there should be a process to deal with this. Not only should the asset then be added to the software, but the cause should also be investigated. Are there assets entering the organization in a different department or by different means that have yet to be added to the asset management process?

Executive Champions

The organizational team should also contain one or more members of the executive staff as a champion to assist in process and procedure changes that will cross through several departments. Larger organizations normally have difficulty with communicating changes and additions to procedures to the correct individuals, while smaller companies seem to resist change. Creating a well thought-out and communicated directive from someone other than security or IT staff will greatly increase the success. This executive member will also be able to see the effects of proper asset management in the form of cost savings and avoidances.

Software Licensing

When it comes to software license management, knowing what you are entitled to have deployed is often more important that what you actually have deployed. More often than not, organizations fail software audits for over-deployment because they can't prove exactly what they have the right to have deployed. Ending up behind on software licensing can be a very expensive mistake. Not only will an updated list of currently installed software eliminate the risk of paying for software that isn't being used, but it also ensures that there are no licensing overage fees or fines.

Define Assets

Define criteria for what constitutes a critical asset—many times they may be the device where critical data lies, as well. It may be a specific type of hardware or appliance such as a head end firewall or fiber switches or certain custom software packages. Discovery and inventory will produce a large asset list. Some assets will require more oversight or management than others.

Documentation

Proper and complete documentation is an integral part of asset management. Creating and maintaining it should be a continual process from day one. Documentation is used to set clear directions and goals, as well as offering a continual reference as needed.

Spend sufficient time creating documentation and provide detailed descriptions of all security projects, including charts and statistics. These documents can be a major advantage when showing management where the security budget went. Another benefit of documentation is the knowledge that will be gained by all parties while creating it. Potential security holes or weaknesses in the program may also become apparent during this process. Every mistake is a learning opportunity; document problems or mistakes so they are not repeated.

What should be documented? There are several levels of documentation depending on the size and scope of an environment. The following sections present a starting point as to what documentation will be beneficial.

Networking Equipment

Many automated scanning tools can provide a detailed overview of networking equipment. A free solution that we would like to suggest is Netdisco (*http:// netdisco.org*). Figure 2-1 shows how Netdisco displays an example router and what ports are configured.

> Netdisco is an SNMP-based L2/L3 network management tool designed for moderate to large networks. Routers and switches are polled to log IP and MAC addresses and map

them to switch ports. Automatic L2 network topology discovery, display, and inventory.[2]

Figure 2-1. Netdisco web interface

Many automated scanning tools can provide a detailed overview of networking equipment, examples of which are outlined in the following lists:

- Hostname
- Licensing information
- Location
- Management IP
- Software, hardware, and firmware versions
- Warranty information

Network

- Default Gateways
- Ingress/Egress point public IP addresses for all sites
- ISP Account Information and Contacts
- Performance baselines of network traffic over a day/week/month period

Servers

- Applications and Roles
- Department or group that manages/supports

---

2 *https://sourceforge.net/projects/netdisco/*

- Hostname
- iLO address
- IP address(es)
- Is remote access allowed?
- Is there PII or other sensitive data?
- OS version
- Open ports
- Performance baselines of CPU, Memory, & Disk
- Warranty Information

Desktops

- Hostname
- Department
- Patch level

Users

Not only should the individual accounts be documented, but also what users have access to each:

- Database Administrator Accounts
- Domain Admins
- Root and Administrator Accounts
- Service Accounts

Applications

- Administrative Users
- Licensing
- Servers and Appliances involved
- Type of Authentication
- Workflow of data (explain further)

Other

- Certificates and Expiration dates
- Domains and Expiration dates

Just as important as the documentation itself is the consistency and organization of the information. Naming in a consistent fashion assists in locating and understanding the roles of assets. For example:

- ORG1-DC1-R2B-RTR3 = Organization 1, Datacenter 1, Row 2, Rack B, Router 3
- SVC_ORG2-SQL10-SNOW = The service account for Organization 2, SQL Server 10, the Snow Application
- ORG3-FL1-JC-AP3 = Organization 3, Floor 1, JC Hall, Wireless Access Point 3

Conclusion

Classify, organize, automate, define, gather, track, monitor, report, document, rinse, lather, repeat. The messy world of asset management can be a daunting task without a solid plan and the understanding that it's not a one-time project. Having as much information in one place as possible about endpoint and infrastructure devices will not only assist in short-term troubleshooting, but also long-term design planning and purchasing decisions.

CHAPTER 3

Policies

Policies are one of the less glamorous areas of information security. They are, however, very useful and can be used to form the cornerstone of security improvement work in your organization. In this chapter we will discuss why writing policies is a good idea, what they should contain, and the choice of language to use.

Why are policies so important? There are a range of reasons:

Consistency
> Concerns about inconsistent approaches from day to day or between members of staff should be vastly reduced in the wake of decent policies. A written set of policies reduces the need to make a judgment call, which can lead to inconsistent application of rules.

Distribution of knowledge
> It is all well and good for *you* to know what the policy is with regards to not sharing passwords with others, but if the entire organization is unaware, then it is not providing you much benefit. Policy documents disseminate information for others to consume.

Setting expectations
> Policies set rules and boundaries; by having clearly defined rules, it becomes equally clear when someone breaks those rules. This enables appropriate action to be taken. Departments like human resources find it difficult to reprimand someone because it "feels like" they may have done something wrong. A clear contravention of a rule is easier to enforce.

Regulatory compliance and audit
> Many industries are regulated or pseudo-regulated, and many have auditors. A criteria common amongst nearly every regulatory compliance or auditing

scheme is the existence of policies. By having a set of policies, you have already ticked a box on the regulatory compliance or audit checklist.

Sets the tone
> The policy set can be used to set the overall tone of a company's security posture. Even if not explicitly laid out, the policy set gives an overall feel as an organization's approach to security.

Management endorsement
> A management-endorsed policy, published within an organization's official document library, lends credibility to the policy set itself and by extension to the security team as well.

Policies are living documents—they should grow with an organization and reflect its current state. Making changes to policy should not be frowned upon; evolution of both the policies themselves and the associated documentation is a positive change. A scheduled annual review and approval process of policies will allow you to ensure that they remain aligned with business objectives and the current environment.

Language

Policies should lay out *what* you, as an organization, wish to achieve in a series of policy statements. Detail as to specifically *how* this is achieved is outlined in procedure and standards documentation. For this reason there is no need to get caught up with complexity and detail. Policy statements should be fairly simple, clear, and use words like "do," "will," "must," and "shall." They should not be ambiguous or use words and phrases such as "should," "try," and "mostly."

For example, a good policy will use statements such as:

> A unique User ID shall be assigned to every user.

As opposed to

> A unique User ID should be assigned to a user.

The use of "should" as opposed to "shall" gives the impression that this is a "nice to have," not a rule. If there are times when a policy can be overridden, then this should be stated as part of the policy statement. This is often achieved by using phrases such as "unless authorized by a manager." Care should be taken not to introduce ambiguity with such statements, however; for example, it must be clear what constitutes "a manager" in this case.

Documents should be designed to be read. There is no need to fill documents with excessively wordy statements or some kind of confusing legalese. Each policy statement can be only a few sentences, often only one, in a bullet point format.

Document Contents

Policy documents should contain a few key features:

Revision control

> At the very least, this should include a version number and an effective date for the document. This allows a user in possession of two versions of a document to quickly establish which is the current version and which is out of date and no longer applicable.

Revision detail

> A brief summary of what has changed since the last revision allows approvers and those already familiar with the policy to quickly understand changes and the new content.

Owner/approver

> Being clear as to who owns and approves any particular document is useful not only for demonstrating that it has been accepted and agreed upon by the appropriate level of management, but it also serves to facilitate feedback and suggestions for updates in future revisions.

Roles and responsibilities

> Defining whose responsibility it is to impliment, monitor, abide by, and update policies ensures that there is little room for ambiguity with regard to roles.

Executive signoff

> By ensuring that executive signoff is clearly marked on each document it is clear to the reader that it is endorsed at the highest level and approved for immediate use.

Purpose/overview

> This provides a brief overview as to what the policy document covers. This is typically only a paragraph and is intended to allow the readers to gauge if they are looking at the correct policy document before they get to the point of reading every policy statement.

Scope

> In all likelihood, the scope section will only be a couple of sentences and will be the same for most policy documents. This explains who the policy document applies to; for example, *"This policy applies to all <Company Name> full-time employees, part-time employees, contractors, agents, and affiliates."* Of course, there could be policies that only apply to a particular subset of readers for some reason, and the scope can be adjusted accordingly.

Policy statements

As discussed earlier, these are the guts of the document—they are the policies themselves.

Consistent naming convention

Consistent naming conventions not only for the documents themselves, but also for artifacts they reference, ensure that they are easy to understand and can be applied consistently across the organization.

Related documents

Cross references to other relevant documents such as standards, policies, and processes allow the reader to quickly locate related information.

For ease of reference during an audit, it is prudent to also include references to sections of any relevant regulatory compliance, standards, and legal requirements.

Topics

For ease of reading, updating, and overall management it is probably easier to produce a set of policy documents rather than a single monolithic document.

Selecting how the policies are broken up is, of course, a matter of determining what is most appropriate for your organization. You may have a favorite security framework, such as ISO 27002, for example, from which you can draw inspiration. Similarly, aligning policy topics with a particular regulatory compliance regime may be more aligned with your organization's objectives. In reality, there are many high-level similarities between many of the frameworks.

SANS, for example, publishes a list of template policies (*http://bit.ly/2mmz3Kl*) that you can edit for your own needs. At the time of writing, its list of topics are:

- Acceptable Encryption Policy
- Acceptable Use Policy
- Clean Desk Policy
- Disaster Recovery Plan Policy
- Digital Signature Acceptance Policy
- Email Policy
- Ethics Policy
- Pandemic Response Planning Policy
- Password Construction Guidelines
- Password Protection Policy
- Security Response Plan Policy
- End User Encryption Key Protection Policy
- Acquisition Assessment Policy

- Bluetooth Baseline Requirements Policy
- Remote Access Policy
- Remote Access Tools Policy
- Router and Switch Security Policy
- Wireless Communication Policy
- Wireless Communication Standard
- Database Credentials Policy
- Technology Equipment Disposal Policy
- Information Logging Standard
- Lab Security Policy
- Server Security Policy
- Software Installation Policy
- Workstation Security (For HIPAA) Policy
- Web Application Security Policy

This is not an atypical list; however, many of the policies listed will not apply to your organization. This is completely fine.

Storage and Communication

The nature of policies and procedures is meant to lend as much standard communication as possible to the organization as a whole. To do this, policies must be easily accessible. There are many software packages that can not only provide a web interface for policies, but also have built-in review, revision control, and approval processes. Software with these features makes it much easier when there are a multitude of people and departments creating, editing, and approving policies.

Another good rule of thumb is to, at least once per reviewal process, have two copies of all policies printed out. As the majority of them will be used in digital format, there will be many policies that refer to and are in direct relation to downtime or disaster recovery procedures. In cases such as these, they may not be accessible via digital media so having a backup in physical form is best.

Conclusion

Policies are important tools used to express the direction of an organization from a security perspective, clearly articulating expectations and providing a level of consistency. They can also be used to explicitly state and enforce rules that have previously been ambiguous or inferred.

Policies are not set in stone forever—they are living documents that can grow and change in line with your organization.

CHAPTER 4

Standards and Procedures

Standards and procedures are two sets of documentation that support the policies and bring them to life. In this chapter we will learn what standards and procedures are, how they relate to policies, and what they should contain.

If we consider the policies of an organization to be the "what" we are trying to achieve, standards and procedures form the "how." As with policies, standards and procedures bring with them many advantages:

Consistency

> Worries about the nuances of the implementation of policies at a technology level are removed and thus consistency applied. By having a written set of standards and procedures, the rules outlined in the policies can be applied equally across the organization.

Distribution of knowledge

> As with policies, it is all well and good for *you* to know how to implement a policy in practice; however, if those elsewhere in the organization are unaware, then it is not providing much benefit. Standards and procedures disseminate this information for others to consume.

Setting expectations

> Policies have already set the rules and boundaries. However, they do not provide the detail required to consistently achieve those goals in the same way every time. Standards and procedures do this.

Regulatory compliance

> Many industries are regulated or pseudoregulated. A criterion common amongst nearly every regulatory compliance scheme is the existence of standards and procedures to accompany the policies. By having a set of standards and procedures, you have already ticked a box on the regulatory compliance checklist.

Management endorsement
> A management-endorsed set of standards and procedures, as with policies, lends credibility to both the documentation set itself, and by extension the security team.

Standards

Standards provide the "how" portion to a policy at a technology viewpoint without specific procedural detail. For example, many policy statements include the requirement that access be authenticated by use of a password.

A standard that provides more detail as to what constitutes a password should accompany this policy statement. For example, it will most likely cover topics such as complexity requirements, the process for changing a password, storage requirements, ability to reuse passwords or otherwise, or any other related detail.

Separating this into two documents—three once we talk about procedures—provides several advantages:

Documents are easier to consume
> A lightweight policy document is easier to navigate and less daunting to read than an all-encompassing policy document the size of a telephone directory.

Lack of repetition
> Using the password example mentioned earlier, having to repeat the need to use complex passwords on each mention of password authentication in ancillary policies will become repetitive and leaves plenty of scope to introduce errors. This way the high-level policies can be read easily, and if further clarification is needed the reader can refer to the appropriate accompanying standard.

Ease of maintenance
> Lack of repetition means that a change in the standard need only be applied in one place for consistent application across the organization. If standards were rolled into the policy documentation, changes would need to take into account all instances of the affected statements. Missing one of these statements could be catastrophic.

Language

As with policies, the language used within standards documentation should be fairly simple, clear, and use words like "do," "will," "must," and "shall." They should not be ambiguous or use words and phrases such as "should," "try," or "mostly."

Unlike policies, however, standards can be more specific and detailed in their guidance. Although being specific about technologies in use, standards remain free of specific procedural detail such as commands. This will be explained when we get to procedures.

For example, in Chapter 3 we used the example:

> A unique User ID shall be assigned to a user.

The accompanying standards documentation would typically include statements such as:

> A User ID is created in the format <first 6 chars of surname><first 2 chars of first-name>, unless this User ID is already in use, in which case...

> A User ID shall only be created after HR approval

> A User ID shall only be created after Line Manager approval

> HR must review and approve user access rights, ensuring that they align with the user's role prior to the User ID being provisioned.

> A record of User ID creation and associated sign-off will be kept in...

> A one-way hash function shall be used for the storage of user passwords. Acceptable hashing algorithms are...

These statements enhance, support, and provide more detail to the associated policy statement.

Documents should be designed to be read. There is no need to fill documents with excessively wordy statements. Each policy statement can be only a few sentences, often only one, in a bullet point format.

Procedures

Procedures take the step made from policies to standards and makes another similarly sized step further along the same trajectory.

Procedures take the detail from standards, which in turn offer guidance based on policies, and provide specific steps in order to achieve those standards at a technology level. This time, the documentation is not intended to describe what we, as an organization, are trying to achieve, but how this is to be implemented at a technology-specific level.

Language

Language is important once more, as ensuring that the desired configuration changes are applied consistently is the ultimate goal. Unlike policies and standards, however, the level of detail will probably depend on corporate culture. For example, it is more appropriate in some organizations to provide an almost keypress-by-keypress level of detail. In others, prescribing which configuration options to make is more appropriate and the administrators are trusted to make a judgment call on which editor they use to make such changes. In most environments the latter is typically sufficient.

Let's revisit the last statement from the standards example, which was:

> A one-way hash function shall be used for the storage of user passwords. Acceptable hashing algorithms are...

The procedure documentation should explain how this is achieved on a specific platform. Because technology platforms differ and procedures are technology-specific, it is entirely likely that there will need to be platform-specific documents created to account for differences between technologies.

For example, to implement platform-specific documentation about FreeBSD on a FreeBSD system, the procedures statement could be something like:

> In order to configure system passwords to use the SHA512 hashing algorithm, edit */etc/login.conf*, and amend the `passwd_format` field to read:
>
> ```
> :passwd_format=sha512:\
> ```

Whereas on a Linux platform the guidance would be:

> In order to configure system passwords to use the SHA512 hashing algorithm, execute the following command with root privileges:
>
> ```
> authconfig --passalgo=sha512 --update
> ```

Both are systems that have a Unix heritage, and both routes ultimately achieve the same goal. However, the precise method at which the goal is reached is clearly articulated to ensure consistency of application across platforms and teams.

Document Contents

As with policies, documentation for standards and procedures should contain a few key features:

Revision control
> At the very least, this should include a version number and an effective date for the document. This allows a user in possession of two versions of a document to quickly establish which version is current and which is out of date and no longer applicable.

Owner/Approver
> Being clear as to who owns and approves any particular document is useful not only for demonstrating that it has been accepted and agreed upon by the appropriate level of management, but it also serves to facilitate feedback and suggestions for updates in future revisions.

Purpose/Overview

This provides a brief overview as to what the policy document covers. This is typically only a paragraph and is intended to allow the readers to gauge if they are looking at the correct policy document before they get to the point of reading every policy statement.

Scope

In all likelihood, the scope section will only be a couple of sentences and will be the same for most policy documents. This explains who the policy document applies to; for example, *"This policy applies to all <Company Name> employees and affiliates."* Of course there could be policies that only apply to a particular subset of readers for some reason.

Policy statements

As discussed earlier, these are the guts of the document—the policies themselves.

Consistent naming convention

Consistent naming conventions not only for the documents themselves, but also for artifacts they reference, ensure that they are easy to understand and can be applied consistently across the organization.

Related documents

Cross references to other relevant documents such as standards, policies, and processes allow the reader to quickly locate related information.

For ease of reference during an audit, it is prudent to also include references to sections of any relevant regulatory compliance, standards, and legal requirements.

Conclusion

As a whole, policies, standards, and procedures offer a high-level administrative overview down to the specific technology and step-by-step implementation. While each has its own functions, they all must be written with the skill level of the reader in mind. A clear and concise set of documentation makes a huge difference in creating a standardized and well-understood environment.

CHAPTER 5

User Education

User education and security awareness as a whole is broken in its current state. It is best to find a way to demonstrate with the right type of metrics that you are successfully implementing change and producing a more secure line of defense. A large portion of the information security industry is focused on perimeter security. However, we are beginning to see a shift from strictly data-level protection to an increase in user-level security and reporting. The security as a process and defense-in-depth mentality must be filtered down and implemented into our user training.

Before you spend money on threat intel that may tell you how better to defend your specific sector, it would be best to start where everyone is being attacked. One of the largest threats today is the targeting of our weakest link: people. According to the 2015 Verizon Data Breach Investigations Report:

> Phishing remains popular with attackers. Campaigns have evolved to include the installation of malware as the second stage of an attack. Our data suggests that such attacks could be becoming more effective, with 23% of recipients now opening phishing messages and 11% clicking on attachments. It gets worse. On average, it's just 82 seconds before a phishing campaign gets its first click.

In this chapter we will demonstrate how to provide more value than the basic training offered in the majority of organizations.

Broken Processes

> The reason that most Security Awareness Training programs fail is because they are *trainings*…not education.[1]

---

[1] David Kennedy, "The Debate on Security Education and Awareness" (*http://bit.ly/2mmMnOL*).

Experience and time in the industry shows that the Computer Based Trainings (CBTs) organizations require their employees to complete annually (or sometimes more often) are comparable to a compliance check box. It is a broken process. The employee is required to complete and pass this training for continued employment. Once the process is complete, the knowledge is either forgotten or greatly reduced. One of the largest proven gaps occurs when end users do not bring the information forward into their day-to-day working lives like they should. This is a large disconnect where it means the most, and it is known as the Ebbinghaus forgetting curve (Figure 5-1). Repetition based on active recall has been demonstrated as effective in other areas for avoiding the curve and, therefore, is the foundational design such awareness programs should be based on. From "The Ebbinghuas forgetting curve" (*http://bit.ly/2mmXCXn*):

> ...basic training in mnemonic techniques can help overcome those differences in part. He asserted that the best methods for increasing the strength of memory are:
>
> 1. Better memory representation (e.g., with mnemonic (*http://en.wikipedia.org/wiki/ Mnemonic*) techniques)
>
> 2. Repetition based on active recall (*http://en.wikipedia.org/wiki/Active_recall*) (especially spaced repetition (*http://en.wikipedia.org/wiki/Spaced_repetition*))

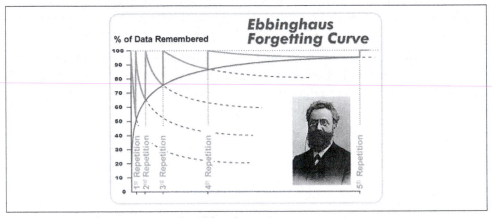

Figure 5-1. Graph representing the Ebbinghaus Curve

There are significant additions and changes that can be made to transform user training into an effective and long-lasting security education.

Bridging the Gap

Repetition is a proven, successful way to bridge the gap of compliance, teaching our users real-life skills and helping secure the infrastructure that we are responsible for protecting. This is best implemented with a comprehensive hands-on security phishing and awareness rewards program. A full program design will provide a maturity that the CBTs do not. While CBTs are a good value-add and can be used to reinforce real-life scenarios, relying on them as a primary means of security awareness training will not provide the value or insight to the first line of defense. By consistently reinforcing the CBTs with a custom-built awareness program, you increase the end user's skills and boost the organization's immunity to phishing and social engineering threat factors.

Building Your Own Program

Building a mature and strategic program from the ground up is achievable with executive support and cultural alignment. An awareness program need not equate to thousands of dollars spent on creating flashy presentations and brown bag luncheons to draw crowds. Teaching by example and rewarding good behavior is what will improve upon the user's awareness:

> The point has never been to make everyone experts in security, it has always been to arm the employees with basic knowledge so that in the event something out of the ordinary occurs, it may help notify the security team.[2]

An important takeaway and key point to remember is that it is not the employees' responsibility to know the difference between a legitimate phish and spam, or to know that they should be hovering over links in emails before clicking. It is our job to have a program that is open enough and easy enough for them to report abnormalities or when something is not quite right. At the end of this chapter you will find a template slideshow for a security awareness program.

Establish Objectives

The direction of an organization's security awareness program should be tailor-fit and reassessed periodically. With the constant changing threat landscape, maturity of user understanding, and a progressing industry, the objectives should be thought of as moving targets. An objective one year of decreased malware removals on desktops may mature past that to increased reporting of phishing/vishing attacks. However, establishing an aggressive set of objectives can result in a failed or unrealistic program. Concentrating on one or two achievable objectives at the beginning of a new program will allow you to accomplish a more specific goal. You can then adjust the target periodically to reflect the organization's and program's maturity.

---

2 Ben0xa, "Security Awareness Education" (*http://bit.ly/2mmJ3mw*).

Establish Baselines

Many organizations do not have formal security awareness training, so establishing a baseline should begin with a live-fire exercise testing the skills and real-world knowledge of a good subset of your users. It should be a standard practice to have a realistic outlook on where your security posture stands in relation to not only technical baselines but also cultural norms. It is important to know how the users currently respond to threats and irregularities. Establishing an engagement with a certified and skilled penetration testing company can help you baseline these responses. By having a third party assess the skills of your users with professional phishing campaigns, you will gain valuable insight into data that you may currently not have.

Scope and Create Program Rules and Guidelines

When the user or employee is being treated essentially as a customer, rules and guidelines should be well thought out and strategized. Miscommunications will only impede the learning process, making succeeding with the program more difficult. Align the rules to be consistent with the organization's culture in order to have a higher adoption rate. Having multiple levels of input will enable you to have clear and concise program instructions and rules, leading to an easier implementation.

Implement and Document Program Infrastructure

You are taught in driver's education to wear your seat belt, look both ways, and adjust your mirrors. The first time you have a close call or, even worse, a real accident, you now have a real-world experience that your mind falls back on each time you make a decision. It is the same with security awareness. The shock of the accident now gives employees pause when future emails show up that may look a little odd and out of place. Afterward, the training teaches them what could possibly be at risk when they click through the illegitimate link. Setting up the phishing attacks to automatically redirect to a website that aligns with the program theme will create a connection between real-life events and the message being presented for education.

Positive Reinforcement

One of the most important parts of building a program is letting users know that it is OK if they fall victim to the attack. This must be a consistent message throughout the education material. The more comfortable users feel reporting the incident, the more cooperation and adoption you will witness. Assure the user that it will always be better coming from an internal training attempt than a real phishing attack, and practice makes perfect. The training should include what to look for and more importantly, how to report something abnormal. With a great first line of defense and solid Incident Response (IR) procedures, you will be far better off securing the human element, which is the weakest security link.

Gamification

Gamification is actually a scientific term that roughly means applying game principles to a situation. The simplest definition of those principles is: 1) Goal establishment, 2) Rules, 3) Feedback, and 4) Participation is voluntary.[3]

Being able to reward good behavior is an essential part of the program as well. Employees should not feel ashamed to come to the right people for help, nor afraid of being reprimanded for making a mistake. Gamification works well in many aspects of life, so why should this be any different? Turn the program into something catchy and a small budget cannot just satisfy your expectations, but exceed them. Making a lottery of gift cards, discounted services, and other items to enforce the brand of the program and put something in the user's hand will reinforce your message.

Define Incident Response Processes

Incident Response looks different in every organization. If you have a current proven method of IR you are already well on your way to including an awareness program into your current structure. Use the newly created program as a case study for testing procedures and policies. This will allow you to flush out any inconsistencies, inefficiencies, or unplanned situations. Assessing each step of the process will give the necessary information to add or change policies to fit the needs of the organization around certain types of attacks.

Gaining Meaningful Metrics

Without knowing the baseline for metrics, you won't know how far your program has improved. Work toward long-term goals regarding the overall security. This will help build metrics into the already forming security program to keep it on track.

> Successful metrics programs include well-defined measurements and the necessary steps to obtain them.[4]

Measurements

There are an abundance of measurements to take throughout a security awareness program. Depending on your program and your goals, they may have to be more tailor-fit totals as opposed to the base set listed here.

Here are some common totals to track:

---

3 Ira Winkler and Samantha Manke, "How to create security awareness with incentives" (*http://bit.ly/2mmPDK4*).

4 Building an Information Security Awareness Program: Defending Against Social Engineering and Technical Threats - Bill Gardner & Valerie Thomas

- Emails sent
- Emails opened
- Links clicked
- Credentials harvested
- Reports of phishing attempts
- Emails not reported on
- Hits on training sites

Tracking Success Rate and Progress

Keeping track of click percentages, phishes reported, and incidents reported is a good start as well as necessary for any complete metric collection. However, charting your gains and losses with structured data over time will give your organization a deeper understanding of progress. Successful education and retained knowledge will be apparent with the increase and decrease of certain measurements and the success of goals set for metrics. Periodic assessment of shifts in metrics should be performed to assist with guidance of the education program's goals and other possible implementations or changes in the current environment's security structure.

Important Metrics

Measures are concrete, usually measure one thing, and are quantitative in nature (e.g., I have five apples). Metrics describe a quality and require a measurement baseline (I have five more apples than I did yesterday).[5]

The metric of how much your security posture has increased in reference to your baseline is the key goal and quality control. Seeing increased reporting changes in suspicious activity on your network should align with a lower amount of malware, DNS queries to blocked sites, or other activity on the network that would lead an analyst to believe the possibility of a targeted attack has been blocked. The ability to link key metrics back to specific departments, buildings, or roles provides the information you need to scope more directed education.

Conclusion

User education can be a massive undertaking, but it will provide a strong layer of defense and monitoring if done correctly. It should not be the first step toward creating a more secure environment, but can greatly increase protection once a strong

---

5 CIO Council, "Performance Metrics and Measures" (*http://bit.ly/2mmPeaa*).

baseline has been created. For the best results, remember to always use a carrot and not a stick. In Appendix A, you can find education templates that can be used for user redirection, instruction, and award rules.

CHAPTER 6

Incident Response

As the name suggests, incident response is the set of processes and procedures that are initiated once a security incident has been declared. In modern-day computing, incidents range from a single compromised endpoint to complete network compromises resulting in massive data breaches. Data breaches and enterprisewide attacks are becoming more and more common, and thus incident response has grown in meaning beyond merely these processes and procedures to encompass an entire discipline within information security.

In this chapter we will discuss the various processes involved in incident response, tools and technology options, and the most common forms of technical analysis that you are likely to need to perform during an incident.

Processes

Incident response processes are an integral component of being able to react quickly in the event of an incident, determine a nonincident, operate efficiently during an incident, and improve after an incident. Having processes in place before an incident begins will pay dividends in the long run.

Pre-Incident Processes

The processes associated with incident response are not merely concerned with what happens during an incident. If there are no processes in place to recognize that an incident is taking place, that the incident response process should be initiated, and those responsible for incident response notified, there is little point in having processes to deal with the incident, as they will never be called upon.

The pre-incident processes do not need to be complex; in fact, they should most definitely not be. The point of these processes is merely to determine if there is a potential incident, and to initiate the incident response process—that's it!

Having been through multiple iterations of internal incident response, we can say that the most effective processes I have worked with include the following:

Leverage existing processes for dealing with events
> Most organizations deal with outages, configuration issues, user-reported issues, and other events. Don't try to set up a parallel set of processes, but leverage what is already there—in all likelihood, the same people who deal with these issues will be the first to hear of an issue anyway. Just modify or supplement existing processes to include calling the incident response contact in the event of an expected incident, much like they already know to call the on-call Unix person when a Linux host fails in the middle of the night.

Define an incident
> If you do not define what you class as an incident, you will either get called for every support call or not get called during a breach of four million records. If it is not simple to define what an incident is, you can opt for wording like, "once a manager has determined that an event is a security incident..." This way you have at least defined that any event will have already progressed beyond triage by first-line support and someone experienced enough to make the determination has made a judgment call.

The result of a pre-incident process is nearly always to initiate the IR process by declaring an incident and calling the contact for incident response.

 An incident turns out to be nothing can always be downgraded again to a standard operations event. It is better to be called for a suspected incident that transpires to be nothing, than to not be called for fear of a false positive.

It is in everyone's best interest to communicate clearly and early on. It not only saves time and effort fixing miscommunication and hearsay issues, but also allows those individuals fixing the downtime or incident the time to fully concentrate on the issue at hand. No downtime is too small for proper communication!

Incident Processes

The processes that take place during an incident, particularly from a technology perspective, cannot be too prescriptive. Incidents, like many operational problems, are far too varied and numerous to prescribe precise courses of action for all eventualities. However, there are some processes that are worth sticking to:

Define an incident manager

This does not have to be the same person for every incident, but should be someone who is senior enough to make decisions and empower others to complete tasks. The incident manager will run the response effort and make decisions.

Define internal communications

Communication between everyone working on the incident to avoid duplication of work, promote the sharing of information, and ensure that everyone is working toward a common goal is key. We would recommend:

- **Open a "war room."** That is, use an office or meeting room to perform the role of center of operations for anyone in the same physical location. This is used as the central point for coordination of efforts.
- **Keep a conference bridge open in the war room.** This allows people who are remote to the physical location to check in, update those in the war room, and obtain feedback. If there is no physical war room, this will often serve as a virtual war room.
- **Hold regular update meetings.** Regular updates allow people to move away, work in a more concentrated fashion, and report back regularly rather than feeling as if they are looked over and reporting back haphazardly. Typically, meeting every hour works well until the situation is well understood.
- **Allocate the task of communicating internally to stakeholders.** Management will typically want to be kept abreast of a larger incident. However, sporadic communication from a number of people can send mixed messages and be frustrating for both management and the incident response team. A single point of communication between the two allows stakeholders to receive frequent, measured updates.

Define external communications

In many cases, but not all, some external communication may be required. Typically, this is because customers or other departments will be affected by the incident in some way. This sort of communication should not be taken lightly as it affects the public image of the organization and internal technology department. If you are considering undertaking any external communications yourself, rather than allowing your corporate communication or PR team to do it, we would suggest you read Scott Roberts' "Crisis Comms for IR" (*http://bit.ly/2mn0Xpx*) blog post on the topic.

Determine key goals

By determining the goals that you wish to achieve in the event of an incident, you can ensure that all actions are taken with these goals in mind. By goals we do not mean simply "fix it," but considerations such as "preserve chain of custody for evidence" or "minimize downtime." This is discussed in more depth in Chapter 7.

High-level technology processes

As mentioned before, it is difficult to account for all eventualities, so being prescriptive with technology-based remedies may be difficult; however, there are some high-level processes that may be in place. For example, there may be policies regarding taking snapshots of affected systems to preserve evidence, ensuring that staff stop logging in to affected systems, or a blackout on discussing incidents via email in case an attacker is reading internal email and will get a tip off.

Plan for the long haul

Many incidents are over in just a few hours, but many last substantially longer, often weeks. It is tempting to pull in all resources to help on an incident in the hopes of a timely conclusion, but if it becomes clear that this is not the case, you should prepare for a longer term course of action. Ensure people are sent away to get rest so that they can come in and cover the next shift, and keep those working fed and watered to prevent fatigue. Try not to burn everyone out, as this can be a game of endurance.

Post-Incident Processes

Once an incident is over, it is very valuable to hold a lessons-learned session. This allows for feedback regarding what worked well and what worked less well. It also allows you the chance to update processes, determine training requirements, change infrastructure, and generally improve based on what you learned from the incident.

It is recommended that this session be held a short time after the incident closes. This offers a few days for people to reflect on what happened, gather some perspective, and recover, without leaving it so long that memories fade or become distorted with time. Using this session to update documentation, policies, procedures, and standards will also allow for updated tabletops and drills.

Outsourcing

Many people do not wish to manage incidents internally, at least not beyond the initial triage point, and would rather bring in external subject matter expertise as required. This is an option that works for many people. However, we would recommend that if this is the route that you decide to take, negotiate contracts, nondisclosure agreements, and service-level agreements before an incident happens. When you are elbow deep in an incident is not the time to be negotiating with a potential supplier about when they can spare someone and what rates you will have to pay.

Tools and Technology

It would be easy to list a large number of technologies that are typically used by incident response professionals, especially in the field of digital forensics. However, a lack of experience in this area can make it easy to misinterpret results, either via a lack of experience with the specific tools or by not understanding the context of what is fully understanding.

Fully understanding an environment, knowing what the various logs mean, knowing what should and should not be present, and learning how to use the tools that are already present can vastly increase the chances of managing an in-progress incident. Mid-incident is not the time to learn how to conduct a forensic investigation; it is better left to someone who has some prior experience in this field. That said, a high level appreciation of what can happen during an incident can be achieved by reviewing some high-level topics. We also discuss some example tools that which can be used to assess what is happening in an environment during an incident.

Log Analysis

The first port of call, as with any type of operational issue, is of course the humble logfile. Application and operating system logfiles can hold a wealth of information and provide valuable pointers to what has happened.

If logs are stored on the host that generated them, you should remain cognizant of the fact that if someone compromises that host, they can easily modify the logs to remove evidence of what is happening. If possible, the logs stored on your Security Information and Event Management (SIEM) platform should be consulted, rather than referring to logs on the target device. This not only reduces the chances of log tampering but also provides the facility the ability to query logs across the whole estate at once, permitting a more holistic view of the situation. A SIEM also has the ability to show if a gap in logs has occurred.

When reviewing logs on an SIEM, it is likely that the SIEM's own log query tools and search language will need to be used. It is also possible that the use of commands such as `curl` or customized scripts will access data via an API.

If the logs are not being accessed on an SIEM, it is recommended to take a copy, if possible, and to analyze them locally with any preferred tools. Personally, we opt for a combination of traditional Unix command-line tools such as `grep`, `awk`, `sed`, and `cut`, along with scripts written for specific use cases.

Disk and File Analysis

Analysis of artifacts on storage devices can also provide clues as to what has happened during an incident. Typically, a disk image will yield more information than purely examining files, as this contains not only the files stored on the disk that are immediately visible, but also potentially fragments of deleted files that remain on disk, chunks of data left in slack space, and files that have been hidden via root kits. Using a disk image also ensures that you do not accidentally modify the original disk, which ensures the integrity of the original should there be legal proceedings of some kind. To obtain a copy of the disk image traditionally means taking a host down and using a tool such as ddfldd (*http://dcfldd.sourceforge.net*) or a commercial equivalent to take an image of the disk, which is saved to another drive and then examined off-line. Unfortunately, this causes downtime.

Disk and File Analysis in Virtual Environments

In most virtualized and some cloud computing environments, taking downtime to image a disk is less of a problem because all the major vendors have various snapshot technologies that can be used to take an image of a guest operating system. However, these technologies will often compress disk images, destroying unused space and losing much of this needed information.

Once a disk image has been obtained, various commercial tools can be used to analyze the filesystem to discover files of interest, construct timelines of events, and other related tasks. In the open source/free space, the old classics The Sleuth Kit (*http://www.sleuthkit.org/sleuthkit/*) and Autopsy (*http://www.sleuthkit.org/autopsy/*) remain favorites.

If a simple recovery of files is all that is desired, PhotoRec (*http://www.cgsecurity.org/wiki/PhotoRec*) is a simple-to-use tool that yields surprisingly good results. Despite the name, it is not limited to photos.

Memory Analysis

Code that is executing, including malicious code, is resident in RAM. If you can obtain a memory dump from a compromised host—that is, a file that contains a byte-for-byte copy of the RAM—then analysis can be performed to discover malicious code, memory hooks, and other indicators of what has happened.

The most popular tool to analyze these RAM dumps is the Volatility Framework (*http://bit.ly/2mn6L26*) (see the wiki on GitHub (*http://bit.ly/2mnfgua*)).

Obtaining RAM dumps will vary from OS to OS and it is a constantly changing field, so we would recommend checking the Volatility documentation for the latest preferred method.

For virtualized platforms, however, there is no need to dump RAM using the OS, as the host can take an image of the virtual memory. Following are the three most common examples of how to achieve this:

QEMU

```
pmemsave 0 0x20000000 /tmp/dumpfile
```

Xen

```
sudo xm dump-core -L /tmp/dump-core-6 6
```

VMWare ESX

```
vim-cmd vmsvc/getallvms
vim-cmd vmsvc/get.summary vmid
vim-cmd vmsvc/snapshot.create vmid [Name] [Description]
  [includeMemory (1)] [quiesced]
```

PCAP Analysis

If you have any tools that sniff network traffic inline or via a span port or inline utilities such as an IDS/IPS or network monitoring device, there is every chance that you could have sample packet capture (PCAP) files. PCAP files contain copies of data as it appeared on the network and allow an analyst to attempt to reconstruct what was happening on the network at a particular point in time.

A vast number of tools can be used to perform PCAP analysis; however, for a first pass at understanding what is contained in the traffic we would recommend using IDS-like tools such as Snort (*https://snort.org*) or Bro Security Monitor (*https://www.bro.org*) configured to read from a PCAP, as opposed to a live network interface. This will catch obvious traffic that triggers their predefined signatures.

Some staples for conducting PCAP analysis include the following tools:

- tcpdump (*http://www.tcpdump.org*) produces header and summary information, hex dumps, and ASCII dumps of packets that are either sniffed from the wire or read from PCAP files. Because tcpdump is command line, it can be used with other tools such as sed and grep to quickly determine frequently occurring IP addresses, ports, and other details that could be used to spot abnormal traffic. tcpdump is also useful because it can apply filters to PCAP files and save the filtered output. These output files are themselves smaller PCAPs that can be fed into other tools that do not handle large PCAPs as gracefully as tcpdump does.
- Wireshark (*https://www.wireshark.org*) is the de facto tool for analysis of PCAP data. It provides a full GUI that allows the user to perform functions such as filtering and tracking a single connection, providing protocol analysis and graphing certain features of the observed network traffic. Wireshark does not, however, handle large files very well, and so prefiltering with tcpdump is recommended.

- tshark (bundled with Wireshark) is a command-line version of Wireshark. It is not quite as intuitive or easy to use, but being on the command line allows it to be used in conjunction with other tools such as grep, awk, and sed to perform rapid analysis.

All in One

If you are familiar with LiveCDs such as Kali in the penetration testing world, then an approximate equivalent for Incident Response is CAINE (*http://www.caine-live.net*). CAINE is a collection of free/open source tools provided on a single LiveCD or USB thumbdrive. It can be booted without prior installation for quick triage purposes.

Conclusion

Incident response is not a prescriptive process from beginning to end. However, there are some key areas that can be process driven, such as communication, roles and responsibilities, and high-level incident management. This allows incidents to be effectively controlled and managed without bogging down technical specialists with complex decision tree processes.

Incident response is an area of information security that most hope they will never have to be involved with; however, when the occasion comes you will be glad that you have prepared.

CHAPTER 7

Disaster Recovery

The terms *disaster recovery* (DR) and *business continuity planning* (BCP) are often confused and treated as interchangeable. They are, however, two different, but related, terms.

Business Continuity pertains to the overall continuation of business via a number of contingencies and alternative plans. These plans can be executed based on the current situation and the tolerances of the business for outages and such. Disaster Recovery is the set of processes and procedures that are used in order to reach the objectives of the Business Continuity Plan.

BCP normally extends to the entire business, not just IT, including such areas as secondary offices and alternate banking systems, power, and utilities. DR is often more IT focused and looks at technologies such as backups and hot standbys.

Why are we talking about DR and BCP in a security book? The CIA triad (confidentiality, integrity, and availability) is considered key to nearly all aspects of Information Security, and BCP and DR are focused very heavily on Availability, while maintaining Confidentiality and Integrity. For this reason, Information Security departments are often very involved in the BCP and DR planning stages.

In this chapter we will discuss setting our objective criteria, strategies for achieving those objectives, and testing, recovery, and security considerations.

Setting Objectives

Objectives allow you to ensure that you are measurably meeting business requirements when creating a DR strategy and allow you to more easily make decisions regarding balancing time and budget considerations against uptime and recovery times.

Recovery Point Objective

The recovery point objective (RPO) is the point in time that you wish to recover to. That is, determining if you need to be able to recover data right up until seconds before the disaster strikes, or whether the night before is acceptable, or the week before, for example. This does not take into account of how long it takes to make this recovery, only the point in time from which you will be resuming once recovery has been made. There is a tendency to jump straight to seconds before the incident; however, the shorter the RPO, the more the costs and complexity will invariably move upwards.

Recovery Time Objective

The recovery time objective (RTO) is how long it takes to recover, taken irrespective of the RPO. That is, after the disaster, how long until you have recovered to the point determined by the RPO.

To illustrate with an example, if you operate a server that hosts your brochureware website, the primary goal is probably going to be rapidly returning the server to operational use. If the content is a day old, it is probably not as much of a problem as if the system held financial transactions for which the availability of recent transactions is important. In this case an outage of an hour may be tolerable, with data no older than one day once recovered.

In this example, the RPO would be one day and the RTO would be one hour.

There is often a temptation for someone from a technology department to set these times; however, it should be driven by the business owners of systems. This is for multiple reasons:

- It is often hard to justify the cost of DR solutions. Allowing the business to set requirements, and potentially reset requirements if costs are too high, not only enables informed decisions regarding targets, but also reduces the chances of unrealistic expectations on recovery times.

- IT people may understand the technologies involved, but do not always have the correct perspective to make a determination as to what the business's priorities are in such a situation.

- The involvement of the business in the DR and BCP plans eases the process of discussing budget and expectations for these solutions.

Recovery Strategies

A number of different strategies can be deployed in order meet your organization's DR needs. Which is most appropriate will depend on the defined RTO, RPO, and as ever, by cost.

Backups

The most obvious strategy for recovering from a disaster is to take regular backups of all systems and to restore those backups to new equipment. The new equipment should be held at a dedicated disaster recovery facility or secondary office, located somewhere where the appropriate connectivity is available and the servers can begin operating right away.

Historically, backups were often to a tape-based medium such as DLT drives, which were physically shipped to another location. However, in recent times the cost of storage and network connectivity has come down, so backups can often be made to a more readily available and reliable media, such as an archive file on a remote hard disk.

Backups will generally have a longer RPO than other strategies, and backups tend not to be continuous but rather a batch job run overnight—and not necessarily every night. The RPO will be, at best, the time of the most recent backup. Additionally, backups frequently fail and so the RPO is in reality the time of your most recent working backup.

The RTO will vary depending on the speed of the backup media and the location of the backup media in relation to backup equipment. For example, if the backup media needs to be physically shipped to a location, this must be factored in.

Warm Standby

A warm standby is a secondary infrastructure, ideally identical to the primary, which is kept in approximate synchronization with primary infrastructure. This infrastructure should be kept a reasonable geographic distance from the primary in case of events such as earthquakes and flooding. In the event of a disaster, services would be manually "cut over" to the secondary infrastructure. The method of doing so varies, but is often repointing DNS entries from primary to secondary or altering routing tables to send traffic to the secondary infrastructure.

The secondary infrastructure is kept in sync via a combination of ensuring that configuration changes and patches are applied to both primary and secondary, and automated processes to keep files synchronized. Ideally the configuration and patching would happen in an automated fashion using management software, however this is often not the case and can cause problems in the event that there are differences.

The RPO is fairly short on a warm standby, typically whatever the frequency of file-system synchronization processes are.

The RTO is however long the cut-over mechanism takes. For example, with a DNS change this is the amount of time to make the change, and for old records to expire in caches so that hosts use the new system. With a routing change, the RTO is at least however long the routing change takes to make and, if using dynamic routing protocols, routing table convergence to occur.

However, this system does rely on having an entire second infrastructure that is effectively doing nothing until such time as there is a disaster.

High Availability

A high-availability system is typically a model like a distributed cluster. That is, multiple devices in distributed locations, which share the load during normal production periods. During a disaster, one or more devices will be dropped from the pool and the remaining devices will continue operation as per normal. In addition, they will continue to process their share of the additional load from the device that is no longer operational.

Due to the nature of high availability, it is typical that all devices in the cluster will be fully synchronized, or very close to it, and for this reason the RPO will be very short.

Many clustering technologies allow for devices to drop out of the cluster and the other devices will automatically adjust and compensate. For this reason, the RTO can also be lower than many other solutions.

Although the RPO and RTO are both advantageous when using a high-availability system, it is not without cost. The cluster needs to have enough capacity to compensate handling the additional load per remaining node. In the event of a disaster, this means running hardware that is not fully utilized in order to have spare capacity. Also, additional investment in areas such as intersite bandwidth will be required. Keeping all devices synchronized to run a clustered solution requires sufficient bandwidth at a low enough latency, which places additional requirements on the infrastructure.

Alternate System

In some cases, using an alternate system is preferential to running a backup or secondary system in the traditional sense. For example, in the case that an internal Voice over IP solution is rendered unavailable due to a disaster, the plan may not be to try to re-instantiate the VoIP infrastructure, but to simply change to using cellular phones until such time as the disaster is over.

This strategy does not always have an RPO per se, as recovery of the existing system is not part of the plan. This is why this type of approach is typically only taken with systems that do not hold data, but provide a service, such as telephones. There is, however, a measurable RTO in terms of the amount of time taken to switch over to using an alternate system.

System Function Reassignment

An approach that can prove to be cost effective is System Function Reassignment, which is a hybrid of other solutions. This is the repurposing of noncritical systems to replace critical systems in the event of a disaster situation. It is not applicable to all environments, and so should be considered carefully before being used as a strategy.

For example, if you already run two datacenters, structure your environments so that for any production environment housed in one datacenter, its test, pre-production, or QA environment is housed in the other datacenter. In this scenario you can have a near production site ready, but not idle, at all times. In the event of a disaster the environment in question will cease to operate as, for example, pre-production, and be promoted to a production environment.

This approach requires that the two environments be separated enough that a disaster affecting one will not affect the other. The state of the other environments should be tightly controlled so that any differences from production are known and easily changed to match that of production state prior to going live.

Dependencies

An important part of developing a strategy for DR and BCP is to understand the dependencies of all of the systems. For example, if you can successfully bring up a fileserver in another location, it does not matter if the staff can connect to it. Servers typically need a network connection, the associated routing, DNS entries, and access to authentication services such as Active Directory or LDAP. Failure to determine the dependencies required for any particular system may lead to missing the RTO for that service.

For example, if you have an email server with an RTO of 1 hour, and yet the network on which it depends has an RTO of 3 hours, irrespective of how quickly the email server is up and running, it may not be resuming operation in any meaningful sense until 3 hours have elapsed.

By mapping out dependencies such as this, it is much easier to identify unrealistic RTOs, or RTOs of other systems or services that need to be improved to meet these targets. Walking through tabletops and drills as mentioned in Chapter 1 will assist in discovering these dependencies.

Scenarios

When developing potential disaster plans, it is often useful to walk through a few high-level scenarios and understand how they impact your proposed plan. This exercise normally works most effectively with representatives from other IT teams who can assist with discussing the implications and dependencies of various decisions.

A few broad categories of scenarios are useful to consider, although which ones you choose to use will probably be dependent upon your own circumstances:

- Hardware failure of mission-critical platform: something that is isolated to a single platform, but that is significant enough to cause a DR incident—for example, the failure of server hardware for the production environment of a key system.
- Loss of a datacenter, potentially temporarily such as during a power outage, or perhaps for more prolonged periods such as a fire or earthquake.
- Pandemic: in the event of a pandemic, services may remain available, but physical access may not be possible, which in turn could prevent certain processes from taking place, such as physically changing backup tapes, users working from home causing extra load up VPN, or other remote access services.

Invoking a Fail Over...and Back

It is all very well having a set of contingency plans in place and having target times by which to achieve them. If you do not know when you are in a disaster situation there is little point to the plans. There should be a process in place to determine what is and is not a disaster, and when to invoke the plan.

There may be a few key, high-level scenarios in which the plan would obviously be put into action. For example, the event of the datacenter being on fire is typically enough to invoke failing over to backup systems. However, care should be taken not to be too prescriptive or else the risk of minor deviations from the situations outlined may cause a failure to invoke the plan. Similarly, not being descriptive enough could cause an inexperienced administrator to invoke a DR plan needlessly. In this case, how do you determine when to invoke the plan? One of the most effective routes is to have a list of named individuals or roles who are authorized to determine when the organization is in a disaster situation and that the plan needs to be executed. The process for anyone who is not authorized to make this determination is to escalate to someone who can, who in turn will make the decision. This way the alarm can be raised by anyone, but the ultimate decision to execute is left to someone suitably senior and responsible.

One often overlooked area of DR and BCP is that as well as failing over to contingency systems, there will need to be a process of switching back again after the disaster has ended. Unlike the initial failover procedure, there is the advantage of being able to schedule the switch and take an appropriate amount of time to do so. Nevertheless, this should be a carefully planned and executed process that is invoked once again by an authorized person. Always remember to include the proper communication during the potential outages as it can be a high-stress time. A downtime is never too big for proper communication to happen.

Testing

Disaster Recovery can be extremely complex, with many of the complexities and interdependencies not being entirely obvious until you are in a disaster situation. Sometimes you'll find that in order to complete the task, a file is required from a server that is currently under several feet of water. For this reason it is advisable—and under some compliance regimes mandatory—that regular DR tests be carried out. Of course, no one suggests that the datacenter be set on fire and attempted to be recovered. Choose a scenario and have the replacement systems brought up within the allotted RTO and RPO. This should be completed without access to any systems or services located on infrastructure affected by the scenario you have chosen.

The test should be observed and notes taken on what worked well and what did not. Holding a post-test debrief with the key people involved, even if the test met all targets, is a valuable process that can yield very useful results insofar as learning what can be improved in preparation for next time. Findings from the debrief should be minuted with clear action items for individuals in order to improve plans and work toward a more efficient and seamless process. A more in-depth look at this topic is covered in Chapter 1.

Security Considerations

As with any process, there are security considerations involved with most plans. These can be summarized into a few key categories:

Data at rest

> Many contingency plans require that data from production systems be duplicated and retained at another site. This is true of both warm standbys and traditional backups, for example. It should always be remembered that this data will have controls placed on it in production in line with its value and sensitivity to the organization. For example, it may be encrypted, require two-factor authentication to access, or be restricted to a small group of people. If equal restrictions are not placed on the contingency systems, the original access controls are largely useless. After all, why would an attacker bother trying to defeat two-factor authentication or encryption on a production system when he can simply access a relatively unprotected copy of the same data from a backup system?

Data in transit

In order to replicate data to a secondary system, it will probably have to be transmitted over a network. Data transmitted for the purposes of recovering from or preparing for a disaster should be treated as carefully as any other time the data is transmitted. The appropriate authentication and encryption of data on the network should still be applied.

Patching and configuration management

It is often easy to fall into the trap of backup systems not being maintained in line with the production environment. This runs the risk of leaving poorly patched equipment or vulnerabilities in your environment for an attacker to leverage. In the event of a disaster, these vulnerabilities could be present on what has become your production system. Aside from the security issues, you cannot be sure that systems with differing configuration or patch levels will operate in the same way as their production counterparts.

User access

During a disaster situation there is often a sense of "all hands to the pumps" in order to ensure that production environments are operationally capable as soon as possible. It should be considered that not all data can be accessed by just anybody, particularly if the data is subject to a regulatory compliance regime such as those that protect personally identifiable healthcare or financial data. Any plans should include the continued handling of this type of data in line with established processes and procedures.

Physical security

Often the secondary site may not be physically identical to the primary site. Take, for example, a company for which the primary production environment is housed in a secure third-party facility's managed datacenter, and the disaster location makes use of unused office space in the headquarters. A lower standard of physical access control could place data or systems at risk should an attacker be willing to attempt to physically enter a building by force, subterfuge, or stealth.

Conclusion

There is no one-size-fits-all solution to DR, although there are several well-trodden routes that can be reused where appropriate. One of the most important aspects of DR planning is to work with the business to understand what their requirements are for your DR solution. By aligning your solution with their expectations, it is easy to measure the success or failure of the system.

CHAPTER 8

Industry Compliance Standards and Frameworks

Businesses may be required to conform to one or more regulatory compliance regimes, which are administered by a variety of governing bodies. Failure to comply with these standards can come with heavy fines or in some cases hindering ability to conduct business (such as preventing the capability of processing credit card transactions). Frameworks differ from regulatory compliance standards by the fact that they are not required for a specific industry or type of data; they are more of a guideline.

The requirement to comply with one standard or the next does provide a few benefits to your organization. Certain standards leave significant room for interpretation, giving you the ability to tie security measures that should be implemented to a portion of that same standard. When compliance is involved there are now social, political, and legal components that can be leveraged to implement security controls and process changes that may not have been possible otherwise. It also may present the opportunity to piggyback off another department that has excess budget for a project.

Industry Compliance Standards

Compliance standards are a minimum, not a complete security program. It is easy and lazy to be just a "check box checker" when going through implementing controls in a compliance list, and it's possible to technically be compliant with a standard and still not have a secured environment. Many standards leave room for the imagination and can be interpreted in different ways. However, following common best practices will lead to compliance as a side effect. The majority of standards listed here are from the United States because international organizations have a whole different set of reporting requirements.

Most organizations will have a compliance officer who may not be in the security department because the majority of regulatory standards are not based on the technology behind information security, but as an overall solution to a greater problem. For example, HIPAA is focused on the safety of patients and patient records, no matter if it is on a piece of paper or a piece of technology.

Payment Card Industry Data Security Standard (PCI DSS)

Payment Card Industry Data Security Standard (PCI DSS) is a standard for organizations that store, process, or transmit credit cards and credit card data. PCI DSS is required by the card brands (MasterCard, Visa, Discover, American Express, and JCB) and is administered by the Payment Card Industry Security Standards Council. PCI DSS was created to increase security controls around cardholder data in an attempt to reduce credit card fraud. Failure to validate compliance can result in fines or other penalties, even including the removal of credit card processing capabilities.

PCI DSS regulates cardholder data (CHD). Cardholder data is any personally identifiable information (PII) associated with a person who has a credit or debit card. This includes the primary account number (PAN), cardholder name, expiration date, or service code.

While PCI DSS does have more information in the full document than other standards, if implemented as-is, an environment will still be insecure if environment context is not taken in consideration. For example, this standard doesn't require network segmentation (only recommends it), and permits the transmission of PCI DSS data of wireless protocols. While PCI DSS does specify that wireless requires a certain level of encryption, that practice is still not recommended to use for transmission. Other portions of the standard are very secure and reinforced by this book, such as, "Do not allow unauthorized outbound traffic from the cardholder data environment to the internet" and, "Implement only one primary function per server to prevent functions that require different security levels from co-existing on the same server. (For example, web servers, database servers, and DNS should be implemented on separate servers.)"

Health Insurance Portability & Accountability Act

Health Insurance Portability & Accountability Act (HIPAA) was enacted in 1996 as law and establishes national standards for electronic healthcare records. It includes any organization that stores or processes ePHI (Electronic Protected Health Information) healthcare providers, health plans, and clearinghouses. Thankfully, we start to see a little more definition regarding technology in the verbiage of this act compared to others we'll cover. There are fifty "implementation specifications," divided into administrative, physical, and technical safeguards. Most of these involve having policies and procedures in place. Addressable specifications involve performing a "risk assessment" and then taking steps to mitigate the risks in a way that's appropriate for your organization. One of the largest HIPAA penalties (*https://www.healthit.gov*) against a small organization was levied not because an event occurred, but because the organization failed to address the possibility that it might. Loss of ePHI can cause significant harm to not only the patients whose data has been compromised, but also the provider and individuals at fault as they are required to report violations to the US Department of Health and Human Services (HHS) and the Federal Trade Commission (FTC). They are also the ones who would be on the receiving end of extremely large fines and possibly even jail time. The HHS provides a breakdown of each portion of the security rule portion of HIPAA (*http://bit.ly/2lOj43g*) and assistance with the implementation of the security standards.

Gramm-Leach Bliley Act

Gramm-Leach Bliley Act (GLBA) is a law that was passed in 1999 to reform and modernize the regulations affecting financial institutions. It is comprised of seven titles, and title five (*http://bit.ly/2lOHVDP*) lists the two paragraphs on information security:

> Title V – PRIVACY Subtitle A - Disclosure of Nonpublic Personal Information Section 501 – Protection of Nonpublic Personal Information (a) PRIVACY OBLIGATION POLICY It is the policy of the Congress that each financial institution has an affirmative and continuing obligation to respect the privacy of its customers and to protect the security and confidentiality of those customers' nonpublic personal information. (b) FINANCIAL INSTITUTIONS SAFEGUARDS In furtherance of the policy in subsection (a), each agency or authority described in section 505(a), shall establish appropriate standards for the financial institutions subject to their jurisdiction relating to administrative, technical, and physical safeguards- (1) to insure the security and confidentiality of customer records and information (2) to protect against any anticipated threats or hazards to the security or integrity of such records; and (3) to protect against unauthorized access to or use of such records or information which could result in substantial harm or inconvenience to any customer.

GLBA compliance is mandatory for financial institutions including banks, mortgage brokers, real estate appraisers, debt collectors, insurance companies, and privacy companies. With such a broad and compact section it also leaves a large amount up to interpretation during implementation. However, there are two documents the Interagency Guidelines and the IT Examiners Handbook that were both created to assist with implementing security practices surrounding GLBA compliance.

Family Educational Rights and Privacy Act

Family Educational Rights and Privacy Act (FERPA) is a federal law that protects the privacy of student education records in both public and private schools, as well as in higher education. As this was enacted in 1974 it has no specific information related to technology, which leaves a large area open for interpretation in regards to information security practices and protections needed. It contains phrasing that should be interpreted as the prohibition of releasing or disclosing any PII (Personally Identifiable Information), directory information, or educational information of students to a third party.

PII can only be disclosed if the educational institution obtains the signature of the parent or student (if over 18 years of age) on a document specifically identifying the information to be disclosed, the reason for the disclosure, and the parties to whom the disclosure will be made.

Directory information is defined as "information contained in an education record of a student that would not generally be considered harmful or an invasion of privacy if disclosed"—for example, names, addresses, telephone numbers, and student ID numbers.

Educational records are defined as "records, files, documents, and other materials maintained by an educational agency or institution, or by a person acting for such agency or institution." This includes students transcripts, GPA, grades, Social Security number, and academic and psychological evaluations.

Sarbanes-Oxley Act

Sarbanes-Oxley Act (SOX) is a law enacted in 2002 to set forth security requirements for all US public company boards, management, and public accounting firms. Portions also apply to privately held companies in regards to withholding or destroying information to impede any federal investigations. SOX has 11 sections and was created to ensure corporate corruption and scandals such as Enron and Worldcom don't happen again. Many organizations that have SOX compliance also abide by either the COSO or COBIT frameworks, which we cover later in this chapter.

The two principle sections that relate to security are Section 302 and Section 404:

- Section 302 is intended to safeguard against faulty financial reporting. As part of this section, companies must safeguard their data responsibly so as to ensure that financial reports are not based upon faulty data, tampered data, or data that may be highly inaccurate.

- Section 404 requires the safeguards stated in Section 302 to be externally verifiable by independent auditors, so that independent auditors may disclose to shareholders and the public possible security breaches that affect company finances. Specifically, this section guarantees that the security of data cannot be hidden from auditors, and security breaches must be reported.

SANS has very in-depth documentation on SOX implementation and audits (*http://bit.ly/2lOCDIG*).

Frameworks

Frameworks are different from compliance standards in that they are not a requirement. They are industry- or technology-specific guidelines created to assist in organizing thoughts, practices, and implementations.

Cloud Control Matrix

Cloud Control Matrix (CCM) is a framework built specifically with cloud security in mind by the Cloud Security Alliance (CSA). It assists in tying together specific cloud security concerns and practices to all major compliance standards and frameworks. CSA also has some great workgroups for specific sectors using cloud solutions.

Center for Internet Security

Center for Internet Security (CIS) not only has a framework for assisting with cyber attacks, but also provides benchmarks, workforce development, and other resources such as whitepapers, publications, newsletters, and advisories. It offers in-depth system-hardening guidelines for specific operating systems and applications. CIS also couples with NIST to combine frameworks for the purposes of securing critical infrastructure, and other cross framework and compliance references.

Control Objectives for Information and Related Technologies

Control Objectives for Information and Related Technologies (COBIT) is a high-level framework created by Information Systems Audit and Control Association (ISACA) to assist in creating secure documentation, implementation, and compliance. COBIT is subdivided into four domains—Plan and Organize, Acquire and Implement, Deliver and Support, and Monitor and Evaluate—and aims to align itself with other more detailed standards. While some frameworks are free, COBIT is available for purchase through its website.

The Committee of Sponsoring Organizations of the Treadway Commission

The Committee of Sponsoring Organizations of the Treadway Commission (COSO) is made up of five organizations: the American Accounting Association, American Institute of CPAs, Financial Executives International, The Association of Accountants and Financial Professionals in Business, and The Institute of Internal Auditors. It aims to provide guidance on enterprise risk management, internal control, and fraud deterrence.

ISO-27000 Series

International Organization for Standardization (ISO) is an independent, non-governmental international organization that has created over 20,000 sets of standards across a variety of industries including food services, technology, and agriculture. Out of these frameworks, the 27000 series (*http://www.27000.org*) has been used for the topic of information security, specifically 27001-27006. ISO standards are also a paid framework.

ISO-27001
> Provides requirements for establishing, implementing, maintaining, and continuously improving an Information Security Management System.

ISO-27002
> Establishes guidelines and general principles for initiating, implementing, maintaining, and improving information security management within an organization.

ISO-27003
> Information Security Management System implementation guidance.

ISO-27004
> Provides guidance on the development and use of measures and measurement for the assessment of the effectiveness of an implemented Information Security Management System and controls.

ISO-27005
> Provides guidelines for information security risk management (ISRM) in an organization.

ISO-27006
> Requirements for bodies providing audit and certification of Information Security Management Systems.

NIST CyberSecurity Framework

The National Institute of Standards and Technology operates as part of the United States Department of Commerce, creating standards for many sections of US infrastructure. This framework was created with both industry and government participation, and it consists of standards, guidelines, and practices surrounding critical infrastructure security. The framework uses common industry business drivers to guide and manage risks, protect information, and safeguard the people using the business's services. It consists of three parts: the Framework Core, the Framework Profile, and the Framework Implementation Tiers, which all put a majority focus on risk management.

Regulated Industries

As mentioned previously, some industries are more heavily regulated than others. The basis of these regulations comes from the sensitivity of data and the likelihood of it being stolen and used for malicious purposes. There is a large black market for stolen data that is used for both credit and identity theft. You've already read about the different regulation types; however, certain sectors are regulated strictly—or at least strict regulations are attempted—for legitimate reasons.

Financial

The financial industry includes thousands of institutions, such as banks, investment services, insurance companies, other credit and financing organizations, and the service providers that support them. They can vary widely in size and the amount of data processed, ranging from some of the world's largest global companies with thousands of employees and many billions of dollars in assets, to community banks and credit unions with a small number of employees serving individual communities.

Some of the major risks the financial sector must be concerned with are account take-overs, third-party payment processor breaches, ATM skimming and other Point of Service (POS) vulnerabilities, mobile and internet banking exploitation, and supply chain infiltration. While all of these risks should be taken into account, the Bitglass (*http://bit.ly/2lOLtGt*) security firm 2016 study shows that between 2006 and 2016, the largest percent of breaches in the financial sector can be attributed to lost or stolen devices (25.6%). Other studies have also pointed out that this sector is one of the most common to see outdated legacy systems throughout organizations, giving would-be attackers an easy foothold once access has been gained.

Government

The government, and specifically in this case, the United States government, has pretty much every type of data imaginable to protect. From the large three-letter acronym agencies such as NSA, FBI, IRS, and FDA to smaller local government offices that contract with their own IT guy, there is an extremely broad landscape covered in this one sector. With the fast changing security landscape it has been seen to hinder progress due to the fact that government organizations can vary greatly from commercial businesses with the process length of approving changes and upgrades, ability and willingness to adopt new technology, and overall atmosphere of personnel.

The breadth of information contained within government agencies means a constant stream of high-profile attacks by organized crime, hacktivists, and state-sponsored agents. One of the biggest breaches in 2015 happened to be the government Office of Personnel Management (OPM), which shed some light onto the department's lack of security. The attack was ongoing for an entire year and an estimated 21.5 million records were stolen. Other data breaches included voting records and information, USPS employee information, IRS tax return data, NSA exploits and attack tools used against foreign adversaries, and other highly sensitive and potentially harmful data.

Healthcare

The healthcare industry at this point in time continues to be one of the least secured industries. Healthcare companies saw a rapid change from a majority of paper records to almost fully electronic patient records, and just like the financial sector, it is riddled with out-of-date legacy devices. For a long time the FDA had strict control over the operating system revision and patch level, restricting the ability for medical devices to be upgraded and still maintain FDA approval. This, coupled with the rapid growth and underestimation of the inherent risk of a large quantity of sensitive medical and patient data stored electronically, creates a largely complicated, insecure environment. While the FDA has relaxed its requirements to allow security patches to be applied, software vendors and organizations have yet to keep up and implement best practice security controls.

Both the Department of Health and Human Services' (HHS) Office for Civil Rights (OCR) and attorneys general have the power to issue penalties for the failure of following HIPAA guidelines and as the result of PHI breaches. Not only can they enforce financial penalties, but can also include criminal lawsuits. In just over the first half of 2016 alone, HHS recorded close to $15 million in HIPAA settlement payments. There are several tiers for both financial and criminal penalties:

Financial

- Tier 1: Minimum fine of $100 per violation up to $50,000
- Tier 2: Minimum fine of $1,000 per violation up to $50,000
- Tier 3: Minimum fine of $10,000 per violation up to $50,000
- Tier 4: Minimum fine of $50,000 per violation

Criminal

- Tier 1: Reasonable cause or no knowledge of violation—Up to 1 year in prison
- Tier 2: Obtaining PHI under false pretenses—Up to 5 years in prison
- Tier 3: Obtaining PHI for personal gain or with malicious intent—Up to 10 years in prison

Conclusion

While obtaining compliance might be a necessity no matter what industry you may be in, ensure that it is not the end goal. If compliance is set as an end goal, an organization can lose sight of its overall security and the bigger picture. Working with well-defined frameworks and best practices while keeping a compliance standard in mind remains the most effective way to secure an infrastructure.

CHAPTER 9

Physical Security

Physical security is often dealt with by the facilities department, especially in larger organizations; thus it is often beyond the remit of the information security team. The security team is responsible for identifying and analyzing possible threats and vulnerabilities and recommending appropriate countermeasures to increase the overall security of a department or the organization as a whole. Physical security is often a feature of regulatory compliance regimes and vendor assessment questionnaires, as well as materially impacting the security of the systems and data that you are tasked with protecting. For this reason, at least a high-level understanding of physical security approaches should be attempted. The physical security aspect should be included in any internal assessments, as well as being in scope for penetration tests.

Social engineering remains to this day a very effective way of accessing the inside of a network. It is within our nature to trust others at their word without verification. The goal of physical security is to prevent an attacker from attempting to mitigate these controls. As is the case with other aspects of information security, physical security should be applied as defense in depth. It is broken into two sections: physical and operational. Physical covers the controls like door locks and cameras, while operational covers employee access, visitor access, and training, just as some examples.

In this chapter you will learn how to manage both the physical and operational aspects of physical security within your environment.

Physical

First and foremost, physical security is composed of the physical properties of your environment.

Restrict Access

The most obvious aspect of physical security is restricting access to the premises or portions of the premises. Physical access controls such as door locks and badge systems prevent unauthorized personnel from gaining access to secure areas where they might be able to steal, interfere with, disable, or otherwise harm systems and data. It is recommended that highly sensitive areas be protected with more than one security control, essentially becoming two-factor authentication for physical assets. Controls that are common to choose from are PIN pads, locks, RFID badge readers, biometrics, and security guards.

In addition to physical controls in the building, some physical security precautions can also be taken at every user's desk:

- Ensure that screens are locked whenever users are not at their desk
- Use computer cable locks where appropriate
- Enforce a clear desk policy, utilizing locking document storage

Access to network jacks, telephony jacks, and other potentially sensitive connectors should be restricted where possible. In public or semi-public areas such as lobbies, jacks should not exposed so that the general public, or visitors, can easily access them. As mentioned in more depth in Chapter 14, where possible, jacks should not be left enabled unless equipment has been authorized for use via that specific jack. These precautions reduce the chance of a physical intruder being able to find a live jack without unplugging something and risking raising an alarm.

Printers and printer discard boxes and piles can be a treasure trove of interesting information. Sensitive documents should stored in a locked receptacle prior to shredding, or be shredded right away.

Video Surveillance

Video surveillance, or closed circuit television cameras, can be useful not only for physical security teams to notice and record incidents of tampering or theft of equipment, but additionally when correlated with other evidence such as user logons and badge swipes. This video evidence can sometimes be used to confirm attribution. For example, the use of a particular user account does not necessarily incriminate the account owner, as the credentials could have been stolen. Video footage of the owner standing at the console is much harder to dispute.

Cameras would typically be located at major ingress and egress points, such as a lobby area as well as, or particularly sensitive areas such as server rooms. Cameras located in positions such that they are able to capture the faces of people when they swipe a badge allow correlation of logs with badging systems to determine if stolen or borrowed badges are being used to hide the identity of a criminal. In order to ensure that cameras are not tampered with, they should be placed out of easy reach and preferably, within a tamperproof physical enclosure.

Surveillance or CCTV (closed-circuit television) cameras should be placed pointing at entrance doors to the building, areas of high importance or sensitivity (e.g., a prescription medicine cabinet or server room door), and wherever else a high risk has been identified. Figure 9-1 shows a good example of how *not* to place surveillance cameras.

Figure 9-1. Inefficient surveillance equipment placement

Authentication Maintenance

Can you see what is wrong with Figure 9-2?

Figure 9-2. I'm just going to assume this key code is 3456 and leave it at that (Thanks to @revrance for the image. RIP.)

This reinforces the need to have audits and to not forget that even if something is functional, it may not be secure. Maintenance also includes changes in staff. In the event that a member of staff ceases to be a member of staff, he too should surrender his badge, along with any keys. Any doors or other assets that are fitted with a physical PIN pad should be changed in accordance with that staff member's previous access.

Secure Media

Controls for physically securing media such as USB flash drives, removable hard-drives, and CDs are intended to prevent unauthorized persons from gaining access to sensitive data on any type of media. Sensitive information is susceptible to unauthorized viewing, copying, or scanning if it is unprotected while it is on removable or portable media, printed out, or left on a desk.

If stored in a nonsecured facility, backups that contain this data may easily be lost, stolen, or copied for malicious intent. Periodically reviewing the storage facility enables the organization to address identified security issues in a timely manner, minimizing the potential risk.

Procedures and processes help protect data on media distributed to internal and/or external users. Without such procedures, data can be lost or stolen, or used for fraudulent purposes.

It is important that media be identified such that its classification status can be easily discernible. Media not identified as confidential may not be adequately protected or may be lost or stolen.

Media may be lost or stolen if sent via a nontrackable method, such as regular mail. Use of secure couriers to deliver any media that contains sensitive data allows organizations to use their tracking systems to maintain inventory and location of shipments. Larger organizations may make use of internal courier services that would need their own security briefing related to their specific role in the company.

Without a firm process for ensuring that all media movements are approved before the media is removed from secure areas, it would not be tracked or appropriately protected, and its location would be unknown, leading to potential loss or theft.

Datacenters

It is important to design physical security into the interior of a datacenter. A variety of situations to plan for range from having co-located equipment to contractors needing physical access to the room, but not the equipment. Use rackable equipment so that locking server racks can be utilized. While they can technically still be moved unless bolted to the floor, the lock on the cabinet itself provides an additional layer of protection. Keys for the racks should remain in a central location to be checked out from and not left in the racks themselves or in the datacenter.

Remote offices are sometimes more difficult to secure as important assets may not have a dedicated datacenter, but instead share space with another department, or be tucked away in a closet somewhere. Normally this equipment is not extremely important, but it is still a potential vector of attack. Equipment like office routers, switches, and maybe a read-only domain controller are all common assets to protect. Many times it is just not feasible to have an entire rack for such a small amount of equipment, but having it in a locked equipment enclosure is a great step to take.

Operational

In addition to the physical properties, there are various operational aspects to physical security.

Identify Visitors and Contractors

Being able to differentiate visitors, staff, and contractors is important so that people can quickly determine an approximate level of trust that they can place on a person with whom they are not already familiar. This ability to quickly differentiate staff from visitors, for example, plays a key role in ensuring that sensitive data is not exposed.

Visitor Actions

All visitors should be signed in and out of the premises, and be escorted to and from the reception area, leaving a permanent record of when they were in the building and who they were visiting, in case this information is required at a later date. Not only should a sign-in/sign-out procedure be required, but any action involving technology, equipment, or potential information gathering should require an employee verification of intent.

Contractor Actions

As contractors by nature will have more access than a normal visitor would, they should be properly identified as well. Proper policy and guidelines should be set on who the contractor works through for identification and access. A proper photo ID should match verification from both the contractor's department and the contracting company. As with permanent staff, appropriate vetting should take place. In the case of contractors, this typically means their agency attesting to background checks on all contractors on your behalf.

Badges

Visitors should be issued a badge that is easily distinguishable from a staff badge, typically displaying the word "visitor" and being a different color than a staff or contractor badge. Visitor badges should be restricted to only the duration of the visitor's stay and surrendered when they sign out. There are also badges that will automatically void after a certain time limit, as seen in Figure 9-3.

 Badges are fairly simple to spoof with time and effort. Recon can be completed by someone malicious to attempt to re-create a legitimate badge.

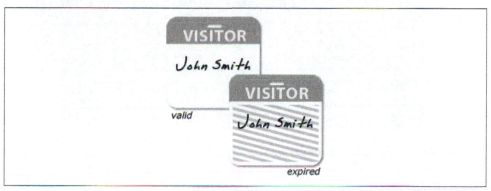

Figure 9-3. Over time some badges will void themselves out

Include Physical Security Training

Employees should not only be trained on the digital aspects of social engineering, but on the physical side as well because these methods can be even trickier to detect. Criminals will often pose as internal personnel, contractors, or as security engineers themselves in order to gain access to POS devices, server rooms, or any other endpoint.

Following are some scenarios and types of potential malicious activities to include in training:

Tailgating
> Employees should be taught that while holding doors open for others is a normal polite response, they should not do this for badge, key, or other restricted access doors. This is an extremely effective way for an unauthorized person to gain access. Often this is one of the more difficult behaviors to address as many companies have positive and people-friendly cultures. Adding signs to reinforce this idea (as seen in Figure 9-4) can be a helpful reminder.

Figure 9-4. Tailgating reminder sign

Badge cloning

RFID keys can easily be cloned with a tool (*http://bit.ly/2lOZJix*) that costs less than $20. As we've recommended elsewhere, highly sensitive areas should be protected with more than one method of authentication. Employees should not allow others to borrow, hold, or "test" their badges at anytime.

Malicious media

While it is recommended that physical communication methods such as USB ports be restricted or disabled and controlled by an endpoint solution, it may not always be possible. In cases where USB ports are enabled and accessible by others, employees should be taught the dangers of this access. Not only can attackers stealthily insert a malicious USB, they may also drop them in public areas with labels such as "Payroll projections 2016" or "Executive Salary Q1," or ask for a document to be printed out. USB drives can be programmed with software to collect information or create reverse shells back to a waiting malicious device, amongst other attacks.

Restricted access

The time and effort to clone a badge isn't needed. Someone can just ask an employee using a predetermined persona and dialogue called a *pretext* to gain access to restricted areas.

Pretexts

Many criminals will try to fool personnel by dressing for the part (for example, carrying tool boxes and dressed in workwear), and could also be knowledgeable about locations of devices. It is important that personnel are trained to follow procedures at all times. Another trick criminals like to use is to send a "new" system with instructions for swapping it with a legitimate system and "returning" the legitimate system to a specified address. The criminals may even provide return postage as they are very keen to get their hands on these devices. Personnel should always verify with a manager or supplier that the device is legitimate, expected, and came from a trusted source before installing it or using it for business.

Conclusion

With the abundance of digital threats that we face day to day, sometimes the old-school physical methods of protection are pushed by the wayside. It is important to keep in mind that the information security team should be actively working with whichever department is in control of physical security to provide feedback on current threats and gaps.

CHAPTER 10

Microsoft Windows Infrastructure

While it may be the bane of every security professional's existence, Microsoft is being used in public and private infrastructures both small and large across the world. It is by far the most in-use operating system and also the most commonly misconfigured. Misconfigurations in Windows operating systems and software contribute to a large amount of security issues and compromises. Exploit Database (*http://bit.ly/2lwTV1C*) currently has over 8,000 exploits running under the Windows platform.

With the staggering amount of verticals that Microsoft currently covers, we will stick to where it comes into play in the enterprise environment and the biggest bang for your buck for security wins. In this chapter we will cover some quick wins such as moving off of older operating systems and turning off open file sharing, as well as in-depth best practices regarding Active Directory, Enhanced Mitigation Experience Toolkit, and Microsoft SQL. Performing these steps significantly decreases the attack surface and detection capabilities (and also might help you sleep better at night).[1]

Quick Wins

There are a few standard no-brainers that we should get out of the way in the beginning.

Upgrade

The first and foremost "quick win" is upgrading endpoints to a supported operating system. While corporations struggle to move off of Windows XP (and shockingly, even older operating systems) the threats keep piling up and the technology forges

---

1 We're not doctors, no guarantee.

on. What makes it that much harder for enterprise environments to make the switch is that many proprietary software packages for different industries were specifically written for XP and Server 2003. Vulnerabilities like MS-08-067, which is an easy remote code execution bug, are still commonly found. Often, situations arise either from a pesky vendor-controlled system or other type of device that leaves you in the unfortunate position of not being able to apply updates. In cases like these the devices should remain off of the network as a matter of policy. If this is not viable, the next secure option would be to have them on private VLANs or an air-gapped network. We cover more on these in Chapter 15.

Another challenge is that security takes a back seat when there is no real communication to stakeholders on the possibility of profit loss. When businesses cling to old technology for whatever reason, their security risk goes up. The lack of support means that you are no longer protected from any new exploits, will not receive fixes for software bugs, or have the ability to take advantage of new features. Paying for prolonged support on defunct technology just delays the inevitable.

Migrating off of a platform that has been in use for such a long period of time has its own costs in the form of many different software upgrades, data migration, and even possibly having to switch to new vendors. However, remaining on an unsupported and outdated version presents the inherent risk of data loss, network outages, breaches, and/or fines. It's difficult to show the full cost of impact prior to these actually happening. As shown in Figure 10-1, XP users are down almost a full 6% in the last year, still holding on at almost 11% market share, even though support ended in April 2014.

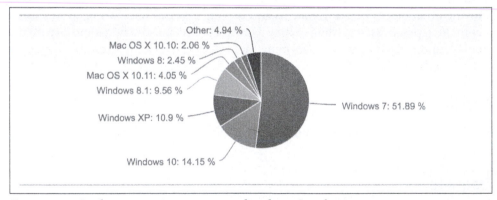

Figure 10-1. Desktop operating system market share Q1 of 2016

Third-Party Patches

Surprisingly, another commonly overlooked protection is some type of software update platform. Windows Server Update Services (WSUS), System Center Configuration Manager (SCCM), and other third-party applications can keep the endpoints up-to-date with the latest security patches. Not only should you worry about regular Windows system patches, but there should also be a focus on outdated versions of commonly exploited software such as Java, Adobe Reader, Firefox, and others that are currently in use.

During the asset management process you will have determined what software exists in the environment. You should also ask yourself if it really needs to be there. Do all endpoints really need Adobe Flash? (Hint: no, they don't.)

Open Shares

Open shares can cause all kinds of security problems. From saved credentials and trade secrets to PII and other sensitive data, file shares can house some extremely important assets. This nmap command should be run on a regular basis to alert on any new open shares (line breaks added for readability):

```
nmap -T4 -v -oA myshares --script smb-enum-shares –script-args
smbuser=MyUserHere,smbpass=MyPassHere -p445 192.168.0.1-255
&& cat myshares.nmap|grep '|\|192'|awk '/[0-9]+\.[0-9]+\.[0-9]+\.
[0-9]+/ { line=$0 } /\|/ { $0 = line $0}1'|grep \||grep -v -E
'(smb-enum-shares|access: <none>|ADMIN\$|C\$|IPC\$|U\$|access: READ)
'|awk '{ sub(/Nmap scan report for /, ""); print }' >> sharelist.txt
```

This can also be accomplished by using PowerShell:

```
$servers = get-content c:\temp\servers.txt
#Provide an account that has rights to enumerate the shares
$cred = get-credential
get-wmiobject Win32_Share -computer $servers -credential $cred |
select __server,name,description,path | export-csv
c:\temp\sharereport.csv -notype
```

Active Directory Domain Services

Active Directory Domain Services (AD DS) is a large part of the foundation of many infrastructure designs. It is a main building block and is relied upon for many things, including authentication, permissions, and asset identification:

> AD DS provides a distributed database that stores and manages information about network resources and application-specific data from directory-enabled applications. Administrators can use AD DS to organize elements of a network, such as users, computers, and other devices, into a hierarchical containment structure. The hierarchical containment structure includes the Active Directory forest, domains in the forest, and organizational units (OUs) in each domain.
>
> —Microsoft Technet

While the structure alone should not be solely relied upon for AD security, it can be used as a good aid and to provide a commonsense structure. Being able to grow and adapt this structure as the organization grows and modifies is essential to prevent the restructuring and redesigning of the layout. From here, we can take a top-down approach to designing the security around the forest.

Forest

> The forest acts as a security boundary for an organization and defines the scope of authority for administrators.
>
> —Microsoft Technet

While many organizations will have one forest with only one domain, there are also environments with large footprints that may have gone through many acquisitions of smaller companies (see Figure 10-2). This can make it difficult to balance the possibly large number of forests that may or may not have security access between other forests or domains.

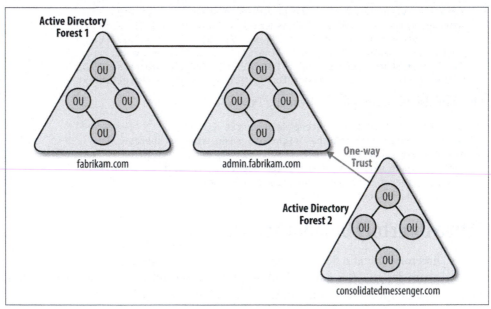

Figure 10-2. A forest can be a collection of domains or a single domain

Cross Domain and Forest Trusts, while helpful, can weaken the security between organizational containers by allowing authentication between resources. They should only be used when the proper stakeholders have recognized the risk associated with them.

The risks surrounding trusts are in the authentication ability from one domain or forest to another. For example, a malicious user with administrative credentials who is located in a trusted forest could monitor network authentication requests from the trusting forest to obtain the security ID (SID) information of a user who has full access to resources in the trusting forest, such as a domain or enterprise administrator. These risks can be mitigated with both SID filtering and selective authentication (*http://bit.ly/2lwZZaD*). Controlling authentication in this way provides an extra layer of protection to shared resources by preventing them from being randomly accessed by any authenticated user in the trusted distributed user forests. Now if one of these user forests is attacked and requires a rebuild, the entire trusting forest won't have to be rebuilt from the ground up.

Domain

Domains should never be considered a security boundary. Any level domain account can query the Active Directory database (*ntds.dit*), which is located on any DC. The functionality exists to pull down the entire structure with everything in it, from computer names to administrator roles, to service accounts. The domain should be used purely as a structural container.

Domain Controllers

What happens if someone steals one of my domain controllers?

There is only one correct answer:

You flatten and then rebuild the entire forest.

—Microsoft TechNet (*http://bit.ly/2lwOxMc*)

Domain controllers are the building blocks of Active Directory Domain Services. They house the Flexible Single Master Operation (FSMO) roles that control the different moving parts that make a domain work. They can be the keys to the castle and should be ferociously guarded.

FSMO roles are the seven special roles that domain controllers can be configured as. The layout of a domain and how many forests there are will dictate where the FSMO roles are best placed. The roles include PDC Emulator, RID Master, Schema Master, Domain Naming Master, Infrastructure Master, Domain DNS Zone Master, and Forest DNS Zone Master. There is also a role called a Global Catalog (GC) that, while not an FSMO role, will still play a part in determining placement of them. There are a few standard rules to abide by to ensure they are placed properly:

Rule 1: The PDC Emulator and RID Master roles should be on the same server by themselves. The PDC Emulator is a large consumer of RIDs and is heavily utilized.

Rule 2: The Infrastructure Master should not be placed on a GC unless there is only one forest or unless every DC in the forest has a GC.

Rule 3: The Schema Master and Domain Naming Master should be on the same server, which should also be a GC.

By default, all roles are placed on the first promoted DC in the forest and can be migrated to additional DCs as they are created.

 At no point in time should a domain controller be a dual-purpose server, be easily accessible, or be treated like a standard workstation.

In datacenters, physical domain controllers should be installed in dedicated secure racks or cages that are separate from the general server population. When possible, domain controllers should be configured with Trusted Platform Module (TPM) chips and all volumes in the domain controller servers should be protected with some type of drive encryption (*http://bit.ly/2lwL7Zv*).

Remote domain controllers can be set up as read-only with only certain parts of the AD structure being replicated. While it may be less likely that you would have an entire server rack dedicated to an offsite DC, there are other options you can take, such as a small form factor server placed inside a locked cage, with the cage somehow bolted into the ground. While it may seem like overkill, many times we've seen DCs sitting in broom closets or break rooms.

OUs

Organizational Units (OUs) can be used for the purpose of delegating rights/permissions to perform certain actions to the objects located in it as well as implementing a well thought-out structure for Group Policy Objects (GPOs).

Groups

There are strict guidelines for what AD groups are and are not used for, because the nesting and assigning of groups can get quite messy. To properly prepare and implement these groups, you should adhere to the following practices:

- Place users into global groups
- Place global groups into domain local groups
- Place domain local groups on the access control lists of the data stored on the servers

If there are multiple domains and universal groups are desired:

- Place global groups containing users into universal groups
- Place universal groups into the domain local groups
- Place domain local groups on the access control lists

In addition to the security benefits of proper user nesting, following this standard can save a significant amount of hassle. When users leave the organization for any reason and their accounts are subsequently deleted, you won't end up with unresolved SIDs all over the place. If you are working through the issue of cleaning this up in your organization, Microsoft has a wonderful tool called SID Walker (*http://bit.ly/2lx1LbI*) that can assist in removing old unresolved SIDs across the network.

Accounts

One of the largest hurdles companies can face is the massive amount of user accounts that are members of the Domain Administrator's Built-In group (or any other type of admin-level group). It is in the best interests of the design and security of the organization to do ample research on each application's access permissions. If you are lucky enough to build a domain from the ground up it is significantly easier, while retroactively performing it is significantly more work. Working with application analysts and vendors on file access, processes, and services will allow only the necessary permissions to be delegated at both an endpoint and server level. This can be accomplished with a variety of tools such as the Microsoft SysInternals Suite, Wireshark, system logs, and application logs.

Many data stakeholders, server administrators, and other high-level access staff may request Domain Admin–level access because honestly, when it's used the application being installed or the task being performed just works. There is no need to know what files are being modified, what is being accessed, or what tasks are being performed when it's just allowed by default by giving the highest access available.

The use of service accounts is highly recommended. Service accounts are just that, accounts that are strictly used for controlling services and will never perform interactive logons. Keep a standard naming convention for these accounts, such as "service-txvbserver-mssql," to allow ease of monitoring and alerting.

Local Administrator Password Solution (LAPS) (*http://bit.ly/2lwLjrQ*) is a free software from Microsoft that will perform random password allocations to local administrator accounts. This provides another added layer of security, making it difficult for an attacker to perform lateral movements from one device to the next.

 A second design flaw to stay away from (or move away from) would be the use of shared user accounts. Shared accounts give zero accountability and can be a security auditing nightmare.

Group Policy Objects

Group Policy Objects (GPOs) are used to centrally manage hardware and software settings in a domain configuration. They are broken up into both local and domain policies and can be applied to specific accounts or containers in a certain order to see differing results. GPOs can be a full-time job to maintain in some domains. With the massive amount of available settings, it can become a hassle and extremely complicated to keep track of them.

It's one of the less glamorous jobs and sometimes is left alone as long as it's somewhat working. Knowing and being able to plot out the order of operations for GPO processing, as well as a deep dive into each policy and setting, can not only improve the security of an organization, but speed up login times as well. While we won't cover much when it comes to the actual design of the AD structure, there are many suitable resources (*http://bit.ly/2lwWelw*) for best practice structure guides.

Instead of starting from scratch attempting to build a secure GPO by going through each individual setting, there are fully configured templates available for use. National Institute of Science and Technology, or NIST (*http://bit.ly/2lwSwrM*), has a secure base set of GPOs that can be downloaded off of its website. A great first step for any organization would be to include these on any base image in the local policy. This will give the added benefit of a standard set of security settings if a computer is either taken off of the domain or somehow not added to it.

The NIST GPOs contain settings such as a standard password security requirements, disabling LM hashes for domain account passwords, disabling the local guest account, and preventing cached user credentials, as well as hundreds of other user and computer settings. They can be found well-laid out and documented on the website, along with the downloads and revision history.

Going one step further, the hands of server and desktop administrators can be forced to follow proper process while performing new installs. While it is not possible to create a GPO linked to the default Computers or Users OU in Active Directory, it is possible to force all newly created accounts to whatever OU makes the most sense. This gives the ability to only allow certain functions that will prompt the helpdesk or other administrator to move the account to the correct location. With a simple command running in an elevated PowerShell session, all of the computers that are joined to the domain will automatically end up in the OU of your choosing. Now this gives the ability to control the new default location of these accounts:

```
redircmp "OU=BOBSTEAM,OU=ALLTHEHACKERS,DC=YAYBLUETEAM,DC=local"
```

EMET

So first things first. A little explanation of the Enhanced Mitigation Experience Toolkit (EMET) from Microsoft straight from its website (*http://bit.ly/2nj7Rt6*):

> The Enhanced Mitigation Experience Toolkit (EMET) is a utility that helps prevent vulnerabilities in software from being successfully exploited. EMET achieves this goal by using security mitigation technologies. These technologies function as special protections and obstacles that an exploit author must defeat to exploit software vulnerabilities. These security mitigation technologies do not guarantee that vulnerabilities cannot be exploited. However, they work to make exploitation as difficult as possible to perform.

EMET works by injecting an *EMET.dll* into running executables to provide memory-level protections and mitigations against common exploit techniques. Nothing is perfect—several individuals have demonstrated how to circumvent EMET; however, it does become much more difficult and has to be built into the exploit.

EMET Bypass

Depending on the version of EMET running, it can be bypassed in several ways. For example, prior to the patch in EMET 5.5, there exists a portion of code within EMET that is responsible for unloading EMET (*http://bit.ly/2lwWz7v*). The code systematically disables EMET's protections and returns the program to its previously unprotected state. One simply needs to locate and call this function to completely disable EMET. In *EMET.dll* v5.2.0.1, this function is located at offset 0x65813. Jumping to this function results in subsequent calls, which remove EMET's installed hooks.

If you are new to EMET, you first need to install it (*http://bit.ly/2lwQV5D*), baseline your applications, and create templates for which types of applications will be covered within it. The big misconception for large organizations is that deploying EMET will break everything. The truth of the matter is that EMET only protects what is specified, tested, and configured within the configuration profile (XML). Applications need to be specifically configured to be protected under EMET.

EMET Support

Microsoft has decided to only support EMET until July 2018, as a majority of its controls are automatically included into newer operating systems. However, we still recommend installing it on Windows endpoints at this time.

Basic Configuration

Once the installation is complete, you should notice an icon on the bottom right of your screen that looks like a lock:

Double-click the lock icon, and the default interface for EMET 5.1 will be displayed, as shown in Figure 10-3.

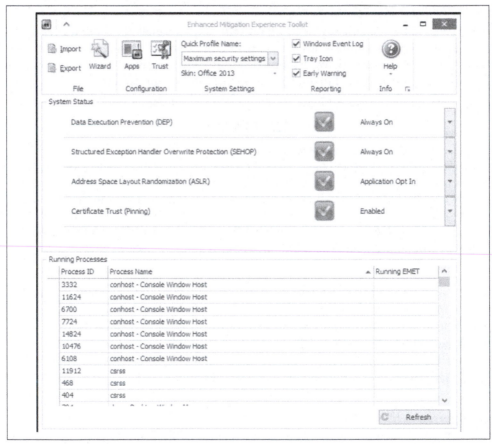

Figure 10-3. EMET 5.1 interface

The lower section of "Running Processes" contains the applications that are currently protected by EMET. By default, EMET will protect common applications such as Java, Adobe, and Internet Explorer. It does not, however, protect anything that is not specified other than these common applications. Since we previously specified "Use Recommended Settings," it will select the default applications just mentioned.

A protected application would have a green check mark under "Running EMET" on the lower righthand side.

Since EMET works by injecting a DLL into the executables memory space, whenever we configure any new process to be protected by EMET, it will require us to close the application or service and restart it. It does not require a full restart, just the services or applications themselves.

In the System Status section of EMET, ensure that DEP is set to Always On, SEHOP to Always On, and ASLR to Application Opt In. The next is certificate trust pinning, which checks certificate security. This setting can be troublesome when deployed to common workstations and endpoints due to the fact that the certificate management field in most of the internet is extremely messed up. This will typically trigger alerts for the end user and cause confusion. You may want to disable this feature for endpoints.

In the top middle of the screen, we recommend configuring the settings for the Quick Profile Name field to Maximum Security Settings.

Next, select the Apps button on the top middle left to open the application window, as shown in Figure 10-4.

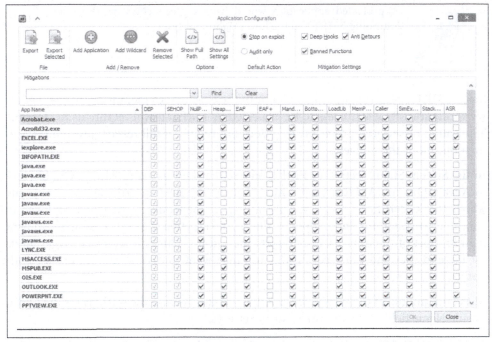

Figure 10-4. EMET 5.1 application configuration

On the top left, ensure that Deep Hooks, Anti Detours, and Banned Functions are selected. These should all be highlighted as these are default configurations of EMET 5.x. Also ensure "Stop on exploit" is selected. The only time you need to deploy "Audit only" is when initial testing is being done and you are experiencing application crashes. EMET will notify you when it blocks something from running versus actually stopping it. The protections can then be fine-tuned to not block a certain protection for normal application functionality.

Custom Configuration

Enterprise users and tech-savvy folks will want to incorporate additional applications for added protection. This is highly recommended for enterprise deployments as it provides uniform configuration. If templates are being created, they should be broken up into two separate categories, one for servers and another for workstations/endpoints.

To add a new application, you can simply select "Add Application" and point EMET to an executable you want protected. Protection mechanisms can be broken up as follows:

Client-side attacks

Applications that can be used against a workstation or server that can be leveraged for remote code execution (RCE). These are typically third-party applications that accept some form of input, whether it's a file or commands. For example, Foxit Software is a PDF reader commonly used as a replacement for Adobe.

Server/service attacks

These are categorized as services, ports, and protocols that could be subject to attack. A little bit of caution is required here because Microsoft's stance has been to protect mostly client-side attacks from exploitation. However, common services are also frequently attacked. EMET can be deployed on services in order to add additional protection. A common deployment scenario that we typically see is placing EMET over IIS, SMTP (transport), RDP, SMB, RPC, and other commonly attacked services.

 Please note that this is not a recommended practice from Microsoft. However, we haven't seen any compatibility issues in our experience by placing EMET on these services.

Once you have determined what applications to add, there's another section that makes it super simple to configure common services that are already running. Exit out of the apps menu and go back to the original EMET home screen. Under the section "Running Processes" is a list of all processes running on the current system. Skim through the processes and identify the services you want to protect. Simply right-click the executable process and select Configure Process. This will automatically add EMET to the applications list for protection.

Enterprise Deployment Strategies

For enterprise users, there are two main deployment methods that work successfully for both small and large organizations. The first is handling configuration changes through patch management software, such as System Center Configuration Manager (SCCM). Changes can be made to the template and the XML pushed to each system through SCCM, when changes are needed for compatibility or enhancements. EMET can also be managed through group policy; however, the group policy settings are limited in nature and do not have the same granularity as utilizing the XML deployment methods.

One major catch is also creating a scheduled task to perform an `EMET_Conf -refresh` upon logon to ensure the latest policies are pushed when a new user logs in to her machine.

The second method, which is a more resilient option, is to automatically refresh EMET policies via a scheduled task and a remote file share. In this case, EMET would be configured completely, tested with a pristine XML, and then exported. This can be done either through the GUI or from inside the EMET directory. The command to run is:

```
EMET_Conf.exe -export EMET_Endpoint_Profile.xml
```

The template will now be exported appropriately. Either select a current GPO from the environment or create a new one for this purpose. Select properties on the GPO, grab the Unique GUID, and document the number (looks something like {343423423-32423432-324324-324-32432}).

Next, go to the sysvol share on a domain controller and navigate to *sysvol\domain \Policies\{my-gpo-guid}*.

Place the *EMET_Endpoint_Profile.xml* file under that group policy object.

Now that you have your profile here, whenever you need to make changes just replace the XML file in this location (either for endpoint or server or both).

> The XML profile name must remain the same since we will be creating a scheduled task that calls the specific file.

Since this is a sysvol share, anyone that is a part of the domain users group will have access to this group policy object and file in order to import it eventually into EMET.

We now need to add a scheduled task to group policy. There are two different options: the first is creating a scheduled task upon logon (the most common deployment) and the other second is having it run at certain intervals (say, every hour). Under the group policy that has been selected, navigate to Computer configuration→Preferences→Control Panel Settings→Scheduled Tasks, and select New Scheduled Task, as shown in Figure 10-5.

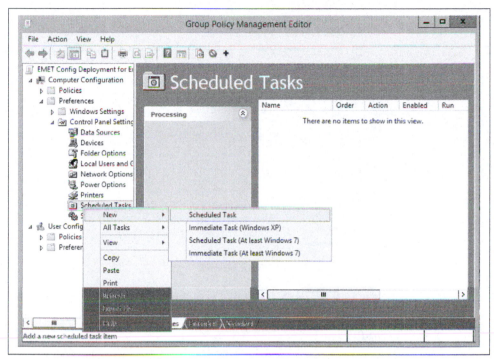

Figure 10-5. Adding a scheduled task

Select a name (in this case, we used "EMET Update"), navigate to the EMET 5.1 program files directory, and select the "EMET_Conf.exe" executable. For arguments, use the --import flag with EMET, which will import the XML file and select your domain controller to pull the group policy from. In this case we used the example of "serverdc1" and provided the path to our GPO, and pointed to the *EMET_Endpoint-Profile.xml* that was just created (see Figure 10-6).

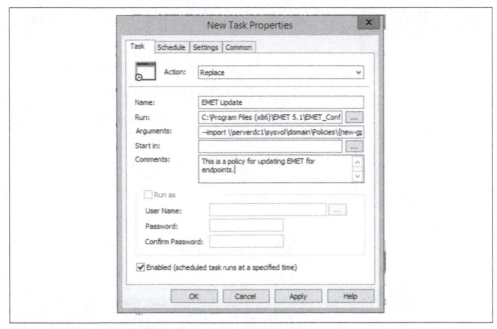

Figure 10-6. New scheduled task

You can also specify when to run this XML file: upon logon, daily, hourly, weekly, or whatever your personal preferences are.

There will now be a scheduled task and whenever the XML file is replaced in that group policy folder it will automatically refresh to the user population without the need to deploy additional packages companywide through something like SCCM.

MS-SQL Server

SQL Servers can be a very easy target for attackers if not configured and patched properly. A wide variety of tools and methods provide privilege escalation and access to database information. In later chapters we will cover certain ways to implement security by obscurity as additional protection, as well as a type of "canary in the coal mine" type of honeypot that will also aid in the overall security monitoring.

When Third-Party Vendors Have Access

It is a common practice to give vendors support access to the database or database server that they support. Some security considerations that are vendor-specific are:

- Require the vendors to use SQL Server's native security instead of one predefined account for all user connections. When only one user account accesses the data, accountability is lost.

- When new applications are purchased, ensure that clients will not be connected to the SQL Server using a login and password stored in a connection string.

- Audit vendor configurations when new applications are purchased.

- Ensure that the vendor does not store unencrypted logins and passwords required by the application in *.sql* files, *.xml* files, *.cfg* files, *.ini* files, or record them in *.log* files.

- Ensure the authentication and activity of vendor accounts are monitored, as well as disabled when not in use.

- Do not allow the vendor to control/use the SA login. A vendor should not require the SA login for equipment that your organization owns.

- Do not store SQL logins and passwords unencrypted in plain text files of any kind.

MS SQL Authentication

SQL Server supports two authentication modes. The mode is selected during installation, but can also be changed later. When authentication modes are changed, all client connections will also need to be changed to the new mode in order for the server to remain operational. The security mode required is determined by the type of client connections used with the application databases on the SQL Server. If all client applications support trusted connections, use Windows Authentication mode. If some clients do not support trusted connections, use Mixed mode:

Windows Authentication mode
> This method relies solely on Windows authentication of the login. Connections using this mode are known as trusted connections. This is the most secure mode, as it does not send logins and passwords over the network unencrypted. Use Windows Authentication mode whenever possible. When Windows Authentication is enabled, Windows credentials are trusted to log on to SQL Server and passwords are not passed across the network during authentication.

Mixed Authentication mode
> Logins can be authenticated by Windows Authentication or by SQL Server Authentication. Mixed mode is available for backward compatibility with legacy systems. In order to access data from a SQL Server database, a user must pass through two stages of authentication—first at the SQL Server level using a SQL login and then at the database level using a database user.

SA User Security

SA is the built-in system administrator account that exists on every MS SQL Server. Because it is well-known and has full rights on the SQL Server, it is often targeted by malicious people. The SA login cannot be deleted. The SA login can be renamed, but that doesn't change its SID (which is always 0x01) and it can still be found. Members of the sysadmin fixed server role have complete control of the SQL Server.

Some general SQL authentication best practices are:

- Have a strong password (as required by the SQL install).
- Limit the number of logins with sysadmin privileges.
- The service account running MS SQL needs to be a sysadmin with a strong password.
- Always run SQL Server services by using the lowest possible user rights, such as a minimally privileged domain account. Many server-to-server activities can be performed only by a domain user account. Avoid granting additional permissions to this account.
- Never connect clients to the database using the SA account in any connection string, ODBC connection, OLE initialization file, etc. This includes interfaces and report writers. Use the least powerful login possible.
- Never store the SA password in a file of any kind other than password safe. No sysadmin password should ever be stored.
- Avoid using the SA login; pull it out for emergencies only.

If Windows Authentication is being used, the SA account is disabled.

Enable it, assign a strong password, disable it again, and set up monitoring of any account activity surrounding its use. Why? A malicious person can easily change the server to Mixed Authentication mode by updating the registry and restarting the SQL service. They then have the ability to change the SA password to one of their choosing.

To change this setting in SQL Server Management Studio, right-click the server and select Properties→Security page. Under Server Authentication, click the radio button for SQL Server and Windows Authentication mode, enter and confirm a strong password, and click OK to save the change. Following this step, go back to the security page and set the authentication mode back to Windows Authentication and click OK to save.

Conclusion

There are countless configuration possibilities across all Microsoft products, however we hope that this will at least cover the low-hanging fruit and give you the ability to tackle the next hurdle in the environment. A great number of commonly scripted offensive attack scenarios can be mitigated by creating a structured and least privileged Microsoft environment. While Microsoft products can be the bulk of an enterprise organization, it is far from the only operating system that you need to consider. We will also cover Linux and Mac operating systems in later chapters.

CHAPTER 11

Unix Application Servers

Application servers are an obvious target for an attacker. They are often a central repository for all manner of data, be it authentication credentials, intellectual property, or financial data. Being so data rich provides an obvious point for a financially motivated attacker to monetize his attack, and for a politically motivated attacker to steal, destroy, or corrupt data.

Of course in a system architected to have many tiers, application servers may not contain data; however, they will contain application code and serve as an ideal pivot point to other systems. They are typically connected to other systems, such as databases, which places a target on the application servers.

For these reasons we should seek to ensure that the servers are built both to perform their desired function with specification and to withstand an attack.

It is always recommended that the infrastructure surrounding an application be configured to defend the server from attack. However, ensuring that a server is as well-defended as possible in its own right is also strongly advised. This way, in the event that any other defensive countermeasures fail or are bypassed—for example, by an attacker using lateral movement from within the infrastructure—the server is still defended as well as is sensibly possible.

The essentials for Windows-based platforms have already been described in Chapter 1, so this chapter will focus on Unix platforms such as Linux, FreeBSD, and Solaris.

The topics covered in this chapter, Unix patch management and operating system hardening principles, are discussed in a deliberately general fashion. Securing Unix application servers, as with most chapters in this book, could be a book unto itself. In order to remain agnostic to the flavor of Unix being used, the topics discussed are deliberately those that are common to most Unix flavors. If you wish to take further precautions and implement features that are common to only a specific few versions, it is certainly worth consulting guides that are specifically written for your operating system.

Keeping Up-to-Date

One of the most effective and yet overlooked aspects of managing Unix servers is patch management. A large number of vulnerabilities in Unix environments occurs either as a result of bugs in software that is installed on a system or bugs in the system itself. Thus many vulnerabilities in an environment can often be remediated purely by keeping a system patched and up-to-date.

Third-Party Software Updates

Unlike Microsoft environments, Unix-based environments typically use a system of package management to install the majority of third-party applications.

Package management and update tools vary depending not only on which flavor of Unix you are running, but also differ depending on distribution you use. For example, Debian Linux and SUSE Linux use two different package management systems, and FreeBSD uses another.

Despite the differences, there are common themes surrounding the package management systems. Typically, each host will hold a repository of packages that are available to install on the system via local tools. The system administrator issues commands to the package management system to indicate that she wishes to install, update, or remove packages. The package management system will, depending on configuration, either download and compile, or download a binary of the desired package and its dependencies (libraries and other applications required to run the desired application), and install them on the system.

The various package management systems are so comprehensive in a modern distribution that for many environments it would be unusual to require anything further. Deploying software via package management, as opposed to downloading from elsewhere, is the preference unless there is a compelling reason to do otherwise. This greatly simplifies the issue of staying up-to-date and tracking dependencies.

The same package management system can be used to perform upgrades. As the repository of available packages is updated, new versions of already installed packages appear in the package database. These new version numbers can be compared against the installed version numbers and a list of applications due for an upgrade to a new version can determined automatically, typically via a single command line.

This ease of upgrade using package management means that unless a robust system of checking for and applying changes is in place for installed applications, the package management system should be used to provide an easy, automated method of updating all packages on Unix application servers. Not only does this remove the need to manually track each application installed on the application servers, along with all their associated dependencies, but it (typically) means that it has already been tested and confirmed to work on that distribution. Of course, individual quirks between systems mean that you cannot be sure that everything will always work smoothly, and so the testing process should remain. However, the testing process may be entered with a good degree of confidence.

To illustrate how this typically works, let's take a look at the Debian Linux method of patching. First, we can update the repository via a single command; in the case of Debian, `apt-get` with the argument update:

```
$ sudo apt-get update
Get:1 http://security.debian.org wheezy/updates Release.gpg [1,554 B]
Get:2 http://security.debian.org wheezy/updates Release [102 kB]
Get:3 http://security.debian.org wheezy/updates/main amd64 Packages [347 kB]
Get:4 http://ftp.us.debian.org wheezy Release.gpg [2,373 B]
Get:5 http://security.debian.org wheezy/updates/main Translation-en [202 kB]
Get:6 http://ftp.us.debian.org unstable Release.gpg [1,554 B]
Get:7 http://ftp.us.debian.org wheezy Release [191 kB]
Get:8 http://ftp.us.debian.org unstable Release [192 kB]
Get:9 http://ftp.us.debian.org wheezy/main amd64 Packages [5,838 kB]
Get:10 http://ftp.us.debian.org wheezy/main Translation-en [3,846 kB]
Get:11 http://ftp.us.debian.org unstable/main amd64 Packages/DiffIndex [27.9 kB]
Get:12 http://ftp.us.debian.org unstable/non-free amd64 Packages/DiffIndex [23B]
Get:13 http://ftp.us.debian.org unstable/contrib amd64 Packages/DiffIndex [102B]
Get:14 http://ftp.us.debian.org unstable/contrib Translation-en/DiffIndex [78B]
Get:15 http://ftp.us.debian.org unstable/main Translation-en/DiffIndex [27.9 kB]
Get:16 http://ftp.us.debian.org unstable/non-free Translation-en/DiffIndex [93B]
Get:17 http://ftp.us.debian.org unstable/contrib Translation-en [48.7 kB]
Get:18 http://ftp.us.debian.org unstable/main Translation-en [5,367 kB]
Get:19 http://ftp.us.debian.org unstable/non-free Translation-en [81.3 kB]
Get:20 http://ftp.us.debian.org unstable/main amd64 Packages [7,079 kB]
Get:21 http://ftp.us.debian.org unstable/non-free amd64 Packages [79.2 kB]
Get:22 http://ftp.us.debian.org unstable/contrib amd64 Packages [53.5 kB]
Fetched 23.5 MB in 13s (1,777 kB/s)
```

Now that the repository is up-to-date we can use the `apt-get` command once again, this time with the argument upgrade, to perform upgrades on any packages that have newer versions available than the one that is currently installed:

```
$ sudo apt-get upgrade
Reading package lists... Done
Building dependency tree
Reading state information... Done
The following packages will be upgraded:
  package-1 package-5
2 upgraded, 0 newly installed, 0 to remove and 256 not upgraded.
Need to get 4.0 MB of archives.
After this operation, 1,149 kB of additional disk space will be used.
```

```
Do you want to continue [Y/n]?
```

Here we can see that the system administrator is told that the example packages "package-1" and "package-5" will be installed. If she selects yes, the system will automatically build and install those packages.

Although this example uses Debian, the process is almost identical across most Unix systems and is covered in the base documentation for every system that we have seen.

Sometimes applications need to be installed outside of the package management system. This can be because it is not included in the package management system, or your organization has particular build and deployment requirements that require a custom build. If this is the case, it is recommended that someone be tasked with monitoring both the new releases of the application and its security mailing. Subscribing to these lists should provide notification of any vulnerabilities that have been discovered, as vulnerabilites in these applications will not be covered by updates addressed automatically by the package management system.

Core Operating System Updates

Many, but not all, Unix systems have a delineation between the operating system and applications that are installed on it. As such, the method of keeping the operating system itself up-to-date will often differ from that of the applications. The method of upgrading will vary from operating system to operating system, but the upgrade methods fall into two broad buckets:

Binary update
    Commercial operating systems particularly favor the method of applying a binary update; that is, distributing precompiled binary executables and libraries that are copied to disk, replacing the previous versions. Binary updates cannot make use of custom compiler options and make assumptions about dependencies, but they require less work in general and are fast to install.

Update from source
    Many open source operating systems favor updates from source, meaning that they are compiled locally from a copy of the source code and previous versions on disk are replaced by these binaries. Updating from source takes more time and is more complex, however the operating system can include custom compiler optimizations and patches.

There are many debates over which system is better, and each has its pros and cons. For the purposes of this book, however, we will assume that you are sticking with the default of your operating system as the majority of arguments center around topics unrelated to security.

Updates to the operating system are typically less frequent than updates to third-party software. Additionally, they are more disruptive, as they typically require a reboot because they often involve an update to the kernel or other subsystems that only load at startup, unlike application updates, which can be instantiated via the restart of the appropriate daemon. Core operating updates are advisable, though as vulnerabilities are often found within both operating systems and applications.

As with any other patch of this nature, it is advisable to have a rollback plan in place for any large update such as one for an operating system. In the case of virtualized infrastructure, this can be achieved simply by taking a snapshot of the filesystem prior to upgrade; thus a failed upgrade can be simply rolled back by reverting to the last snapshot. In physical infrastructure this can be more problematic, but most operating systems have mechanisms to cope with this issue, typically by storing a copy of the old binaries and replacing them if required.

Nevertheless, patches to the operating system are often required in order to close security gaps, so you should have a process defined to cope with this. As with applications, the effort to upgrade the operating system is lower the more up-to-date a system already is, so we recommend remaining as current as is reasonable, leaving only small increments to update at any one time.

Hardening a Unix Application Server

The next area to discuss is that of hardening the servers. This is the art of making the most secure configuration possible, without compromising the ability of the system to perform its primary business functions.

This can be a particularly difficult balancing act as restricting access to user and processes must be tempered with the fact that the server must still perform its primary function properly and system administrators must still be able to access the system to perform their duties.

Disable services

Every service (daemon) that runs is executing code on the server. If there is a vulnerability within that code, it is a potential weakness that can be leveraged by an attacker; it is also consuming resources in the form of RAM and CPU cycles.

Many operating systems ship with a number of services enabled by default, many of which you may not use. These services should be disabled to reduce the attack surface on your servers. Of course you should not just start disabling services with reckless abandon—before disabling a service, it is prudent to ascertain exactly what it does and determine if you require it.

There are a number of ways to ascertain which services are running on a Unix system, the easiest of which is to use the ps command to list running services. Exact argument syntax can vary between versions, but the `ps ax` syntax works on most systems and will list all currently running processes. For minor variations in syntax on your operating system, check the manual page for `ps` using the command `man ps`.

Services should be disabled in startup scripts (rc or init, depending on operating system) unless your system uses systemd, in which case you can refer to the following discussion on systemd. Using the `kill` command will merely stop the currently running service, which will start once more during a reboot. On Linux the commands are typically one of: `rc-update`, `update-rc.d`, or `service`. On BSD-based systems, you typically edit the file */etc/rc.conf*. For example, on several flavors of Linux the `service` command can be used to stop the `sshd` service:

```
service sshd stop
```

To start `sshd` (one time):

```
service start sshd
```

And to disable it from starting after a reboot:

```
update-rc.d -f sshd remove
```

Some Linux distributions have moved toward using `systemd` as opposed to SysV startup scripts to manage services. `systemd` can be used to perform other administrative functions with regards to services, such as reloading configuration and displaying dependancy information. To stop `sshd` (one time):

```
systemctl stop sshd
```

To enable `sshd` upon every reboot:

```
systemctl enable sshd
```

And to disable `sshd` upon further reboots:

```
systemctl disable sshd
```

Older Unix operating systems may use `inetd` or `xinetd` to manage services rather than rc or init scripts. `(x)inetd` is used to preserve system resources by being almost the only service running and starting other services on demand, rather than leaving them all running all of the time. If this is the case, services can be disabled by editing the *inetd.conf* or *xinetd.conf* files, typically located in the */etc/* directory.

File permissions

Most Unix filesystems have a concept of permissions—that is, files which users and groups can read, write, or execute. Most also have the SETUID (set user ID upon execution) permission, which allows a nonroot user to execute a file with the permission of the owning user, typically root. This is because the normal operation of that command, even to a nonroot user, requires root privileges, such as `su` or `sudo`.

Typically, an operating system will set adequate file permissions on the system files during installation. However, as you create files and directories, permissions will be created according to your umask settings. As a general rule, the umask on a system should only be made more restrictive than the default. Cases where a less restrictive umask is required should be infrequent enough that chmod can be used to resolve the issue. Your umask settings can be viewed and edited using the umask command. See man umask[1] for further detail on this topic.

Incorrect file permissions can leave files readable by users other than whom it is intended for. Many people wrongly believe that because a user has to be authenticated to log in to a host, leaving world or group readable files on disk is not a problem. However, they do not consider that services also run using their own user accounts.

Take, for example, a system running a web server such as Apache, nginx, or lighttpd; these web servers typically run under a user ID of their own such as "www-data." If files you create are readable by "www-data", then, if configured to do so, accidentally or otherwise, the web server has permission to read that file and to potentially serve it to a browser. By restricting filesystem-level access, we can prevent this from happening—even if the web server is configured to do so, as it will no longer have permission to open the file.

As an example, in the following, the file test can be read and written to by the owner _www, it can be read and executed by the group staff, and can be read by anybody. This is denoted by the rw-, r-x, and r-- permissions in the directory listing:

```
$ ls -al test
-rw-r-xr--  1 _www  staff  1228 16 Apr 05:22 test
```

In the Unix filesystem listing, there are 10 hyphens (-), the last 9 of which correspond to *read*, *write*, and *execute* permissions for *owner*, *group* and *other* (everyone). A hyphen indicates the permission is not set; a letter indicates that it is set. Other special characters appear less often; for example, an S signifies that the SETUID flag has been set.

If we wish to ensure that *other* can no longer see this file, then we can modify the permissions. We can alter them using the chmod command (o= sets the *other* permissions to nothing):

```
$ sudo chmod o= test
$ ls -la test
-rw-r-x---  1 _www  staff  1228 16 Apr 05:22 test
```

Note that the "r" representing the read permission for *other* is now a "-"[2].

---

1 Type man umask at the command prompt of almost any Unix system.

2 For further reading on this topic, consult your system manual for the commands chmod, chgrp, chown, and ls.

Host-based firewalls

Many people consider firewalls to be appliances located at strategic points around a network to allow and permit various types of connection. While this is true, most Unix operating systems have local firewall software built in so that hosts can firewall themselves. By enabling and configuring this functionality, the server is not only offered some additional protection should the network firewall fail to operate as expected, but it will also offer protection against hosts on the local LAN that can communicate with the server directly, as opposed to via a network appliance firewall.

Typical examples of firewall software in Unix systems are IPTables/NetFilter, ipchains, pf, ipf, and ipfw, the configuration and use of which will vary from platform to platform. The end goal, however, is the same: to create a ruleset that permits all traffic required to successfully complete the server's tasks and any related administration of the server—and nothing else.

One point to note is that using a stateful firewall on a host will consume RAM and CPU with keeping track of sessions and maintaining a TCP state table. This is because a stateful firewall not only permits and denies packets based on IP address and port numbers alone, but also tracks features such as TCP handshake status in a state table. On a busy server, a simple packetfilter (i.e., permitting and denying based on IP addresses, port numbers, protocols, etc., on a packet-by-packet basis) will consume way fewer resources but still allow an increased level of protection from unwanted connections.

Managing file integrity

File Integrity Management tools monitor key files on the filesystem and alert the administrator in the event that they change. These tools can be used to ensure that key system files are not tampered with, as in the case with a rootkit, and that files are not added to directories without the administrator's permission, or configuration files modified, as can be the case with backdoors in web applications, for example.

There are both commercial tools and free/open source tools available through your preferred package management tool. Examples of open source tools that perform file integrity monitoring include Samhain and OSSEC. If you are looking to spend money to obtain extra features like providing integration with your existing management systems, there are also a number of commercial tools available.

Alternatively, if you cannot for whatever reason install file integrity monitoring tools, many configuration management tools can be configured to report on modified configuration files on the filesystem as part of their normal operation. This is not their primary function and does not offer the same level of coverage, and so is not as robust as a dedicated tool. However, if you are in a situation where you cannot deploy security tools but do have configuration management in place, this may be of some use.

Separate disk partitions

Disk partitions within Unix can be used not only to distribute the filesystem across several physical or logical partitions, but also to restrict certain types of action depending on which partition they are taking place on.

Options can be placed on each mount point in */etc/fstab*.

 When editing */etc/fstab* to make changes, the changes will not take effect until the partition is either remounted using the umount and/or mount commands or following a reboot.

There are some minor differences between different flavors of Unix with regards to the options, and so consulting the system manual page—using man mount—before using options is recommended.

Some of the most useful and common mount point options, from a security perspective, are:

nodev

Do not interpret any special dev devices. If no special dev devices are expected, this option should be used. Typically only the */dev/* mount point would contain special dev devices.

nosuid

Do not allow setuid execution. Certain core system functions, such as su and sudo will require setuid execution, thus this option should be used carefully. Attackers can use setuid binaries as a method of backdooring a system to quickly obtain root privileges from a standard user account. Setuid execution is probably not required outside of the system-installed *bin* and *sbin* directories. You can check for the location of setuid binaries using the following command:

```
$ sudo find / -perm -4000
```

Binaries that are specifically setuid root, as opposed to any setuid binary, can be located using the following variant:

```
$ sudo find / -user root -perm -4000
```

ro

Mount the filesystem read-only. If data does not need to be written or updated, this option may be used to prevent modification. This removes the ability for an attacker to modify files stored in this location such as config files, static website content, and the like.

noexec

Prevents execution, of any type, from that particular mount point. This can be set on mount points used exclusively for data and document storage. It prevents an attacker from using this as a location to execute tools he may load onto a system and it can defeat certain classes of exploit.

chroot

chroot alters the apparent root directory of a running process and any children processes. The most important aspect of this is that the process inside the chroot jail cannot access files outside of its new apparent root directory, which is particularly useful in the case of ensuring that a poorly configured or exploited service cannot access anything more than it needs to.

There are two ways in which chroot can be initiated:

- The process in question can use the chroot system call and chroot itself voluntarily. Typically, these processes will contain chroot options within their configuration files, most notably allowing the user to set the new apparent root directory.
- The chroot wrapper can be used on the command line when executing the command. Typically this would look something like:

```
sudo chroot /chroot/dir/ /chroot/dir/bin/binary -args
```

For details of specific chroot syntax for your flavor of Unix, consult man chroot.[3]

It should be noted, however, that there is a common misconception that chroot offers some security features that it simply does not. Chroot jails are not impossible to break out of, especially if the process within the chroot jail is running with root privileges. Typically processes that are specifically designed to use chroot will drop their root privileges as soon as possible so as to mitigate this risk. Additionally, chroot does not offer the process any protection from privileged users outside of the chroot on the same system.

Neither of these are reasons to abandon chroot, but should be considered when designing use cases as it is not an impenetrable fortress, but more a method of further restricting filesystem access.

Mandatory Access Controls

There are various flavors of Unix that support Mandatory Access Controls (MAC), some of the most well-known being SELinux (*http://selinuxproject.org*), TrustedBSD (*http://www.trustedbsd.org*), and the grsecurity (*https://grsecurity.net*) patches. The

---

3 Type man chroot at the command prompt of almost any Unix system.

method of configuration, granularity, and features of Mandatory Access Controls vary across systems; however, the high-level concepts remain consistent.

MAC allows policies to be enforced that are far more granular in nature than those offered by traditional Unix filesystem permissions. The ability to read, write, and execute files is set in policies with more fine-grained controls, allowing a user to be granted or denied access on a per-file basis rather than all files within the group to which they belong, for example.

Using MAC with a defined policy allows the owner of a system to enforce the principles of least privilege—that is, only permitting access to those files and functions that users require to perform their job and nothing more. This limits their access and reduces the chances of accidental or deliberate abuse from that account.

MAC can also be used with enforcement disabled; that is, operating in a mode in which violations of policy are not blocked, but are logged. This can be used in order to create a more granular level of logging for user activity. The reasons for this will be discussed later in Chapter 20.

Conclusion

Keeping Unix application servers secure does not necessarily require the purchase of additional infrastructure or software. Unix operating systems as a whole are designed to have a large number of useful tools available to the user out of the box, with package management systems to provide supplemental open source tools.

A large number of vulnerabilities can be mitigated simply by keeping patches up-to-date and ensuring that a sensible configuration is used.

CHAPTER 12

Endpoints

Endpoints, devices that an end user operates such as a desktop, laptop, tablet, or cell-phone, are increasingly becoming a target for malicious individuals who seek to compromise a network. With an increasingly mobile workforce, growing numbers of knowledgeable workers, and rapidly falling prices for storage, the availability of vast quantities of data that are either stored on endpoints or available to endpoints via the repositories that they access (i.e., shared drives) is becoming more and more substantial by the day.

In what may appear to be a counterintuitive response to this increased availability of data, demands are high for ease of access to that data to be increasingly low friction, often in the name of productivity or agility of the organization.

Endpoints are, of course, also the location at which most people conduct activities such as web browsing, instant messaging, reading email, and clicking any random links or attachments that seem appealing to them at the time. The number of vectors available to attack the endpoint is large, and they are filled with targets for whom security is not necessarily the number one priority.

This has unsurprisingly led to endpoints being increasingly targeted, not only by malware and ransomware, but in more precise spearphishing and hacking campaigns.

In this chapter we will explore steps you can take on most endpoint devices to drastically reduce the chances of an endpoint being compromised, and to minimize the impact to you should this ever happen.

Keeping Up-to-Date

As with the server estate, ensuring that patches are installed on endpoints is critical to limiting the number of bugs, and thus vulnerabilities, on any one system. By minimizing the number of vulnerabilities on endpoints, the number of technology-based options open to an attacker are reduced. The same can be said of automated attacks by certain types of malware.

The method of patching will vary from platform to platform; indeed, it will vary depending on the style of management used by an organization. A "bring your own device" (BYOD) system of device selection and management will be very different from a more traditional set up whereby an employer will provide and manage a device in terms of hardware, operating system, and often applications.

Microsoft Windows

Ever since the launch of Windows 95, Microsoft has provided the Windows Update service, which has undergone a number of different incarnations, but ultimately serves the purpose of distributing patches to endpoints in a semi-automated way. This website allows desktop PCs running Microsoft Windows to download updates and patches based on which version of the operating system is being run. However, this service has been mostly aimed at the consumer and BYOD markets and has often been rather self-service, with the user being provided the opportunity to decline and defer updates, and no visibility provided to system administrators with regards to the deployment status of various patches.

Microsoft has, in the past, provided what are effectively enterprise versions of this system in the form of Systems Management Server (SMS), Microsoft Operations Manager (MOM), and Windows Server Update Services (WSUS), to allow systems administrators to deploy patches to workstations within the environment without relying on Windows Update or Microsoft Update. These systems are, however, no longer the standard.

At the time of writing Microsoft recommends the use of Windows Update for Business (*http://bit.ly/2lYsI4f*) for endpoints running Windows 10. You can use either Group Policy or Mobile Device Management (MDM) solutions to configure devices to use the Windows Update for Business service, as opposed to the consumer-style Windows Update service.

macOS

macOS clients can be centrally patched using the Software Update Service (*https://support.apple.com/en-ca/HT202030*) in macOS Server. This is achieved by using a configuration profile that directs the client on which update server to use, as opposed to using the general-use update server provided by Apple across the internet.

The Profile Manager tool (*https://support.apple.com/profile-manager*) is distributed by Apple and can be used to configure a number of configuration options for iOS and macOS devices in your estate. It is not a central management system, per se, but can be used to deploy policies.

For unmanaged devices—that is, devices for which you have not installed a configuration profile—the change of update server can be made manually using the following command:

```
sudo defaults write /Library/Preferences/com.apple.SoftwareUpdate
  CatalogURL http://my.update.server.tld:8088/index.sucatalog
```

It is worth remembering that as with other operating systems, macOS allows users with suitable privileges to install software outside of this ecosystem, and as such, they will not be automatically patched via a system such as this. In these types of cases, the onus may well be on the user to perform regular updates and to ensure that the system is functioning as expected.

One of the most popular methods of distributing third-party software to macOS hosts is homebrew (*http://brew.sh*). Users of this system can update their repository by running the command:

```
brew update
```

And then upgrade any packages that have been updated in the repository by running the command:

```
brew upgrade
```

Unix Desktops

As is often the case, Unix desktops vary depending on Unix flavor, and between distributions within each flavor. But there are some high-level approaches that can be researched for suitability depending on the environment:

- Use similar management tools to those that may be used for Unix servers to run commands on desktops causing the local package management software to perform the desired upgrades. Management tools such as Puppet (*https://github.com/puppetlabs/puppet*) and Ansible (*https://github.com/ansible/ansible*) can be used to centrally automate these tasks.

- Ensure that desktops are configured to run the automatic update and upgrade processes, if available, via a scheduled job, typically via cron.

- Entrust patching to the desktop owner.

Third-Party Updates

Not all software will be managed by the operating system's own update mechanisms. Users with suitable privileges can install third-party software that is not covered by the central patch management systems previously described. Thankfully, an ever-increasing number of applications are implementing automatic or semi-automatic update mechanisms to aid users with this process. The use of these automatic update systems is often more of a challenge with regard to user education than it is for technology. Security teams spend a lot of time telling users not to click on things—unless it's a patch, in which case they should really really click on them.

Users should accept updates and thereby keep applications patched and up-to-date; however, they should be taught not to blindly click Accept on everything, as this will naturally expose them to several types of social engineering attacks, such as FakeAV malware, for example. It is recommended that users update their applications, but be aware of how to discern a valid update as opposed to a browser popup.

Applications that do not have an automatic update mechanism should be monitored for new releases, typically by subscription to mailing lists and such, as well as applying upgrades manually as new releases become available.

Keeping an inventory of applications installed within the environment is worthwhile. This way in the event of an advisory being released for software, it is immediately apparent if you have a problem, how large it is, and how many desktops will need to be visited in order to mitigate it. This sort of information is typically kept in your asset register, as mentioned in Chapter 2.

Hardening Endpoints

As with servers (discussed in Chapters 10 and 11), hardening is the art of making the most secure configuration possible, without compromising the ability of the system to perform its primary function. Patching, as mentioned, is the first critical step to hardening an endpoint, but there are other steps that should be taken in order to reduce the opportunity for compromise.

Disable Services

Every service (daemon) that runs is executing code on the endpoint. If there is a vulnerability within that code, it is a potential weakness that can be leveraged by an attacker. It also consumes additional resources in the form of RAM and CPU cycles.

Many operating systems ship with a number of services enabled by default, many of which you may not use. These services should be disabled to reduce the attack surface on your servers. Of course, you should not just start disabling services with reckless abandon—before disabling a service it is prudent to ascertain exactly what it does and if it is required.

On Microsoft systems, there is a GUI-based administration tool within Control Panel that can be used to list, start, and stop services, either temporarily or permanently. There is also a command-line option to list running services, which is:

```
sc query type= service
```

Services can also be stopped or started from the command line. For example, to stop the Task Scheduler, which as it happens, you should *not* do, you can type:

```
sc stop "Task Scheduler"
```

And to start it again:

```
sc start "Task Scheduler"
```

This only stops and starts a service for the duration that the endpoint is booted up, however. To permanently enable or disable a service you should use the following command:

```
sc config "Task Scheduler" start= disabled
sc stop "Task Scheduler"
```

In addition to the built-in commands, there are other Microsoft tools that will provide a more in-depth view into services and their hooks into the operating system. Both Process Explorer and Process Monitor from the Sysinternals suite of products can assist in research into service and process activities.

There are a number of ways to ascertain which services are running on a Unix system, the easiest of which is to use the `ps` command to list running services. Exact argument syntax can vary between versions, but the `ps ax` syntax works on most systems and will list all currently running processes. For minor variations in syntax on your operating system, check the manual page for `ps` using the command `man ps`.

Services should be disabled in startup scripts (rc or init, depending on operating system) unless your system uses `systemd`, in which case you can refer to the following discussion on `systemd`. Using the `kill` command will merely stop the currently running service, which will start once more during a reboot. On Linux the commands are typically one of `rc-update`, `update-rc.d`, or `service`. On BSD-based systems, you typically edit the file */etc/rc.conf*. For example, on several flavors of Linux the `service` command can be used to stop the `sshd` service:

```
service sshd stop
```

To start `sshd` (one time):

```
service start sshd
```

And to disable it from starting after a reboot:

```
update-rc.d -f sshd remove
```

Some Linux distributions have moved toward using systemd as opposed to SysV startup scripts to manage services. Systemd can be used to perform other administrative functions with regard to services, such as reloading configuration and displaying dependancy information. To stop sshd (one time):

```
systemctl stop sshd
```

To enable sshd upon every reboot:

```
systemctl enable sshd
```

And to disable sshd upon further reboots:

```
systemctl disable sshd
```

Older Unix operating systems may use inetd or xinetd to manage services rather than rc or init scripts. (x)inetd is used to preserve system resources by being almost the only service running and starting other services on demand, rather than leaving them all running all of the time. If this is the case, services can be disabled by editing the *inetd.conf* or *xinetd.conf* files, typically located in the */etc/* directory.

macOS is based upon FreeBSD, a Unix system, and thus the ps and kill commands work in the same fashion as previously described. The preferred route is to use the launchctl command to control launchd, which can be invoked with the list, stop, or start arguments to stop or start enabled services.

To disable a service, use the command:

```
launchctl disable <servicename>
```

It should be noted that there are a wide range of options when using launchctl, so it is recommended that you consult man launchctl before proceeding.

Desktop Firewalls

With an ever-growing mobile workforce, using a desktop firewall is becoming more of a necessity. The days of a workforce whose IT footprint is confined to the office environment are long gone for most organizations. The last time an employer gave me a desktop that was an actual desktop was 2002. Ever since then, irrespective of industry vertical or company size, my "desktop" has always been a laptop, even if it remained permanently at a desk. This means that users' main computing device, the one that probably holds a large volume of your corporate information on it, is at best being plugged into home networks with partners, housemates, and children's devices, and most likely into public wifi hotspots in hotels and coffee shops.

Of course, a firewall is far from a panacea, but being able to block all ingress connections—and ideally, blocking egress connections also—is very beneficial when on an untrusted network. Ingress filtering blocks those attempting to connect to the endpoint. By blocking egress connections, applications that are unsafe to use on a shared network, such as those that use unencrypted protocols, can also be blocked.

Windows systems have included a built-in firewall capability of one sort or another since Windows XP. We would hope that you are running something more recent than Windows XP, and so we should assume that this option is available to you. If you're running a Windows system that is older than XP, then you have quite a number of other problems to address, and your endpoints should not be connecting to public WiFi at all.

The location of the administration interface varies from version to version, but it is consistently within Control Panel. In Windows 10, the current version of Windows at the time of writing, the interface is located in Control Panel→System and Security→Windows Firewall.

Since Leopard, macOS has included an application firewall that, rather than operating on IP addresses and port numbers, allows you to configure settings based on an application. For example, you could specify that the web browser can make connections, but that the PDF reader cannot. The administrative interface is located in System Preferences→Security and Privacy→Firewall.

Linux-based desktops will almost without exception have a host-based firewall available to them, although this will vary between distributions. The default for Ubuntu, for example, is "Uncomplicated Firewall" or ufw. Details on how to use ufw can be found by using the command `man ufw`. Other Linux flavors and Unix systems could use any one of a range of firewalls. It is recommended that specific documentation be consulted for determining the type of firewall per distribution.

Full-Disk Encryption

As we just discussed in "Desktop Firewalls" on page 118, the workforce is increasingly mobile due to the replacement of traditional desktop systems with laptops, which people carry around with them. This means that organizational data is also increasingly mobile, which of course is accompanied by the risk of a laptop being stolen or left somewhere.

Another change in desktop computing is the cost, capacity, and physical size of storage. This has led to large capacity disks being commonplace within the desktop environment, meaning that members of staff can store large volumes of data, which is often sensitive.

The combination of these trends means that the scope for potentially losing large volumes of data has increased dramatically.

For this reason, among many others, it is recommended to run a full-disk encryption solution in order to protect the hard disk or solid state disk in laptops and desktops.

Modern hardware and operating systems are optimized for the use of full-disk encryption, so after the initial encryption of the drive, a performance overhead is not something that is noticeable in most cases. Modern full-disk encryption implementations are fairly transparent to the user, typically only requiring an additional boot-time password after initial encryption of the disk has taken place.

Forensics

It should be obvious, but for the sake of clarity, encrypting the storage on a laptop will, by design, render the data on it unreadable to anyone but the owner who is configured to decrypt the data. Thus, if you rely on the ability to perform disk forensics, for example, you should consider other solutions that include the option for centrally controlled keys to allow forensic examination by your team.

Current versions of most operating systems come with bundled full-disk encryption solutions that should serve perfectly well unless you have a requirement for centrally managed keys or the ability to use specific configuration, such as altering the cryptographic characteristics.

Windows includes a tool called BitLocker, which can be found in Control Panel→System and Security→BitLocker Drive Encryption. Enabling BitLocker is simply a case of clicking to enable and following the onscreen prompts.

On OSX there is a similar tool called FileVault. To enable FileVault use the administrative interface located in System Preferences→Security & Privacy→FileVault, and again click to enable and follow the onscreen prompts.

Full-disk encryption on Linux platforms is typically more difficult to accomplish after the installation of the operating system, so the documentation for the specific distribution should be consulted. However, if a new system is being installed, this is often as simple as an install-time checkbox (this is certainly the case in recent versions of Ubuntu, for example).

Locked Screens, Sleeping, and Hibernating

Full-disk encryption works by leaving the filesystem on the disk encrypted at all times, with a key stored in memory. This key is then used by a driver for the disk, which reads encrypted data from the disk, decrypts its memory using the key, and then passes the decrypted data to the operating system and applications. The OS and applications are, to all intents and purposes, completely unaware that the data is encrypted on the drive.

This decryption key is itself encrypted on the drive, but is decrypted using the passphrase entered by the user at encryption time, and again at each bootup. This allows for the key used to decrypt data on the disk to be substantially larger than the passphrases used by humans.

There is, however, one issue with this model—the key to decrypt the disk must remain in memory at all times. Memory is only cleared when the host is shut down. During normal operation, locked screen, sleep mode, and hibernate mode, the memory is retained. This means that leaving a laptop on the lock screen will not necessarily protect it from an attacker.

This is not any different than normal operation on a network. However, users often expect that when a host screen is locked or in sleep mode (for example, when it's left unattended in a hotel room), it is safe from a physical attacker. There are attacks which can be used to dump the memory over one of the ports on an endpoint, and from that memory dump the decryption keys can be acquired.

Endpoint Protection Tools

Endpoint protection tools, such as antivirus, are often a contentious point, especially with regards to their effectiveness versus any potential new vulnerabilities that they can introduce into a system while performing their tasks. At the same time they are fixing issues, they are themselves running additional code on a host which can, and does, contain bugs.

A general rule of thumb is that until you are suitably advanced in matters of security to make this determination for yourself, you are probably better off running the software than not. Antivirus, anti-malware, and other endpoint protection tools are far from complete coverage, but they do catch low-hanging fruit, and they in turn reduce the noise in the data that you are analyzing, which in turn makes it easier to spot other issues that could have been lost in the noise.

Mobile Device Management

Mobile device management (MDM) is the generic term used to describe a number of possible technologies that can be used to provide centralized management of mobile devices—typically smartphones, but also including tablets and other mobile computing devices.

An MDM is used to enforce policy on a device, typically taking the form of a server running MDM software, which has been configured as an MDM on the mobile device prior to delivery to the user. Examples of policies that can be enforced are:

- Enforce PIN/password
- Enforce VPN use
- Application installation
- Remote erase
- Enforce configuration options (ban or enforce the use of certain applications or configuration options)

Unlike many other technologies mentioned in this book, there are not any prevalent open source MDM solutions. There are, however, a number of commerical solutions. The largest differentiators between solutions, other than cost, are which devices are supported, and which sort of policies you wish to enforce upon each device type. Before purchasing a solution, it would be advisable to understand which devices you are going to support and what you would like to manage on them. This will instantly narrow down the number of contenders to evaluate.

Endpoint Visibility

Endpoint visibility tools allow the collection of key data on how an endpoint is operating. Details such as which network connections it has open, running processes, open files, and so on, can be helpful information for many reasons. This information can often be used to detect compromised hosts, malware, or members of staff deliberately acting in a malicious way. When aggregated across the enterprise, it can not only be used for detection and blocking purposes, but also potentially to reconstruct lateral movement and data exfiltration in the event of a larger compromise.

Endpoint visibility can be a potentially contentious topic, however, as to the expectation of privacy employees have within your organization. This often comes down to a number of factors: the organization itself, the industry vertical, the country in which you are located, and a number of other similar cultural factors. It is often wise to speak to human resources prior to deploying endpoint visibility tools in order to ensure that they are permissible under the contract of employment. Having staff trust the security team is crucial to being effective, and this small act can pay large dividends later on.

Various tools are available, however OS Query (*https://osquery.io/*) is a well-established and respected open source tool that supports Windows, macOS, and Linux out of the box.

Other Endpoints

Not only should endpoints with full operating systems be considered, but also other devices such as printers and heating, ventilation, and air conditioning (HVAC) systems that interact with heating, cooling, and other infrastructure equipment.

Printers will ship with default passwords and may store Active Directory credentials on them for authenticating to LDAP to send scanned/printed documents to file shares. Printers are inherently insecure and can also often be coaxed into providing LM hashes. It is best to lock down logins that printers use as well as segmenting them as much as possible.

SCADA systems are not only insecure, but can also be extremely fragile when interacting with modern technology. The third-party vendors that supply or manage the systems may have security protocols specific to their devices or they may have a backdoor into the system that has zero security. Any SCADA equipment should be treated just like any other part of the network—documented, secured, and tested as a precautionary measure.

Other items to consider:

- Heating and ventilation control systems
- IP-enabled cameras
- IP-enabled thermostats
- Door locking systems
- IP telephony systems

Centralization

One of the goals with endpoint management is to centralize resources as much as possible. Central management consoles, central authentication systems, centralized logging, and centralized file stores all bring economies of scale, ease of management, consistency of configuration, minimization of management overhead, and typically a simplified architecture. By aiming for a centralized infrastructure that makes sense for your organization, life will be made easier both for yourself and for the end user.

Conclusion

Endpoints are the new go-to system for an attacker as remote or mobile workforces grow, and access to often-sensitive company data becomes more ubiquitous. Securing these endpoints is a must for any organization. There are several fairly simple steps you can take to vastly reduce the risk of compromise and to increase the chances of detection if it does occur. Patching, hardening, and using endpoint tools are achievable goals for most organizations.

CHAPTER 13

Password Management and Multifactor Authentication

The use of passwords in regards to technology has been around since the early 1960s, when the first shared environment was born. MIT's Compatible Time-Sharing System was the first multiuser computer. At this early stage there was little-to-no password security, as previously only physical security was used to limit access. The CTSS passwords in theory were only accessible by the administrators, but an admin error in the late '60s caused widespread display of all users' plain text passwords during login after the message-of-the-day file was swapped with the password file. Oops!

Passwords have come a long way since then and some professionals even have the opinion that they are useless. While we do agree that some password implementations can be incredibly insecure, they can also add another layer of security. Passwords can be the keys to the kingdom and they aren't going anywhere any time soon. There are many ways to ensure that the transmission and storage of passwords are securely implemented. In this chapter, you'll learn how best to manage passwords and go a little bit behind the scenes on how they work.

Basic Password Practices

Simple password hashes can be cracked in less than a second with some trivial knowledge. Password cracking software such as John the Ripper support the cracking of hundreds of types of hashes using brute force or rainbow tables. Brute force attacks often use dictionary files, which are large text files containing thousands upon thousands of plain text passwords that are commonly used and have been stripped from data breaches and other sources. Both the tool and the dictionaries are readily available on the internet.

Let's start with some basic math surrounding the length and complexity of passwords. The times listed are approximate and wouldn't take into consideration if a service doesn't allow certain characters:

- 8 characters at only lowercase equals 26^8. Extremely easy, will crack in < 2 minutes.

- 8 characters at upper- and lowercase equals 52^8. Still not the best, will crack in < 6 hours.

- 8 characters at uppercase, lowercase, and numbers equals 62^8. A little better, will crack in < 24 hours.

- 10-character passphrase with uppercase, lowercase, numbers, and symbols 94^{10}. Approximately 600 years.[1]

Rainbow tables are a relatively modern twist on the brute-force attack as the cost of storage has become cheaper, allowing for a processing time/storage trade-off. A rainbow table contains a list of precomputed and stored hashes and their associated cleartext. A rainbow table attack against a password hash does not rely on computation, but on being able to look up the password hash in the precomputed table.

While long and complex passwords won't matter if the backend encryption is weak or there has been a breach involving them, it will protect against brute-force attacks.

Teaching users and requiring administrators to create complex passwords is an overall win for everyone. One way of making secure passwords easier to remember is using phrases from books, songs, expressions, etc., and substituting characters. They then become a passphrase instead and are inherently more secure. For example:

Amanda and Lee really love their password security = A&LeeR<3TPS

Another learning opportunity for end users, and possibly even an enterprise-wide shift in process, would be to not trust others with passwords. Helpdesk staff should not be asking for passwords, ever, period. Users should be educated to the fact that no one in the organization would ask for their password, and to do the right thing and report anyone who does. The idea of keeping passwords to yourself doesn't only apply to humans. Internet browsers store passwords encoded in a way that is publicly known, and thus easy to decode. Password recovery tools, which are easily available online, enable anyone to see all the passwords stored in the browser and open user profiles.

---

1 Random ize, "How Long Would It Take to Hack My Password" (*http://random-ize.com/how-long-to-hack-pass/*).

Password Management Software

In this day and age we have passwords for everything. Some of us have systems that make remembering passwords easier, but for the majority of users it isn't feasible to expect them to remember a different password for each piece of software or website. Don't make the mistake of reusing passwords for accounts. In the increasingly likely event that a website with stored password hashes gets hacked, attackers will inevitably start cracking passwords. If passwords are successfully cracked, particularly those associated with an email address, attackers will probably attempt to reuse those credentials on other sites. By never reusing passwords, or permutations on passwords, this attack can be thwarted. Whether it is a personal account or an enterprise account, passwords should not be reused. Sites and services with confidential or powerful access should always have unique complex passwords.

Password reuse is a common problem that can be solved by using a password manager. There are many different options from free to paid versions of password management software. Password management implementations vary, from the rudimentary password-storing features in most browsers to specialized products that synchronize the saved passwords across different devices and automatically fill login forms as needed. Perform significant research to come up with the best fit for your organization. Some questions that should be asked when looking into the software include:

- Are there certain passwords that need to be shared among admins such as for a root or sa account?
- Will you be using two-factor authentication to log in to the password manager? (Hint: you should.)
- Do you want to start with a free solution that has fewer features, or with a paid version that will allow more room to grow, and better ease of use? You may want to start with the free version and then decide later if it makes sense to move to something more robust. Take note that many free versions of software are for personal use only.
- Is there a one-time cost or a recurring fee?
- Should the system have a built-in password generator and strength meter?
- Is there a need for it to auto-fill application or website fields?
- Does the password manager use strong encryption?
- Does it have a lockout feature?
- Does it include protection from malicious activity, such as keystroke logging— and if so, which kinds of activity?

In all cases, the master password should be well protected; it's best to memorize it rather than write it down, although writing it down and keeping it in a secure location is also an option. It's never a bad idea to have a physical copy of major user accounts and passwords written down or printed out in a vault in case of emergency. Before deciding on a password manager, read reviews of the various products in order to understand how they work and what they are capable of doing. Some reviews include both strengths and weakness. Perform analysis as well by reading background information on vendors' websites. When a password manager has been chosen, get it directly from the vendor and verify that the installer is not installing a maliciously modified version by checking an MD5 hash of the installer. If a hash is not available, request one from the vendor; if the vendor cannot provide a verification method, be skeptical. Although moving to a password manager (*http://bit.ly/2lYEiff*) may take a little effort, in the long run it is a safe and convenient method of keeping track of the organization's passwords and guarding specific online information.

Password Resets

Password reset questions when not using 2FA (or when using it when poorly implemented) can be a surefire way for an attacker to get into an account and cut the user off from accessing it. Answers to the questions "What is your mother's maiden name?" "What city were you born in?" or "Where did you graduate high school?" are added onto an account for "security" purposes. The majority of answers to these questions are easily found on the internet, guessed, or even socially engineered out of the user.

When designing a system that allows password resets, try to not use standard everyday questions that are easily guessed. A method of ensuring the security questions are not brute forced would be to supply false information. The answer to "What is the name of your elementary school?" could be "Never gonna give you up" or "Never gonna let you down." The answers can then be stored away in a password manager as it would be incredibly hard to remember the answer that has been supplied.

Password Breaches

According to the 2016 Verizon Data Breach Incident Report, 63% of confirmed data breaches involved weak, default, or stolen passwords and 76% of network intrusions were carried out by compromised user accounts. Looking at some numbers of overall breaches in 2015, the numbers of unique accounts are staggering (see Table 13-1).

Table 13-1. 2015 Identity Theft Resource Center: Data Breach Category Summary (http:// bit.ly/2lYyfrj)

Totals for Category	# of Breaches	# of Records	% of Breaches	% of Records
Banking/Credit/Financial	71	5,063,044	9.1%	2.8%
Business	312	16,191,017	40.0%	9.1
Educational	58	759,600	7.4%	0.4%
Government/Military	63	34,222,763	8.1%	19.2%
Medical/Healthcare	276	121,629,812	35.4 %	68.4%

Good password security will allow you to minimize the impact of the consistent breaches on personal accounts, as well as making it less likely that the enterprise will have a breach.

Encryption, Hashing, and Salting

There is a common misunderstanding of these three terms. It will be extremely helpful to understand what encryption, hashing, and salting mean and the difference between them. All three can be involved with password implementations and it's best to know a little about them and how they work.

Encryption

Encryption has been around for an awfully long time. The Egyptians used it to create mystery and amusement, and the Romans used it to send secret messages. Encrypting a password consists of applying an algorithm that scrambles the data, and then a key can be used that returns the scrambled data to it's original state. ROT13 is one of the simplest examples of a substitution cipher. It basically replaces each letter with one 13 places away in the alphabet:

Amanda and Lee are awesome = Nznaqn naq Yrr ner njrfbzr

ROT13 is obviously a weak cipher, but it is useful to illustrate the key point here: encrypted data is reversible to anyone who knows the key; in this case it is that the shift size is 13. It is like that by design. There is no point encrypting a secret message if the person at the other end is unable to decipher it. Therefore, it is useful in situations such as VPNs, HTTPS traffic, and many other forms of communication. Other common encryption algorithms include Triple DES, AES, RSA, and Blowfish.

Hashing

Hashing is different from encryption in that once the data is encoded, it cannot be decoded. The lossy nature of the algorithms makes reversal mathematically impossible; however, brute forcing all possible variants of the source material and hashing it until a match is found is a technique that can yield results, as is the case with password brute forcing. Unlike encryption, for most algorithms, the output is always of a fixed length.

Using our phrase from before and the MD5 algorithm, we get:

```
Amanda and Lee are awesome = 2180c081189a03be77d7626a2cf0b1b5
```

If we try a longer phrase we get:

```
Amanda and Lee are awesome at creating examples =
51eba84dc16afa016077103c1b05d84a
```

The results are both the same length. This means that multiple inputs could result in the same output, which is called a collision. Collisions are unavoidable when using the same hashing algorithm on a large data set, but can be useful for comparing the validity of other types of data. MD5 is also a hashing algorithm that can easily be cracked.

Hashing is useful when storing things that do not need to be read back, but would like to have the capability of checking validity. Passwords are the primary example. Instead of storing the cleartext, the hashed version is stored. Then, when someone types in their password, the same hashing algorithm is applied and compared with what is located in the database, which looks for a match. Hash functions can also be used to test whether information, programs, or other data has been tampered with.

The important factor for hashing algorithms is that they only work one way. The only way to work out the original value is to use brute force by trying multiple values to see if they produce the same hash.

This is particularly problematic with passwords, which are generally short and use commonly found words. It would not take a modern computer extensive time to run through a large dictionary (or use existing rainbow tables (*http://en.wikipedia.org/wiki/Rainbow_table*)) and figure out the hashed result of every common password. This is where salting comes in.

Salting

Salting works by adding an extra secret value to the input, extending the length of the original password.

In this example the password is Defensive and the salt value is Security.Handbook. The hash value would be made up from the combination of the two: DefensiveSecurity.Handbook. This provides some protection for those people who use common words as their password. However, if someone learns the salt value that is used, then they just add it to the end (or start) of each dictionary word they try in their attack. To make brute forcing attacks more difficult, random salts can be used, one for each password. Salts can also be created from multiple parts, such as the current date-time, the username, a secret phrase, a random value, or a combination of these. Bcrypt, for example, is a hashing algorithm that includes the use of unique salts per-hash by default.

There are many insecure encryption and hashing algorithms currently in use that should be upgraded to stronger methods. NIST (*http://bit.ly/2lYGL9G*) recommends the following upgrades:

- Upgrade MD5 to use SHA512 (or above)
- Upgrade SHA1 to use SHA512
- Upgrade DES/3DES to use AES3

Depreciated encryption/hashing includes:

- SHA-1
- 1024-bit RSA or DSA
- 160-bit ECDSA (elliptic curves)
- 80/112-bit 2TDEA (two key triple DES)
- MD5 (never was an acceptable algorithm)

For security through the year 2030, NIST recommends at least SHA-224, 2048 bits for RSA or DSA, 224-bit EDCSA, and AES-128 or 3-key triple-DES be used.

Password Storage Locations and Methods

Many locations and methods of password storage are typically insecure by default. The following lists some higher profile and more common insecure methods of password storage. Ensure the vulnerabilities are patched, are not using the processes, and are alerting on the possible implementation of the items listed.

- A high-profile Linux vulnerability in 2015 with the Grand Unified Bootloader (grub2) allowed physical password bypass by pressing the backspace button 28 times in a row. Grub2, which is used by most Linux systems to boot the operating system when the PC starts, would then display a rescue shell allowing unauthenticated access to the computer and the ability to load another environment.
- Set proper authentication settings in MS Group Policy. The default GPO settings have the LM hash enabled, which is easily cracked:
  - Navigate to Computer Configuration→Policies→Windows Settings→Local Policies→Security Options.

— Enable the setting "Network Security: Do not store LAN Manager hash value on next password change."

— Navigate to Computer Configuration→Policies→Windows Settings→Local Policies→Security Options.

— Enable the setting "Network Security: LAN Manager Authentication Level" and set it to "Send NTLM response only."

— Navigate to Computer Configuration→Policies→Windows Settings→Local Policies→Security Options.

— Enable the setting "Network Security: LAN Manager Authentication Level" and set it to "Send NTLMv2 response only\refuse LM."

- A well-known vulnerability within Windows is the ability to map an anonymous connection (null session) to a hidden share called IPC$. The IPC$ share is designed to be used by processes only; however, an attacker is able to gather Windows host configuration information, such as user IDs and share names, and edit parts of the remote computer's registry.

  — For Windows NT and Windows 2000 systems navigate to HKEY_LOCAL_MACHINE → SYSTEM → CurrentControlSet → Control → LSA → RestrictAnonymous.

  — Set to "No Access without Explicit Anonymous Permissions." This high-security setting prevents null session connections and system enumeration.

- Baseboard Management Controllers (BMCs), also known as Integrated Lights Out (ILO) cards, are a type of embedded computer used to provide out-of-band monitoring for desktops and servers. They are used for remote access to servers for controlling the hardware settings and status without having physical access to the device itself. The card provides system administrators the ability to connect through a web browser as long as the unit has power running to it. The ILO allows the powering on of the device, changing settings, and remote connection into the desktop of the OS. Often, the default password on the cards are not changed.

  — The protocol that BMC/ILOs use is also extremely insecure (*http://bit.ly/ 2abU9om*). Intelligent Platform Management Interface (IPMI) (*http://bit.ly/ 2lYGJyT*) by default has often used v1 of the protocol and has cipher suite zero enabled, which permits logon as an administrator without requiring a password. So not only should default passwords be of concern, so should taking steps to protect against this critical vulnerability by upgrading the ILOs to v2 or greater and changing default passwords. There are specific modules in Metasploit that will allow scanning of the network for ILO cards with vulnerabilities (the Metasploit scanner in this case is auxiliary/scanner/ipmi/).

- As covered in Chapter 14 using centralized authentication when possible, such as Active Directory, TACACS+, or Radius, will allow you to have less overall instances of password storage to keep track of.

Password Security Objects

In Windows Server 2008, Microsoft introduced the capability to implement fine-grained password policies (FGPP) (*http://bit.ly/2lYtuOr*). Using FGPP can be extremely beneficial to control more advanced and detailed password strength options. There are some cases when certain users or groups will require different password restrictions and options, which can be accomplished by employing them.

Setting a Fine-Grained Password Policy

Fine-grained password policies can be difficult to set up and manage, so it is important that a long-term plan is created for deploying them.

Some important prerequisites and restrictions to setting a fine-grained password policy include the following:

- The domain *must* be Windows Server 2008 Native Mode. This means *all* domain controllers must be running Windows Server 2008 or later.
- Fine-grained password policies can only be applied to user objects and global security groups (not computers).[2]

If an Automatic Shadow Group (*http://bit.ly/2lYq0vs*) is set up, password policies can be applied automatically to any users located in an OU.

To create a password security object (PSO), follow these steps:

1. Under Administrator Tools, open ADSI Edit and connect it to a domain and domain controller where the new password policy will be set up.

---

2 "AD DS: Fine-Grained Password Policies" (*http://bit.ly/2lYAPO8*)

If this option does not appear, go to "Turn Windows Features On or Off" and make sure the "AD DS and AD LDS Tools" are installed.

PSOs can also be created with LDIFDE as well as ADSI Edit. However, these instructions are for ADSI Edit.

2. Double-click the "CN=DomainName", then double-click "CN=Password Settings Container", as shown in Figure 13-1.

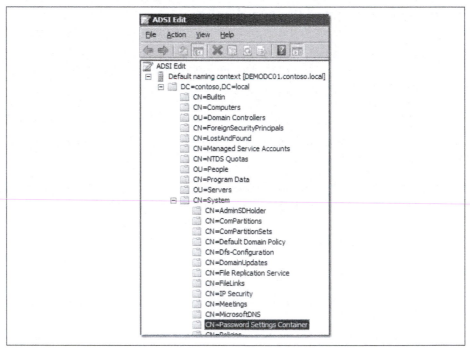

Figure 13-1. ADSI Edit

3. As shown in Figure 13-2, right-click "CN=Password Settings Container". Click "New" and then "Object…"

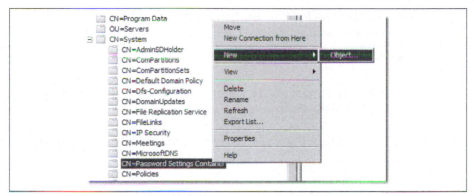

Figure 13-2. Creating a new object

4. Click Next.

5. Type the name of the PSO in the Value field and then click Next.

6. Set ms.DS-PasswordSettingsPrecedence to 10. This is used if users have multiple Password Settings Object (PSO) applied to them.

7. Set msDS-PasswordReversibleEncryptionEnabled to FALSE.

 You should almost never use TRUE for this setting.

- Set msDS-PasswordHistoryLength to 24, This will be the number of passwords that are remembered and not able to be reused.

- Set msDS-PasswordComplexityEnabled to TRUE.

- Set msDS-MinimumPasswordLength to 8.

- Set msDS-MinimumPasswordAge to 1:00:00:00. This dictates the earliest a password can be modified with a format of DD:HH:MM:SS.

- Set msDS-MaxiumumPasswordAge to 30:00:00:00. This dictates the oldest a password can be. This will be the password reset age.

- Set msDS-LockoutThreshold to 3 to specify how many failed logins will lock an account.

- Set msDS-LockoutObservationWindow to 0:00:30:00. This value specifies how long the invalid login attempts are tracked. In this example, if four attempts are made over 30 minutes, the counter will reset 30 minutes after the last failed attempt and the counter of failed attempts returns to 0.

- Set msDS-LockoutDuration to 0:02:00:00. This identifies how long a user remains locked out once the msDS-LockoutThreshold is met.
- Click Finish.

The Password Settings Object (PSO) has now been created and the ADSIEdit tool can be closed. Now to apply the PSO to a users or group:

1. Open Active Directory Users and Computers and navigate to System→Password Settings Container.

Advanced Mode needs to be enabled.

2. Double-click the PSO that has been created, then click the Attribute Editor tab. Select the msDS-PSOAppliedTo attribute and click Edit, as shown in Figure 13-3.

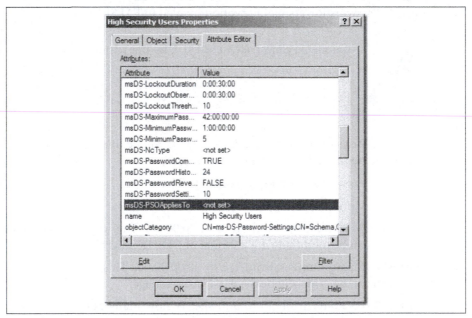

Figure 13-3. msDS-PSOAppliedTo attribute

3. Click the Add Windows Account button (Figure 13-4).

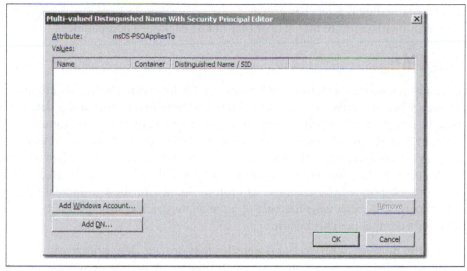

Figure 13-4. Adding a Windows account

4. Select the user or group this PSO will be applied to and click OK, as in Figure 13-5.

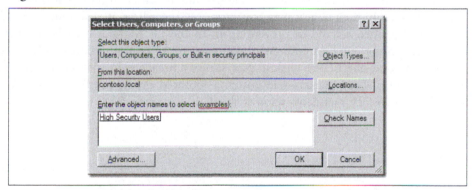

Figure 13-5. Selecting user or group for the PSO

Multifactor Authentication

Multifactor Authentication (MFA) or two-factor authentication (2FA) uses two separate methods to identify individuals. 2FA is not a new concept. It is a technology patented in 1984 that provides identification of users by means of the combination of two different components. It was patented by Kenneth P. Weiss (*http://bit.ly/2lYJQ9Q*) and has been slowly gaining popularity throughout the years. Some of the first widely adopted methods of 2FA were the card and PIN at ATMs. Now that the need to protect so many digital assets has grown, we are struggling to implement it in environments and with software that may or may not be backward compatible.

Why 2FA?

Basically, password strength doesn't matter in the long run. Passwords are no longer enough when it comes to the sheer volume and sensitive nature of the data we have now in cyberspace. With the computing power of today, extensive botnets that are dedicated to password cracking, and constant breaches, you can no longer rely on only a password to protect the access you have. So why compromise when it comes to the security of data, access to systems, or the possibility of giving an attacker a foothold into corporate infrastructure? On top of doing your best to increase password complexity, 2FA is an essential part of a complete defense strategy—not just a bandaid for a compliance checkmark.

While the number of services and websites that provide 2FA is increasing, we rarely think about it in our own enterprise environments. A surprising number of companies and services decide to implement 2FA only after a large-scale or high-visibility breach. Figure 13-6 shows the widely known AP Twitter hack that brought the stock market down in April 2013 (Figure 13-7). Twitter started offering 2FA in August of that same year, less than four months later. While it can be argued that this specific hack, being a phishing attack, may have occurred regardless, it is still likely that 2FA could have lended a hand in preventing it. In the J.P. Morgan breach, the names, addresses, phone numbers, and email addresses of 83 million account holders were exposed in one one of the biggest data security breaches in history. J.P. Morgan's major mistake? The attackers had gotten a foothold on an overlooked server that didn't have two-factor authentication enabled.

Figure 13-6. False tweet from the hacked @AP Twitter account

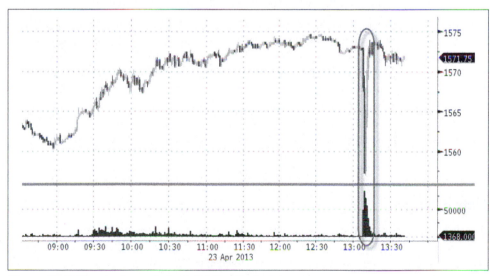

Figure 13-7. The stock market crash after the tweet

2FA Methods

There are three different methods of authentication to consider when implementing a type of 2FA:

1. Something you know, such as a password, passphrase, pattern, or PIN. This is current the standard when it comes to single authentication.

2. Something you have, which would be a physical device that you would carry on you, in your wallet, or even on a keychain. These physical devices can come in the form of a token, a card with a magnetic strip, an RFID card, or your phone, which could use SMS, push notifications through an application, or even a phone call. Some popular options are the RSA tokens, yubikeys, Duo Security, or Google Authenticator.

3. Something you are. A biometric reading of a unique part of your body, such as your fingerprint or retina, or even your voice signature.

These are all methods of authentication that you and only you should be in possession of.

SMS Now Deprecated as a Secure Standard

At the time of this writing, NIST released a special publication (*http://bit.ly/2lYz2su*) declaring that "If the out of band verification is to be made using a SMS message on a public mobile telephone network, the verifier SHALL verify that the pre-registered telephone number being used is actually associated with a mobile network and not with a VoIP (or other software-based) service. It then sends the SMS message to the pre-registered telephone number. Changing the pre-registered telephone number SHALL NOT be possible without two-factor authentication at the time of the change. OOB using SMS is deprecated, and will no longer be allowed in future releases of this guidance."

How It Works

2FA is based on several standards. The Initiative for Open Authentication (OAUTH) was created in 2004 to facilitate collaboration among strong authentication technology providers. It has identified HOTP (hash-based one-time passwords), TOTP (time-based one-time passwords), and U2F (Universal 2nd factor) as the appropriate standards. They are used as out-of-band authentication (OOBA) wher, for example, the first factor would traverse the local network and the secondary factor would then be performed over the internet or a cellphone connection. Providing different channels for the authentication methods significantly increases the difficulty for attackers to gain authenticated access to the network or devices.

Threats

There are various ways that 2FA may fail to be the necessary security blanket, especially when it comes to poor implementation.

Company A decides that it wants to implement 2FA by using the push notification or phone call method. A criminal or pentester comes along to break in by either phishing, using passwords from a recent breach, or a password brute-forcing technique. Somehow they end up with a legitimate username/password combo, but they should be stopped from authenticating because of the 2FA, right? Well in this case, the user gets the phone call or application alert that they have gotten so many times in the past. This notification doesn't tell the user what they are supposedly logging in to, so as a force of habit they acknowledge the alert or answer the phone call and press the # key. Boom, the bad guy or pentester is in. There have also been case studies where attackers have used password reset options to bypass 2FA. It all boils down to how the implementation has been designed.

So the principle idea behind "something you have" can take on different forms. In this situation it's technically 2FA, and allows Company A to be compliant but it is still not leveraging the security potential of the software. If Company A were to have that second form of authentication include a code as opposed to a single click or button, it would have been both secure and compliant.

There are many other threats that we won't get into right now. The bottom line is that passwords alone are weak, and adding 2FA strengthens that authentication method to be more secure. In the words of Bruce Schneier (*http://bit.ly/2nj2bPQ*):

> Two-factor authentication isn't our savior. It won't defend against phishing. It's not going to prevent identity theft. It's not going to secure online accounts from fraudulent transactions. It solves the security problems we had ten years ago, not the security problems we have today.

Two-Factor Authentication is just another piece of the security puzzle. It's not our savior for sure, but it is an essential part of defense in depth.

Where It Should Be Implemented

2FA is here to stay and can significantly increase network security. We recommend that it be implemented wherever possible. If there is any type of remote access in your organization, such as VPNs, portals, or email access, 2FA should be used as part of the authentication. And not just for administrators, but vendors, employees, consultants—everyone. By implementing a solution in an organization, remote and local access to firewalls, servers, applications, and critical infrastructure can be secured.

Your data is worth protecting. We also suggest that you use it on a personal level for your home accounts such as email, social media, banking, and other services, where offered.

Conclusion

As much as we hear that passwords are dead, password management will be a necessary evil for a long time to come, so securing them as much as possible will be in your best interest. Many security topics can lead you down a never-ending rabbit hole, and password security and cryptology are no different. Here are some great references if you would like to know more about the inner workings of password storage and cryptography:

- Password Storage Cheat Sheet (*http://bit.ly/owasp-cheat*), Cryptographic Storage Cheat Sheet (*http://bit.ly/2lYv6rA*)
- Guide to Cryptography (*http://bit.ly/2lYv82G*)
- Kevin Wall's Signs of broken auth (& related posts) (*http://bit.ly/2lYRjWr*)
- John Steven's Securing password digests (*http://bit.ly/2lYISdT*)
- IETF RFC2898 (*http://bit.ly/2lYKRih*), RFC5869 (*http://bit.ly/2lYzyXd*)
- scrypt (*http://bit.ly/2lYGmUU*), IETF Memo: scrypt for Password-based Key Derivation (*http://bit.ly/2lYGGCZ*)
- Open Wall's Password security: past, present, future (*http://bit.ly/2lYDNCj*)

These (*http://bit.ly/2lYDNCj*) should provide some additional insight for anyone interested in more in-depth cryptography.

CHAPTER 14

Network Infrastructure

It is easy to focus our attention on application and operating system security, and to overlook fundamental building blocks of an environment such as the network infrastructure. We should always be cognizant that attacks against this infrastructure can be very effective. Networks can be attacked for the purposes of disruption, such as Denial of Service (DoS) attacks, which cause unexpected outages. Networks can also be attacked as a means of redirecting the flow of traffic on a network to achieve goals such as bypassing security technologies or steering traffic toward compromised systems, which could be used by an attacker for the interception or modification of traffic elsewhere in the network.

A well-designed and maintained network will hamper an attacker's efforts to move laterally within a network or to exfiltrate data, and it will aim to keep him contained within a particular area of the network in the event that a breach should occur.

In this chapter we will discuss good practices you can employ within your environment to harden network infrastructure against a range of attacks.

Firmware/Software Patching

As with other infrastructure, network equipment runs software or firmware, and that requires patching to stay up-to-date in the same way that servers, desktops, and your cellphone do. There is often a tendency to incorrectly believe that firmware contains special properties that somehow make it less susceptible to vulnerabilities. In most respects that matter, firmware is just the same as software except that it is loaded from chips as opposed to other media, such as hard disks. Many types of network equipment do not separate into various abstraction layers such as operating system, device drivers, and applications in the way that desktops and servers do. Network devices are nevertheless running what is essentially software, which exhibits many of the same flaws as desktops and servers; firmware should be considered in a very similar way to a server operating system when it comes to patching. Patches should be tested, approved, and deployed under your internal change control processes, but they should also be deployed as swiftly as is appropriate to close security holes and remain on a vendor-supported version.

Unlike Windows or Unix systems, however, patches are often delivered as a single large image that updates software for the entire device, rather than subcomponents such as drivers or applications, as you may find in a desktop or server operating system. This means that upgrades are often not a vector to a previous version that updates key files, but are more akin to overwriting an entire disk with a complete fresh image with only your own configuration remaining.

Automated and scheduled updates for network infrastructure are more unusual, so a more manual approach to vetting and installing patches is often required. This is not necessarily a bad thing, as core network infrastructure components updating automatically is probably something that most organizations would be as comfortable with as they are with the same approach on desktops and servers.

The method of deployment will vary from vendor to vendor, as will the requirements around backing up configuration beforehand, and the amount of time required for an update. It is recommended that the vendor documentation be consulted to ensure that requirements are met and the correct procedure is followed. Typically, vendors will issue release notes, which contain details of key changes and bugs, including security vulnerabilities that have been fixed for any given release. Consulting the release notes prior to performing any upgrades is strongly advised.

On consumer-grade equipment, the process is generally as simple as downloading a binary package from a website, verifying the signature, and installing via a web interface by uploading to the relevant form. On enterprise-grade equipment, the task is somewhat more complicated. The specific vendor's documentation should be consulted when upgrading software or firmware, although depending on the update processes for major networking infrastructure manufacturers, the process is generally one of preparation and upgrade.

Here are the steps to prepare:

1. Select the correct system image for download from the network equipment manufacturer. Images are often specific to hardware and license, as well as the version of the software or firmware you wish to run.
2. Verify prerequisites. Some software versions will require that the existing software version be of a particular minimum version, for example. RAM, storage, and other hardware requirements may need to be met for successful installation of software of firmware.

3. Verify the signature of the image. Unlike operating systems for general-purpose computers, many network devices do not have a built-in channel for download and verification of software and firmware images. Thus, where possible, the digital signatures of firmware/software patches should be manually verified prior to using the image in an update. This is typically either via cryptographic signature or file hash.
4. Backup existing configuration. Although it is generally not possible to back up entire network devices, it is generally the case that the configuration can be backed up to another location. Unlike servers and desktops, network infrastructure does not really store data, and the configuration is typically all that is needed to restore normal operation in the case of an update that loses previously stored information.

And here are the steps for upgrading:

1. Copy the verified image to the device. Many network devices have a certain amount of flash storage onboard. Copying the image prior to upgrade avoids issues with updating over the network, as network outages can leave a device with a partial image.
2. Upgrade. This is the process of replacing the running image with the new image. Typically this is a single command that overwrites the existing software or firmware with the new copy.
3. Reboot. Due to the nature of network devices, in-suite upgrades are often impossible and a reboot onto the new version will probably be required.
4. Verify successful operation. Ensure that the equipment is functioning as expected. If not, consult the running configuration and compare against the backup copy.

Device Hardening

Hardening network devices is an effective way to drastically reduce the risk of compromise or abuse of a network device and by extension, your environment.

Services

Although not as configurable as a server with regards to running services, networking infrastructure will typically run services of sorts for remote management, time synchronization, telemetry data, etc.

As with hardening a server or desktop, disabling unused services on network infrastructure reduces the opportunity for an attacker to find a flaw in code that is listening on the network and use it to their advantage.

Ideally the device configuration and management interfaces should make it clear which services are running; however, this is not always the case. In this situation we can use other tools, prior to moving into production, to determine which services appear to be running. For example, by using a portscanner like nmap, we can determine which TCP and UDP ports are listening on equipment and make educated inferences to determine which services may be running.

To scan all TCP ports we use the command:

```
nmap -sT -p1-65535 10.0.10.1/32
```

-sT

> Sets the scan type to TCP connect. nmap has many scanning options, many of which are used to circumvent poor firewalling or ACLs. However, if you are on the same network as the equipment being scanned and it is using no counter-measures of its own, you can connect using a true TCP handshake and obtain more accurate results.

-p1-65535

> Tells nmap to scan ports in the range 1 to 65535—i.e., all of them. This can be more time consuming, but will give a more complete view, especially if the vendor has taken a not-unusual approach of running additional management interfaces on higher ports.

10.0.10.1/32

> The target to scan, in this case the host 10.0.10.1. The /32 is CIDR notation for a single host. Entire networks can be scanned by using the correct CIDR notation for a wider range.

This will produce something like the following output:

```
$ nmap -sT -p1-65535 10.0.10.1/32
Starting Nmap 7.12 ( https://nmap.org ) at 2016-01-01 00:00 UTC
Nmap scan report for targethost (10.0.10.1)
Host is up (0.00043s latency).
Not shown: 1021 closed ports
PORT    STATE SERVICE
23/tcp  open  telnet
80/tcp  open  http
443/tcp open  https
```

In this case, we can see that ports 23, 80, and 443 are open. Typically these ports are assigned to telnet, HTTP, and HTTPS. This is not an entirely unusual set of results. It is most likely that telnet is used for command-line remote administration, while HTTP and HTTPS are used to present the same web-based management interface both with and without encrypted transport.

In this example we would consider how the host should be administered. If the command line is to be used exclusively, then disabling the HTTP and HTTPS interfaces is likely to be worthwhile, as this will remove the opportunity to pass data to the code that runs the internal web server, thus reducing the attack surface available to an attacker. In this case, it would also be advisable to determine if the device is capable of using an encrypted protocol, such as ssh, as opposed to the cleartext telnet. Assuming ssh is available, it is advisable to enable ssh and disable telnet.

This process can be repeated, substituting the -sT for -sU to scan all the UDP ports. UDP ports are likely to highlight SNMP and time synchronization services.

SNMP

SNMP, or Simple Network Management Protocol, is a protocol that has many uses. The most common use is for collecting telemetry data such as bandwidth usage per interface, CPU usage, memory consumption, etc. SNMP can also be used to obtain more sensitive configuration data and, if using the "private community string," to reconfigure devices remotely.

SNMP Community Strings

Access to SNMP is granted via *community strings*, which are essentially just passwords. By default, these are set to "public" for read only access and "private" for read/write access.

The number one configuration change to make with regards to SNMP is to change the community strings to something other than the defaults. There are three main reasons for this:

- Data that can be obtained, even via the public community string, is often very sensitive and at the very least will leak information about your organization's network architecture. This sort of information is very useful for attackers in determining other targets within your network and avoiding defenses. Data that is available ranges from IP addressing information through to, in some cases, user credentials stored in the configuration.

- The private community string allows an attacker to reconfigure devices. If an attacker can control your organization's network infrastructure, then your defenses are no longer effective, and you may not even know about it.

- SNMP produces vastly disproportionate output compared to its input. And so an open (i.e., default credential) SNMP service can be used by others as an amplifier for DoS attacks.

DDoS Amplification

DDoS Amplification is a technique whereby an attacker who wishes to attack host X will find an amplifier (i.e., a host whose output is larger than the input) host Y. By spoofing (faking) network packets to appear to come from host X to host Y, host Y will send disproportionately larger responses back to host X thinking that it is the originator of the request. This means that host X is flooded with more traffic than the attacker produced originally, thus amplifying the attack.

SNMP has three versions: v1, v2c, and v3. From a security perspective, v1 and v2c are functionally the same, with most modern devices automatically using v2c as opposed to v1. If, however, the option for v3 is available, it is advisable to make use of it as both encryption and authentication are features that become available, keeping data secure in transit and reducing the risk of attacks against the simpler community string model.

Encrypted Protocols

Network equipment is often not as mature as server operating systems when it comes to the use of cryptography. This means that encrypted management is not always available, or is not enabled by default.

In the earlier example we saw that not only were both HTTP and HTTPS configured for use in the web interface, but that the command line used telnet as opposed to ssh. This is not an unusual situation.

Of course this sort of issue will vary from vendor to vendor, but it is worth checking the documentation to determine if encrypted versions of management protocols can be used. Needless to say, login credentials will pass over that channel and protecting login credentials to network equipment is key to keeping them secure.

Management Network

Networking equipment typically allows configuration that restricts access to configuration and management functions to a single physical network interface.

It is advisable to build a dedicated management network and configure all devices to restrict access to their management consoles to network interfaces that are connected only to the management network.

Access to the management network can be exclusively through a bastion host, meaning that no management consoles are placed on either public or internal networks, other than for those with credentials to access the bastion host. By restricting access to these interfaces, an attacker would have to compromise the management network before she could attempt to compromise the management interface of the device.

Bastion Hosts

Bastion hosts (or jump boxes) are specifically hardened servers placed on a network that serve as the single point of entry to that network. They typically have a very minimal and locked-down build, with an above-average level of auditing enabled. Only access to these hosts will grant access to the networks that they are on, thus providing a single point of management and enforcement for access to the management network.

Routers

All of the preceding advice is applicable to routers. However, there are some router-specific security considerations worth discussing in more depth.

Routers typically contain options to provide some rudimentary packet filtering in the form of Access Control Lists (ACLs). ACLs are very much like simplified firewall rules, which allow a router to drop packets based on simple criteria such as IP addressing information. ACLs are typically not stateful nor particularly intelligent so as not to impact routing performance, but they do serve some useful purposes:

- Other than for management purposes, there is typically no reason for traffic to be destined to a router's own IP address. ACLs can drop all traffic to the router unless it originates from specific networks authorized to manage the router, for example, a network operations center or bastion host.
- ACLs can provide coarse filters for other equipment or networks, for example dropping traffic directed to, as opposed to through, firewalls.
- Fragmented packets have a history of causing issues for security devices and so attackers can use fragmentation to circumvent tools such as Intrusion Detection Systems. By dropping fragmented packets, this sort of technique is limited to only a local LAN. However, the implications of such an ACL on your network should be understood prior to implementation of such a measure, as some networks will have legitimate fragmented packets.

Routers may, depending on vendor and default configuration, ship with dynamic routing protocols such as Interior Gateway Protocol (IGP), Routing Information Protocol version 2 (RIPv2), Enhanced Interior Gateway Routing Protocol (EIGRP), or Open Shortest Path First (OSPF). These protocols, if used properly, can dynamically determine the fastest routing path between two hosts and to route around failed devices, links, and network segments. However, if improperly configured, an attacker can leverage such protocols to route traffic via a malicious device that he controls for the purposes of eavesdropping or launching a man-in-the-middle attack.

The specific intricacies of each protocol could be a chapter in its own right, but as with services, it is recommended that routing protocols that are not used by your network be disabled to remove the possibility of abuse. The correct configuration of dynamic routing protocols will be something that is not only specific to vendors, but also to the architecture of your network.

Switches

As with routers, the previous advice is equally applicable to switches, only there are some switch-specific configuration options that may be of use.

For the most part, even managed layer-2 switches are fairly simplistic devices when compared to routers and firewalls. A managed layer-2 switch is a network switch that can be configured with features such as supporting multiple VLANs, SNMP monitoring, VLAN trunking, span ports, and other settings not available on a basic unmanaged switch. Switches have much higher port density than other devices and are used to directly connect devices to the network, and so they have some additional options that are useful:

Virtual Local Area Networks (VLANs)
> As the name suggests, these are virtualized broadcast domains that can be used to provide logical segmentation. Many performance improvements can be achieved with VLANs, but from a security perspective they can be used to contain groups of devices together and restrict broadcast protocols such as DHCP from reaching other hosts. However, it should be noted that VLANs are not as secure as physical segmentation and should not be considered a security boundary in the same way, as there are still attacks that can make use of VLAN hopping attacks.

Port security
> Can be used to prevent an attacker from gaining access to a network by unplugging a legitimate device and plugging in a malicious device in its place. This can be achieved with static MAC address-based controls or dynamic controls, which allow any MAC address on first physical connection to a port, but do not allow that MAC address to change without administrator authorization.

802.1X
> A standard for providing port-level authentication. The difference between this and, for example, Windows authentication is that when Windows authentication is used, the host is already on the network and authenticates against Active Directory. Failure to authenticate will not permit access to Windows resources, but at an IP level the host is already on the network and can send and receive

traffic. With 802.1X, the host has to authenticate in order for the network port to be connected to the rest of the network.

Egress Filtering

Egress filtering refers to filtering outbound traffic—that is, traffic originating from your internal network destined to another network, such as the internet. But why would you want to filter network traffic exiting your network? Aren't all of the bad people and viruses on the internet trying to get in from the outside? (No.)

Even if we discount the issues surrounding the insider threat, egress filtering is a very useful, cheap, underused technique. Not only could internal traffic heading outbound be worthy of blocking, it could be a useful indicator that there is an active breach that you should address:

- Malware command and control traffic typically originates from infected desktops "calling home" to command and control infrastructure. By restricting outbound traffic only to protocols and IP addresses that are expected as part of normal use, command and control infrastructure running on other ports and IP addresses will be unavailable to the malware. Not only this, but by reviewing logs of dropped traffic it is possible to determine which hosts internally may be infected with malware and are worthy of further scrutiny.
- Data exfiltration attempts by someone trying to steal data from a compromised host can often take the form of outbound connections from the internal network. Data theft often takes place using network resources, as opposed to being copied to removable media. By blocking access to all but the expected resources, data exfiltration can be made more difficult to achieve. Again, by reviewing logs of dropped traffic, it may be possible to spot failed attempts at data exfiltration.

IPv6: A Cautionary Note

IPv6, the successor to IPv4, has been in existence for quite some time, but it is often considered by many to not be in use because of the lack of adoption by many ISPs on internet connections, without the use of a tunnel broker. However, the major operating systems all ship with both IPv4 and IPv6 stacks, and have for some time. This means that most networks are unwittingly running a dual IPv4 and IPv6 stack without the knowledge of the network administrators. Furthermore, many security devices are not yet fully IPv6 aware.

Without configuration, IPv6-enabled hosts will configure themselves onto the fe80::/10 prefix and will be able to communicate on, at least, the local LAN using native IPv6.

If devices are prebuilt to use a tunneling protocol such as Teredo, 6in4, 6to4, or 6rd, then they may well have not only internet access using IPv6, but internet access that is effectively unfirewalled and unmonitored. Why is this? Your network equipment will most likely only see IPv4 traffic and not inspect inside the tunnel to see the true IPv6 destination, and thus access controls and monitoring facilities will be ineffective. This, if it is not clear, is bad.

Teredo, 6in4, 6to4, and 6rd

Teredo, 6in4, 6to4, and 6rd are the four flavors of tunneling protocol allowing the use of IPv6 addresses transported over IPv4 to a tunnel broker. This allows the use of IPv6 when connected to an ISP that only supports IPv4.

The preference, of course, is to take control of the situation and to run an IPv6 network yourself to avoid this situation. However, this is not a minor undertaking and is at least a book in its own right.

Egress filtering may take care of the tunneling portion of the problem, but the issue remains that many network security devices may not be capable of properly detecting or preventing IPv6-based attacks. There is no panacea, as many devices are still catching up, so self-education and vigilance are required until such time as IPv6 becomes the de facto standard in networking protocols.

TACACS+

When the word TACACS is mentioned, it most likely means TACACS+, which has replaced TACACS and XTACACS.

TACACS+, or Terminal Access Controller Access-Control System Plus, provides AAA architecture for networking equipment.

AAA

AAA architecture refers to:

- Authentication
- Authorization
- Accounting

By setting up a TACACS+ server, networking equipment can make use of central authentication, which, as with server and desktop operating systems, brings with it all the benefits of a single point of provisioning and deprovisioning of users. Additionally, the accounting features provide centralized storage of accounting data in a central logging repository.

 Both centralized authentication and central logging are discussed elsewhere in this book.

Conclusion

Network infrastructure is often considered to be "just plumbing," as it often will not directly serve requests to applications. However, the underlying integrity of the network is core to the security of other components.

By following good practices such as patching, hardening, enabling encryption, and filtering connections, you can vastly reduce the risk posed to the rest of your environment.

CHAPTER 15

Segmentation

Segmentation is the process of compartmentalizing a network into smaller zones. This can take many forms, including physical, logical, networking, endpoints, and more. In this chapter we will cover several verticals and walk through segmentation practices and designs to help aid in the overall environment design. Unfortunately, many environments have little design in place and can be extremely flat. A flat network contains little-to-no segmentation at any level.

Network Segmentation

Both network segmentation and design are comprised of physical and logical elements. Any physical aspects are going to either require the use of equipment already in the environment or additional capital for purchasing new devices (or both). Logical segmentation will require sufficient knowledge of your specific network, routing, and design. Both take many design elements into consideration.

Physical

Network segmentation should start, when possible, with physical devices such as firewalls and routers. Effectively, this turns the network into more manageable zones, which when designed properly can add a layer of protection against network intrusion, insider threats, and the propagation of malicious software or activities. Placing a firewall at any ingress/egress point of the network will offer the control and visibility into the flowing traffic. However, it isn't acceptable to just place the firewall in line with no ruleset or protection in place and assume that it will enhance security.

Within this visibility, several advantages are obtained:

- The ability to monitor the traffic easily with a packet capture software or continuous netflow appliance.
- Greater troubleshooting capability for network-related issues.
- Less broadcast traffic over the network.

As well as adding a physical device to ingress/egress points of the network, strategically placing additional devices among the environment can greatly increase the success of segmentation. Other areas that would benefit exist between the main production network and any of the following:

Development or test network
There may be untested or nonstandard devices or code that will be connected to this network. Segmenting new devices from the production network should not only be a requirement stated in policy, but also managed with technical controls. A physical device between such a large amount of unknown variables creates a much needed barrier.

Network containing sensitive data (especially PII)
Segmentation is required in a majority of regulatory standards for good reason.

Demilitarized zone (DMZ)
The DMZ is the section of servers and devices between the production network and the internet or another larger untrusted network. This section of devices will likely be under greater risk of compromise as it is closest to the internet. An example of a device in this zone would be the public web server, but not the database backend that it connects to.

Guest network access
If customers or guests are permitted to bring and connect their own equipment to an open or complimentary network, firewall placement segments corporate assets from the unknown assets of others. Networks such as this can be "airgapped" as well, meaning that no equipment, intranet, or internet connection is shared.

Logical

Logical network segmentation can be successfully accomplished with Virtual LANs (VLANs), Access Control Lists (ACLs), Network Access Controls (NACs), and a variety of other technologies. When designing and implementing controls, you should adhere to the following designs:

Least privilege
Yes, this is a recurring theme. Least privilege should be included in the design at every layer as a top priority, and it fits well with the idea of segmentation. If a

third-party vendor needs access, ensure that her access is restricted to the devices that are required.

Multi-layered

We've already covered the physical segmentation, but data can be segmented at the data, application, and other layers as well. A web proxy is a good example of application layer segmentation.

Organization

The firewall, switch, proxy, and other devices, as well as the rules and configuration within those devices, should be well organized with common naming conventions. Having organized configurations also makes it easier to troubleshoot, set additional configurations, and remove them.

Default deny/whitelisting

The design and end goal for any type of firewall (application, network, etc.) should be to deny everything, followed by the rest of the rules and configurations specifically allowing what is known to be legitimate activity and traffic. The more specific the rules are, the more likely that only acceptable communications are permitted. When implementing a firewall in post-production, it would be best to begin with a default allow while monitoring all traffic and specifically allowing certain traffic on a granular basis until the final "deny all" can be achieved at the end.

Endpoint-to-endpoint communication

While it's convenient for machines to talk directly to each other, the less they are capable of doing so the better. Using host-based firewalls gives the opportunity to lock down the specific destinations and ports that endpoints are permitted to communicate over.

Egress traffic

All devices do not need access to the internet, specifically servers! Software can be installed from a local repository, and updates are applied from a local piece of software. Blocking internet access when it is not required will save a lot of headache.

Adhere to regulatory standards

Specific regulatory standards such as PCI DSS and HIPAA briefly mention segmentation in several sections and should be kept in mind during the design. Regulatory compliance is covered more in depth in Chapter 8.

Customize

Every network is different and the design of yours should take that into consideration. Identifying the location of varying levels of sensitive information should be a main agenda contributing to your design. Define different zones and customize based on where the sensitive information resides.

VLANs

A virtual area network (VLAN) allows geographically distributed, network-connected devices to appear to be on the same LAN using encrypted tunneling protocols.

The main security justification for using VLANs is the inherent security to the network by delivering the frames only within the destined VLANs when sending broadcasts. This makes it much harder to sniff the traffic across the switch, as it will require an attacker to target a specific port, as opposed to capturing them all. Furthermore, when utilizing VLANs it is possible to make the division according to a security policy or ACL and offer sensitive data only to users on a given VLAN without exposing the information to the entire network. Other positive attributes of VLAN implementation include the following:

Flexibility
Networks are independent from the physical location of the devices.

Performance
Specific traffic such VoIP in a VLAN and the transmission into this VLAN can be prioritized. There will also be a decrease in broadcast traffic.

Cost
Supplementing the network by using a combination of VLANs and routers can decrease overall expenditures.

Management
VLAN configuration changes only need to be made in one location as opposed to on each device.

> VLAN segmentation should not solely be relied on, as it has been proven that it is possible to traverse multiple VLANs (*http://bit.ly/ 2lAGIor*) by crafting specially crafted frames in a default Cisco configuration.

There are a few different methodologies that can be followed when customizing the approach to VLAN planning. One common method is to separate endpoints into risk categories. When assigning VLANs based on risk level, the data that traverses it will need to be categorized. The lower-risk category would include desktops, laptops, and printers; the medium-risk category would include print and file servers; and the high-risk category would include domain controllers and PII servers. Alternatively, VLAN design can be based on endpoint roles. All separate VLANs would be created for desktops, laptops, printers, database servers, file servers, APs, and so on. In a larger environment, this method tends to make more sense and create a less complicated network design.

 Remember, just because all of these VLANs are currently present and configured, doesn't mean they need to show up at every site. VLAN pruning can be configured to only allow certain ones to cross physical devices.

ACLs

A network access control list (ACL) is a filter which can be applied to restrict traffic between subnets or IP addresses. ACLs are often applied by equipment other than firewalls, often network routers.

Expensive firewalls cannot always be installed between segments; for the most part it is just not necessary. All data entering and leaving a segment of a network should be controlled. ACLs are applied to the network to limit as much traffic as possible. Creating exact matches of source and destination host, network addresses, and port rather than using the generic keyword "any" in access lists will ensure that it is known exactly what traffic is traversing the device. Have an explicit deny statement at the end of the policy to ensure the logging of all dropped packets. Increased granularity increases security and also makes it easier to troubleshoot any malicious behavior.

NACs

"Network access control (NAC) is an approach to network management and security that enforces security policy, compliance and management of access control to a network."[1]

NAC uses the 802.1X protocol, which is part of the IEEE 802.1 group of protocol specifications. One of the key benefits of 802.1X is that it provides authentication at the port level, so devices are not connected to the network until authenticated. This differs from more traditional approaches, such as domain logon, whereby a host is on the network with an IP address and is capable of making connections before the authentication process begins.

NACs are amazing when implemented correctly and have solid processes surrounding their use. They make us particularly happy as they combine asset management with network security. The captive portals that pop up after you've connected to the wireless signal at a hotel or airport are usually run by a NAC. They can separate

---

1 Techopedia, "What is Network Access Control?" (*http://bit.ly/2lAxNDA*)

unknown and known devices onto their own VLANs or networks depending on a variety of categories.

NACs are implemented for a variety of reasons. Here is a list of some common reasons and examples:

- Guest captive portal: Mr. Oscaron walks into your lobby and needs to use your guest connection. After agreeing to your EULA, he is switched from the unroutable internal network to a guest access VLAN that only has access to the internet on port 80 or 443 and is using DNS filtering. This enables him to access needed resources without the ability to easily perform any malicious activity.

- Initial equipment connection: Installing new equipment from a third-party vendor has its inherent risks. For example, Mr. Wolf from your third-party vendor Moon Ent is required to plug in a PC as a part of a new equipment purchase and installation. This device happens to be running a very old version of Java and has malware that the vendor isn't aware of. The NAC enables you to give this new PC access to a sectioned-off portion of the network for full vulnerability and antivirus scanning prior to addition to a production network.

- Boardrooms and conference rooms: While you do want to turn off all unused ports by default, doing so in a conference room can be difficult due to the variety of devices that may require connection. For example, all 20 Chris's from the company are showing up for a meeting with a vendor for a presentation. The NAC offers the ability for the vendor to be on a separate network with access to a test environment, but only after a full antivirus scan and check against outdated vulnerable software. Most have automated detection and restriction of non-compliant devices, based on a configured policy set.

- Bring your own device (BYOD) policies: Now that we are in an age where most people have one or more devices capable of wireless with them, BYOD is something that many organizations struggle to implement securely. A NAC can be used in conjunction with the data stored within an asset management tool to explicitly deny devices that are foreign to the network.

VPNs

A virtual private network (VPN) is a secure channel specifically created to send data over a public or less secure network utilizing a method of encryption. VPNs can be utilized to segment sensitive data from an untrusted network, usually the internet.

This section will assume the reader has a general understanding of how VPNs work and focus more on baseline security practices surrounding them.

Many devices will allow an insecure VPN configuration. Following these guidelines will ensure a secure setup:

- Use the strongest possible authentication method
- Use the strongest possible encryption method
- Limit VPN access to those with a valid business reason, and only when necessary
- Provide access to selected files through intranets or extranets rather than VPNs

Two main types of VPN configuration are used in enterprise environments: IPsec and SSL/TLS. Each has its advantages and security implications to take into consideration.

Here are the advantages of an IPSec VPN:

- It is an established and field-tested technology commonly in use.
- IPSec VPN is a client-based VPN technology that can be configured to connect to only sites and devices that can prove their integrity. This gives administrators the knowledge that the devices connecting to the network can be trusted.
- IPSec VPNs are the preferred choice of companies for establishing site-to-site VPN.
- IPSec supports multiple methods of authentication and also demonstrates flexibility on choosing the appropriate authentication mechanism, thereby making it difficult for intruders to perform attacks like man-in-the-middle, etc.

Security considerations of an IPSec VPN:

- They can be configured to give full access to all intranet resources to remote users. While users feel as if they are at the office, a misconfigured connection can also open the door to a large amount of risk. Steps should be taken to ensure that users only have access to what they need.
- Depending on the remote network (if traveling to customers/clients/etc.), it may be impossible to use an IPSec VPN due to firewall restrictions at the site you are connected to.

Advantages of SSL/TLS VPN:

- SSL/TLS VPNs allow for host integrity checking (the process of assessing connecting devices against a preset security policy, such as the latest OS version or OS patch status, if the antivirus definitions are up-to-date, etc.) and remediation. This addresses the first security consideration in the following list; however, it has to be enabled to effectively assess endpoints.

- They can provide granular network access controls for each user or group of users to limit remote user access to certain designated resources or applications in the corporate network.

- They supports multiple methods of user authentication and also integration with centralized authentication mechanisms like Radius/LDAP, Active Directory, etc.

- They allow the configuration of secure customized web portals for vendors or other restricted users to provide restricted access to certain applications only.

- They have exhaustive auditing capabilities, which is crucial for regulatory compliance.

Security considerations of a SSL/TLS VPN:

- SSL/TLS VPNs support browser-based access. This allows corporate resources to be accessed by users from any computer with internet access after proper authentication. This opens the potential for attack or transmittal of a virus or malware from a public device to the corporate network.

- They open the possibility for data theft. As they are browser-based, information can be left in the browser's cache, cookies, history, or saved password settings. There is also a higher possibility of keyloggers being present on noncorporate devices.

- There have been known man-in-the-middle attacks to the SSL protocol.

- Split-tunneling, or the ability to access both corporate and local networks simultaneously, creates another entry point for security vulnerabilities. If the proper security measures are not in place, the opportunity is available to compromise the computer from the internet and gain access to the internal network through the VPN tunnel. Many organizations do not allow split-tunneling for this reason.

Physical and Logical Network Example

In Figure 15-1, the majority of the designs previously discussed have been implemented. Although there is a very small chance that this could be a live working environment, the basics have been covered. Live environments should be inherently more complex, with hundreds or sometimes thousands of firewall rules.

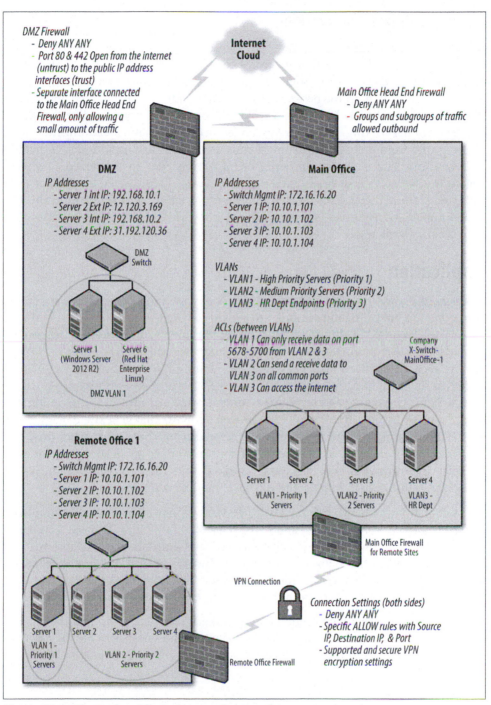

DMZ Firewall
- Deny ANY ANY
- Port 80 & 442 Open from the internet (untrust) to the public IP address interfaces (trust)
- Separate interface connected to the Main Office Head End Firewall, only allowing a small amount of traffic

Internet Cloud

Main Office Head End Firewall
- Deny ANY ANY
- Groups and subgroups of traffic allowed outbound

DMZ

IP Addresses
- Server 1 int IP: 192.168.10.1
- Server 2 Ext IP: 12.120.3.169
- Server 3 Int IP: 192.168.10.2
- Server 4 Ext IP: 31.192.120.36

DMZ Switch

Server 1 (Windows Server 2012 R2)
Server 6 (Red Hat Enterprise Linux)

DMZ VLAN 1

Main Office

IP Addresses
- Switch Mgmt IP: 172.16.16.20
- Server 1 IP: 10.10.1.101
- Server 2 IP: 10.10.1.102
- Server 3 IP: 10.10.1.103
- Server 4 IP: 10.10.1.104

VLANs
- VLAN1 - High Priority Servers (Priority 1)
- VLAN2 - Medium Priority Servers (Priority 2)
- VLAN3 - HR Dept Endpoints (Priority 3)

ACLs (between VLANs)
- VLAN 1 Can only receive data on port 5678-5700 from VLAN 2 & 3
- VLAN 2 Can send a receive data to VLAN 3 on all common ports
- VLAN 3 Can access the internet

Company X-Switch-MainOffice-1

Server 1   Server 2   Server 3   Server 4

VLAN1 - Priority 1 Servers   VLAN2 - Priority 2 Servers   VLAN3 - HR Dept

Remote Office 1

IP Addresses
- Switch Mgmt IP: 172.16.16.20
- Server 1 IP: 10.10.1.101
- Server 2 IP: 10.10.1.102
- Server 3 IP: 10.10.1.103
- Server 4 IP: 10.10.1.104

Server 1   Server 2   Server 3   Server 4

VLAN 1 - Priority 1 Servers

VLAN 2 - Priority 2 Servers

Remote Office Firewall

Main Office Firewall for Remote Sites

VPN Connection

Connection Settings (both sides)
- Deny ANY ANY
- Specific ALLOW rules with Source IP, Destination IP, & Port
- Supported and secure VPN encryption settings

Figure 15-1. Physical and logical network example

Software-Defined Networking

While SDNs are neither a cheap nor easy solution for segmentation, we still feel that they deserve a short explanation. As technology advances and we start to drift away from needing a hardware solution for everything, the concept of "micro-segmentation," where traffic between any two endpoints can be analyzed and filtered based on a set policy, is becoming a reality. SDNs can be looked at like the virtual machines of networking. In a software-defined network, a network administrator can shape traffic from a centralized control console without having to touch individual switches, and deliver services to wherever they are needed in the network, without regard to what specific devices a server or other device is connected to. The key technologies are functional separation, network virtualization, and automation through programmability. However, software-defined network technologies can carry their own security weaknesses.[2]

Application

Many applications, as perceived by the end user, have multiple application components that are linked together in order to provide a single experience to the end user. The easiest example of this is a simple web application—an application that is consumed by the user in the form of a browser-based interface delivered over HTTPS. In reality, such an application is not a singular chunk of code executing in isolation, rather in the most basic form there will be a web server such as Nginx or Apache to handle HTTPS requests and serve static content, which in turn uses a scripting language such as Python, Ruby, or PHP to process requests that generate dynamic content. The dynamic content may well be generated from some user data stored in a database such as MySQL or Postgresql. Of course, a larger application may be more complex than this with load balancers, reverse proxies, SSL accelerators, and so on. The point is that even a simple setup will have multiple components.

The temptation, particularly from a cost perspective, may be to run something like a LAMP (Linux, Apache, MySQL, and PHP) stack all on one host. Perceived complexity is low because everything is self-contained and can talk on localhost with no obstruction, and costs are low because only one host is needed. Putting aside discussions as to the performance, scalability, and ease of maintenance of this type of solution, security does not benefit from such a setup. Let's examine another example.

Let's say that we have an application that uses the LAMP stack, and that the application allows your customers to log in and update their postal address for the purposes of shipping products to them. If there is a flaw in one of the PHP scripts, which, for

---

2 Avi Chesla, "Software Defined Networking - A New Network Weakness?" (*http://bit.ly/2lAF06L*), *Security Week*, accessed March 7, 2017.

example, allows an attacker to gain control of the web server, then it is quite possible that the entire application would be compromised. They would, on the same disk, have the raw files that contain the database, the certificate files used to create the HTTPS connections, and all the PHP code and configuration.

If the application components were separated onto different hosts, a compromise of the web server would of course yield some value for an attacker. However, keep these in mind:

- There would be no access to raw database files. To obtain data from the database, even from a fully compromised host, they would need to execute queries over the network as opposed to just copying the database files. Databases can be configured to only return a set maximum number of responses; similarly, they would be restricted only to records that the PHP credentials could access. Raw access to files could have provided access to other data stored there also.
- SSL keys would not be accessible as they would most likely be stored on a load balancer, SSL acceleration device, or reverse proxy sitting between the web server and the internet.

These are some significant gains in the event of a compromise, even in a very simple application. Now consider some of the applications that you access, perhaps those that hold sensitive data such as financial information or medical records, and the regulatory requirements surrounding the storage and transmission of such data. You should see that segregating application components is a necessary aspect for application security.

Roles and Responsibilities

Segmenting roles and responsibilities should occur at many levels in many different ways in regard to users and devices. You are encouraged to design this segmentation with what works best for you and your environment. However, no individual should have excessive system access that enables him to execute actions across an entire environment without checks and balances.

Many regulations demand segregation of duties. Developers shouldn't have direct access to the production systems touching corporate financial data, and users who can approve a transaction shouldn't be given access to the accounts payable application. A sound approach to this problem is to continually refine role-based access controls. For example, the "sales executive" role can approve transactions but never access the accounts payable application; no one can access the developer environment except developers and their direct managers; and only application managers can touch production systems.

Whenever possible, development and productions systems should be fully segregated. At times a code review group or board can be of use to determine if development code is production ready. Depending on the footprint size of the organization, the same developers working on code in the development environment may also be the ones implementing it into production. In this case, ensure the proper technical controls are in place to separate the environments without hindering the ability of the end result. The developer shouldn't have to rewrite every bit of code each time it is pushed to production, but it shouldn't be an all-access pass either.

Ensure that environment backups, backup locations, and the ability to create backups are not overlooked. Obtaining a physical copy of backup media can prove to be an extremely valuable cache of information in the hands of someone malicious. Approved backup operators should be identified in writing with the appropriate procedures.

While the security or technology department may be the groups involved with creating structured access groups, they are not always the ones who should be making the decisions, at least not alone. This should be a group effort comprised of information stakeholders and management.

Not only should system access be of concern, but permission levels locally and domain-wide should also be taken into account. Much of this has been covered in Chapters 10 and 11 in regard to Windows and Linux user security. Some others include:

- Generic administrative accounts should be disabled and an alerted on if they are used.
- Database administrators are the hardest position to control. DBAs should only have DBA authority, not root or administrator access.
- Administrators and DBAs should have two accounts for separate use: one with elevated rights and one with normal user rights. The normal account is used to perform everyday functions such as checking email, while the account with elevated rights is only used for administrator-type activity. Even going as far as having a separate endpoint for administrative activities would be a fantastic idea as the PCs can then be monitored closely as well as the user accounts.

It is also in your best interest to separate server roles. As mentioned before, having an SQL database on the same server as an application leads to a much likelier successful attack. Some smaller applications can share servers when the risk associated has been determined to be acceptable. There are some server roles that should always remain isolated such as AD Domain Controllers, Mail Servers, and PII Servers.

Conclusion

Segmentation can span almost every aspect of an information security program, from physical to logical and administrative to documentation. With each design decision, sit back and look at the details. Should or can the design be more segmented? What benefits or hurdles would the segmentation create for users or attackers? There is always going to be a balance between a certain level of security and usability.

CHAPTER 16

Vulnerability Management

Contrary to what some vendors' marketing material would have us believe, a huge quantity of successful breaches do not occur because of complex 0-day vulnerabilities, lovingly handcrafted by artisanal exploit writers. Although this does happen, a lack of patching, failure to follow good practices for configuration, or neglecting to change default passwords are to blame for a far larger number of successful attacks against corporate environments. Even those capable of deploying tailor-made exploits against your infrastructure will prefer to make use of these types of vulnerabilities.

Vulnerability management is the terminology used to describe the overall program of activities that oversees vulnerability scanning and detection through to remediation. This is a program that ultimately raises the security of your network by removing potential flaws.

Vulnerability assessment is a different discipline than penetration testing, typically carried out by different people; however, the term is often used interchangeably by those who are not aware of the differences.

Unlike penetration testing, vulnerability assessment is automated or semiautomated, continuous, and less focused on bespoke systems and applications. Vulnerability assessment tools generally search for flaws such as missing patches, outdated software, common configuration errors, and default passwords. Vulnerability scans ideally operate on an ongoing basis, rather than a one-time or annual assessment.

Issues that are often discovered by a vulnerability assessment tend to be known issues found in widely distributed software, and so vulnerabilities in your own code are less likely to be discovered by a vulnerability scanner. That is the role of penetration testing and code analysis. Vulnerability scanners do not attempt to adapt to the environment; rather, they attempt to enumerate an environment, discovering which software is installed, which versions of software, what some of the configuration options are, and if any default accounts remain with the default password.

In this chapter we will discuss vulnerability scanning at a technology level, and how this can form part of a larger program designed to better manage vulnerabilities across your environment—and ultimately improve the overall security of your systems.

How Vulnerability Scanning Works

Of course the exact techniques used by a vulnerability scanner will vary from tool to tool, especially in an industry like information security where techniques fall in and out of favor fairly quickly.

In the simplest form, a vulnerability scanning tool will attempt to determine the information that it requires by probing the target and trying to solicit a response that will allow it to determine some detail about the software running on the host and its configuration. How this is achieved will vary depending on whether the type of scan is authenticated or unauthenticated.

Authenticated versus Unauthenticated Scans

Vulnerability scans can be both authenticated and unauthenticated; that is, operated using a set of known credentials for the target system or not.

This is because authenticated scans typically produce more accurate results with both fewer false positives and false negatives.

An authenticated scan can simply log in to the target host and perform actions such as querying internal databases for lists of installed software and patches, opening configuration files to read configuration details, and enumerating the list of local users. Once this information has been retrieved, it can look up the discovered software, for example, and correlate this against its internal database of known vulnerabilties. This lookup will yield a fairly high-quality list of potential defects, which may or may not be further verified before producing a report depending on the software in use and its configuration.

An unauthenticated scan, however, will most likely not have access to a helpful repository of data that details what is installed on a host and how it is configured. Therefore, an unauthenticated scan will attempt to discover the information that it requires through other means. It may perform a test such as connecting to a listening TCP socket for a daemon and determining the version of the software based on the banner that several servers display. This technique can be easily demonstrated against an SMTP server using telnet, for example:

```
$ telnet my.example.com 25
Trying 192.168.1.25...
Connected to my.example.com.
Escape character is '^]'.
220 my.example.com ESMTP Exim 4.82 Ubuntu Tue, 01 Jan 2016 00:00:00 +0100
```

In this example an unauthenticated scanner would typically assume that the SMTP server is running Exim version 4.82 on Ubuntu. The scanner would then compare this server to an internal database of vulnerable SMTP servers and output a report based on whether or not this version was listed to be susceptible to any vulnerabilities.

However, there is nothing to say that the administrator of the server isn't really running a much older or vulnerable version of Exim, or any other mail server for that matter, and is just displaying a false banner via a configuration option in order to hamper this sort of profiling. This could have been achieved in Exim with this simple configuration option:

```
smtp_banner = "${primary_hostname} ESMTP Exim 4.82 Ubuntu $tod_full"
```

Ideally, the toolset would use the version in the banner as a best current guess, but conduct other tests to determine if that is the true version. For example, different mail servers and different versions of the same mail server may act differently with regard to supported features, the ordering of header information, or other nuances that can be used to fingerprint a system. This, however, is not always the case; it depends on the toolset. In lieu of tools that automatically complete these tasks, it often falls to the person reviewing the results to verify them, or to at the least make decisions with the knowledge that there is a chance of incorrect results being gathered this way.

As described earlier, an authenticated scanner will log in to the host and execute commands to determine the correct version of the software installed, not just make assumptions based on the banner.

Authenticated scans not only remove ambiguity from results of this nature, but can often highlight issues that are not discoverable from an unauthenticated scan. For example, a local privilege escalation vulnerability via an installed command-line tool would most likely not be visible by probing services that are listening for network connections via an unauthenticated scan. These sorts of vulnerabilities are still important to discover and remedy, and when combined with another exploit such as a remote code execution vulnerability, would create a remote root vulnerability. That is, vulnerability #1 is used to remotely execute a command as an unprivileged user, and that command executes an exploit against vulnerability #2 to escalate from an unprivileged user to a privileged user such as root in Unix and Administrator in Windows.

If authenticated scans can reduce both false positives and and false negatives, why is there even an option for unauthenticated scans? There are a couple of reasons.

While it is true that authenticated scans are more accurate, there is one risk that should be highlighted before running headlong into using them. They are authenticated, which means that they, by definition, will have access to some sort of authentication credential, be that username and password combination, ssh keys, or something else. These credentials need to be managed as well as any other credentials would be. It is therefore sensible to set up dedicated credentials just for the scanning server to use. If possible, schedule these credentials to only be active during pre-authorized scanning windows; that is, they should be disabled during times that scanning is not scheduled to take place to minimize the chance of abuse. If this is not possible, ensure that an audit log of login times and IP addresses is produced, and that this audit log is reviewed to ensure that login times and locations align with those of the scheduled scanning time.

The results of unauthenticated scans are what attackers would see, assuming that they do not already have credentials for your systems, and so even if not a completely true representation of vulnerabilities, unauthenticated scans can provide insight to what is available from an attacker's perspective.

 There have been instances of legacy applications and network equipment encountering performance issues, and in some instances crashing during a a simple port scan, nevermind a full vulnerability assessment. For this reason scans should take place during a prearranged engineering window, and under change control.

After a couple of successful scans it will become easier to make the case for regular scans to take place on a predetermined schedule.

Using some trial runs to place people at ease, we have managed to take organizations from being unable to run scans at all to having a fully automated scan that tests a different area of the network each day, recurring every week. That organization is now never more than a week out of date for vulnerability data regarding any host.

Vulnerability Assessment Tools

As with most other security disciplines, there are many tools available for vulnerability assessment, both free and commercial. The value that each tool brings is entirely dependent on your particular environment and the staff that will be operating the tools. When selecting a tool or tools to use, the key areas to consider are:

Coverage for your particular technology stack
> Many vulnerability assessment tools will have gaps in coverage, especially for more esoteric systems. For example, in my case, one of the leading commercial

solutions that had thorough coverage for Windows and Linux systems had a gaping hole when it came to AIX systems. A guess as to which system we were running in our environment is left as an exercise for the reader. Some tools are aimed at very specific areas, such as web applications. While useful in their specific area due to the focus, such tools often tend to not give much visibility into operating system issues, and should be used in tandem with other tools to provide the appropriate coverage.

Automation

Some tools are heavily automated, run on a schedule, self update, and can effectively be left to run with only minimal maintenance on a day-to-day basis, producing reports as scheduled. Others are almost guided penetration-testing tools that require specific technical knowledge to obtain reasonable results. Picking the right tool based on experience, technical knowledge, and how much time you have to operate the tool is essential. Most organizations tend to lean toward a general-use tool for vulnerability assessments, and favor regular penetration tests, code review, and code analysis to find weaknesses in these areas.

Scope

Vulnerability scanners come with a wide range of features, and it is worth determining what the scope of your vulnerability assessments will be when assessing possible tools. For example, some will focus on missing operating system patches, while others will have more options with regard to web application scanning. Some will use auto discovery, while others will need to be told which IP addresses are in vulnerability assessment. You can make more informed decisions regarding which tool is most appropriate for you.

 Additional results can be gained by using the guided penetration test–type tools, if used by an experienced operator. A better use of time, however, is probably to use automated tools to capture low-hanging fruit such as missing operating system patches and older versions of software, and undertake a full penetration test via an external company to uncover issues in bespoke applications.

Vulnerability Management Program

The vulnerability management program is not only a matter of technology, it is comprised of the policies, processes, and procedures that are used to discover vulnerabilities, and see them through to remediation. After all, what is the point in discovering flaws in your system if you are not going to fix them?

Working on the assumption that if you are reading this, you probably do not have a vulnerability management program in place at this point, we are going to need to catch you up before we move on to business as usual.

Program Initialization

If you have existing infrastructure but no vulnerability management program in place, it is incredibly likely that when you run your first scan you are going to end up reading a very long report. This can be a daunting experience filled with red lines on graphs. Fret not—with some pragmatic planning and prioritization this is a manageable task.

Let's assume that the results of your first scan have highlighted vulnerabilities across a wide range of hosts, with a wide range of criticality ratings from low to critical, and that you probably have a mixture of different operating systems in the mix. The normal methods of prioritization, outlined in "Business as Usual" on page 175, may not be practical. If you can skip directly to the business-as-usual process, you should, as it permits the use of better prioritization techniques.

Let's break down the vulnerabilities in the report by the operations team who will most likely have the access to systems required, and the appropriate job responsibilities to deploy fixes. Typically this is either by technology type (Linux team, Windows team, network team, etc.) or by function (finance servers, IT servers, human resources servers, etc.). Now you have a separate list of fixes for each team to implement.

Next let's try to create batches of multiple fixes or instances of fixes that can be deployed during a single change or engineering window to maximize the number of fixes that can be deployed at any one time. The easiest two approaches are:

- Look for vulnerabilities that occur frequently throughout your environment. By patching the same vulnerability or making the same configuration change over and over across the entire environment, certain tasks such as pre-implementation testing can be performed only once, reducing the amount of time needed to roll out the fix. The remediation steps are likely to be repeated identically on each host that it is deployed to, leading to a predictable outcome on each host and less friction for those who are making the changes.
- Pick a particular host of group or hosts and attempt to address all, or at least many, patches on that host or group. Although the range of patches is more varied than in the previous option, there is only one host or group of hosts to raise change requests for, manage outages for, and to monitor throughout the process. This will result in fewer reboots because, hopefully, a single reboot can be used to roll in multiple patches, and you may only have one team that needs to work to deploy all the patches.

Once the patches are grouped using whichever system works best for your particular organization, you should prioritize (see "Remediation Prioritization" on page 175) the batches of remediation work to ensure that the most important changes are implemented as quickly as possible.

By using one of these approaches, it is possible to deploy large numbers of patches during an engineering window. By repeating this process regularly, it should be possible to catch up to a point whereby you can move to the business-as-usual phase.

Business as Usual

Unlike the program initiation phase, which is often predominantly comprised of "catching up" remediation activities in bulk patching, config change, or upgrade cycles, operating vulnerability management as a business-as-usual process relies upon a more systematic approach to handling vulnerabilities. The process should look something like:

- Discover vulnerabilities within your environment. This is typically via a combination of scheduled automated scans, vendor announcements, and scheduled releases.
- Prioritize remediation activities in order to determine the priority order and timeline to remedy each vulnerability.
- Assign remediation activities as appropriate. In many organizations there may be separate teams to manage different systems.
- Track and monitor remediation activities. This will often happen through a check of change control tickets and ensuring that items are not present during the next scheduled vulnerability scan, indicating that they have been fixed successfully.

Remediation Prioritization

It is all very well having a long list of vulnerabilities that require remediation, but the reality is that for most people the ability to remediate everything quickly is purely aspirational. Not only is there the issue of time and resources, to carry out work, but also problems with obtaining a maintenance window, raising change control tickets, patch testing, and all manner of other potential issues. For us mere mortals there is a need to prioritize the work in order to ensure that the more important vulnerabilities are addressed in the most timely manner, while less important issues can wait a little longer. This brings us to the important factor in prioritization: what *is* "important"?

Typically this is the point in the book where you will find a 3x3 or 5x5 matrix with differing levels of panic along each axis to tell you how to deal with your vulnerabilities. Ultimately what these diagrams come down to is having a repeatable process to determine how quickly a vulnerability should be remediated that works for your organization.

Nearly every system of vulnerability prioritization, matrix or otherwise, will use the severity rating placed on the vulnerability as one of the metrics. The severity rating is often derived from a combination of the impact of successful exploitation *without any context of your environment*, and the "likelihood" of exploitation. Likelihood is typically comprised of factors such as complexity, preconditions, if user interaction is required, and other items that could influence the likelihood of a successful attack.

Ultimately, all these methods of determining priority are based on determining when each item should be patched. Use what works for and is relevant to your organization.

Severity Ratings

There are multiple systems used to calculate severity ratings. The most common is probably the Common Vulnerability Scoring System, or CVSS (*http://bit.ly/2lASvDi*). However, some vendors, such as Microsoft, will produce their own severity ratings (*http://bit.ly/2lAJHxu*).

Ratings

Unless you are someone who is versed in risk and risk language, or you have a particular interest in the field, it is probably advisable to accept the vendor-supplied rating and continue. The need to set a completely accurate severity rating is not always present. For the purposes of this exercise, the severity rating serves to provide approximate categorization.

As alluded to earlier, the missing element from the vendor-supplied severity rating is context. A vulnerability present on a standalone PC with no sensitive data and no network connection is going to have a very different potential impact to the same vulnerability discovered on an internet-facing web server; context makes all the difference. If your infrastructure is suitably small you may be able to prioritize based on vendor rating alone, but context can provide further granularity in order to prioritize more effectively. This context typically forms, in one way or another, the other axis of the aforementioned matrix.

There are multiple ways that you could add context, and relevance will depend on your organization. Some examples are:

Sensitivity
    The more sensitive the data held on the device, the higher the priority. This is mostly driven by breach-type scenarios whereby loss of personal or financial data is a worst-case scenario both from a regulatory and PR point of view.

Volume of hosts
    If all hosts are even, then this approach can work well, as a vulnerability affecting 300 hosts will be more important than one that affects only 5 hosts. In reality, however, most hosts are not created equal.

Exposure

That is, how likely it is that a host be exposed to an attacker. For example, an internet-facing host will probably have a higher exposure than one on an internal network.

Having determined how you are going to rate each vulnerability, the final step is to set timelines for remediation to ensure a consistent approach. For example, an internet-facing, critical vulnerability should be remediated within 1 day, while a low criticality rating affecting only desktops could wait 30 days. Mapping out your strategy with timelines brings consistency, which in turn makes it easy to set expectations and to track progress of remediation activities. Meeting the timeline could be part of internal SLAs or KPIs for teams and is a relatively easy metric to track.

An example, which should of course be modified to your own needs, could be Table 16-1.

Table 16-1. Vulnerability remediation time table

	Isolated LAN	Internal LAN	Partner Facing	Internet Facing
Critical	7 days	2 days	1 day	1 day
High	7 days	5 days	3 days	3 days
Medium	14 days	7 days	5 days	5 days
Low	21 days	7 days	14 days	14 days

Risk Acceptance

In the case that a vulnerability cannot be mitigated, either within the agreed timelines or at all, there is a process known as risk acceptance.

Risk Acceptance

Security professionals wince, quite rightly, at the mention of risk acceptance. Although this may seem quite obvious, experience has borne out that this bears repeating, quite possibly twice.

When a risk is "accepted" via a process, it does not, in reality, disappear. Software is still vulnerable, the risk is still present on the system, and an attacker can still make use of it. Merely, a suitably senior member of staff has acknowledged the existence of the vulnerability and accepted responsibility for the decision to permit its continued existence in the environment.

This is only a "fix" on paper.

(Read this just one more time.)

Risk acceptance is, as it sounds, the process of a member of staff of predetermined seniority being able to document acceptance of a risk. That is, he agrees that for whatever reason, the risk is permitted to remain within the environment and that he accepts responsibility for this decision. Typically this is for reasons such as software interdependence, which means that remediating a vulnerability will cause some sort of other issue, or that upgrades require the procurement of a license, for example.

Risk acceptance should be used as a last possible measure, and all acceptances should have an expiry placed on them and not remain in perpetuity. This helps to ensure that risks are reviewed, revisited, and hopefully remediated instead of living on forever in an accepted and perpetually renewed-acceptance state. Even a vulnerability that is expected to remain for a long period of time should only have a short acceptance period, which is reviewed and reissued upon expiry if needed. This ensures that its continued existence is a cognizant decision, with a named individual responsible for that decision.

Conclusion

A vulnerability management program allows you to assess, log, and remediate vulnerabilities within your environment using a largely automated set of processes and tools. By following even a simple such program, the issues responsible for a large number of breaches, unpatched systems, and simple configuration errors will be drastically reduced.

CHAPTER 17

Development

As we have discussed in previous chapters, any code that is executed on a system can contain errors, and if these errors can be leveraged by an attacker then this becomes a vulnerability in the system. This is, of course, something that we do not want.

The aim of securely developing code is, somewhat obviously, to reduce the chances of this occurring, and to reduce the impact if it does.

Secure coding insofar as particulars within any one language is a large and complex field, far too expansive to cover in its entirety within this book. However, we have covered the high-level concepts so that you can understand enough of the topic to be able identify specific areas that are useful for you to go and research separately.

Language Selection

Anyone who codes with any regularity is probably aware that a variety of programming languages are available. She is probably also aware that the choice of programming language can have an effect on a number of areas, including ease of development, speed of execution, availability of libraries, resources required, operating system compatibility, and a wide array of other factors that contribute to the decision. One of the lesser considered factors is the impact upon security.

Of course, the choice cannot be entirely about security. Failure to meet other business objectives for the sake of security alone tends to lead to organizations going out of business (unless the purpose of the business is security). But security should be a factor, especially when other requirements leave several options open.

In the interests of keeping this section from spilling over into an insane number of pages and trying to characterize every language, we have selected some common examples to illustrate the main themes and characteristics. If you are running a development department, you should conduct your own research into your language options, however these examples should serve as guide to the types of features to consider.

0xAssembly

Assembly is about as close to the hardware as you can get, and with that power comes enormous scope for error. In comparison to other languages, writing directly into assembly provides very few checks that what you are asking the processor to execute makes any sense or will work. The potential issues this can create are far beyond those of a simple off-by-one error in other languages.

Assembly is made further complicated by having no abstraction from the processor, and so unlike most other languages, needs to be written with specific knowledge of the type of processor being used.

Thankfully, with the exception of a few key disciplines, assembly is a very unlikely choice of language that you will face unless you are already experienced.

/* C and C++ */

C, and to a lesser degree, C++, are the next best thing after assembly for being close to the hardware but without the burden of needing to deal with nitty gritty like processor registers. C and C++ are written in an ASCII file that is compiled into a binary executable. They offer familiar statements such as if and else for flow control. A lot of code at the operating system layer is written in C, C++, or a combination. Prime examples of this are the Linux and BSD kernels.

At compile time, a modern compiler will perform some basic checks against the code. However, the very features that provide the power to C and C++ are also their downfall. For example, both languages allow the use of pointers—variables that point to another location in memory that holds a variable, or another pointer, as opposed to holding a value themselves. Features such as the ability to use pointers, leaving lots of scope for "unchecked buffers," "use after free," "double free," and other memory-related conditions as pointers that are not managed properly can easily end up pointing to the wrong location in memory. These conditions in turn lead to entire classes of bugs that are much more difficult to introduce when using other languages.

GO func()

GO, often referred to as GOLANG, is also a compiled language, but one that is much more modern and with more protections traditionally offered within scripting languages rather than compiled languages. It is a garbage-collected language, meaning that unlike C, C++, or assembly, GO is designed to manage memory (mostly) automatically rather than leaving it in the hands of the developer, closing many of the bugs that cna be introduced in languages that run closer to the bare metal.

Pointers still exist, but pointer arithmetic does not. Additionally, accessing an out-of-bounds memory location results in a panic, reducing the impact of their presence as the code will simply stop rather than exhibiting unknown, potentially dangerous behaviors. This makes accidentally introducing an exploitable buffer overflow very difficult.

GO is also very strongly typed—that is, every object is of a known type at compile time. Variables cannot be cast to another type; rather, they need to be type switched, which is a safer operation from the perspective of introducing vulnerabilities to the system.

#!/Python/Ruby/Perl

Scripting languages such as Python, Ruby, and Perl are written into a human-readable file that is parsed by an interpreter at run time, rather than being compiled into an executable binary. The interpreter internally translates each statement into a series of precompiled routines and executes those. Typically, there is very little in the way of memory management required of the developer with variable sizes automatically growing, garbage collection being automated, and such. This removes many of the flaws associated with memory-related vulnerabilities. Of course if there is a flaw in the interpreter itself, then problems will manifest across all scripts. However, they are equally all positively affected by a successful patch of said buggy interpreter.

It does not, of course, remove all bugs. For example, interpreted languages, by virtue of their flexibility and ease of development, fall foul of other vulnerabilities. The ease with which data can be consumed can often lead to failure to correctly parse input. Suffering from unexpected function behaviors and lazy management of data due to automated memory management are both common flaws in interpreted scripts.

<? PHP ?>

Strictly speaking, PHP should fall into the same category as Python, Ruby, and Perl as it too is interpreted and has many of the same advantages and disadvantages. However, PHP deserves a special mention because it is often derided for security issues in many common scripts.

Some of the negative press toward PHP is not because the interpreter itself contains vulnerabilities per se, but that the nature of the language makes it incredibly easy for developers to implement flaws into their code without realizing it. This has, in turn, led to many issues in a wide range of popular PHP-based applications.

For example, vulnerabilities have been introduced into PHP-based applications because a programmer will dynamically generate the filename for a server-side include based on some user input, without realizing that the function to include files also permits remote includes as an argument. A prime example of this is having the name of a theme stored in a cookie, which dynamically loads a locally included file to present that theme to the user. However, PHP is flexible in that if a URL is provided to the include argument, it will perform a remote include. This means an attacker can craft a cookie to provide a theme name that is a URL to a script that he controls, which causes a remote include of a file of his choice and subsequently runs his code.

Secure Coding Guidelines

When you work on a project alone or in a small group it can seem pointless to have secure coding guidelines. However, once you move into a larger development team, outsource components of development, or have rotations in staffing, the necessity becomes clear. Secure coding guidelines not only educate less experienced staff with regard to expectations surrounding the level of code quality in areas such as input validation and memory management, but also provides a level of consistency across the entire code base.

Secure coding guidelines are in many ways like policies, standards, and procedures as they pertain to code.

For example, with regard to validation of user input, the following statements could be applicable, depending on the environment:

- User-supplied input is defined as data that is received over a network, from a file, from the command line, from interactions with the GUI, or from a peripheral device.
- User input must never be processed without prior validation.
- Validation includes:
    — Data is of the expected type (e.g., numeric, alphanumeric, binary blob)
    — Data is of the length expected
    — Data is within the range expected
    — Data is received in conjunction with other data that passes validation
- Data that fails to correctly validate will be discarded, along with any other data, valid or not, received in the same transaction.

Additionally, coding guidelines may stipulate that specific libraries or code snippets should be used for commonly occurring tasks to ensure further consistency across the codebase.

Similar guidelines should be included for a wide range of commonly occurring areas such as the use of cryptography, database access, memory management, network communication, error handling, authentication, audit trails, and access management. There may be further guidelines within specific types of applications. For example, a web application will almost certainly require guidelines with regard to session management and differences between requirements on client-side and server-side components.

Testing

Once code has been written it should be tested before being released into production. This is a fairly well-understood process from the perspective of quality assurance, performance, and meeting functional requirements. However, many forget that security testing should also be performed in order to prevent detectable bugs from making their way into a production environment.

There are many subtle variants on types of testing, and which one is most appropriate and will yield the most results will vary depending on the environment. For example, the average lifespan of a release can vary from minutes in a continuous deployment environment to years in some more traditional configurations. The amount of time consumed by any particular testing methodology could easily be a factor if rapid turnaround to production is a factor.

Automated Static Testing

Static testing is a type of analysis whereby the code is not executed as part of the testing process, but rather source code is analyzed by specialist tools that search for a number of programming flaws that can often lead to the introduction of a vulnerability.

This kind of testing is quick and fairly easy to set up, but it is prone to false positives and can often require someone who understands secure development practices. This understanding gives her the ability to explain to the development team why the issues highlighted are a problem and to determine which of the findings are false positives.

The types of issues that are easily highlighted are often of the ilk of memory bugs, such as buffer overflows, and the use of unsafe functions. Static testing does not normally fare well with "design" type issues, such as the incorrect use of cryptography, flaws in authentication mechanisms, and replay attacks, as these flaws are due to implementation choices, not code that is operating in an unexpected manner.

Automated Dynamic Testing

Dynamic testing is performed by executing the application in real time and analyzing how the running code operates under various conditions. Rather than trying to formulaically "understand" the operation of the application based on the content of the source code, dynamic testing will apply various inputs. These inputs in turn create outputs and internal state changes, which are used to determine potential flaws in the executing code.

This type of testing is more complex and time consuming to set up compared to static testing. It may lack complete coverage, as no source code visibility means that some areas of the application may not be tested due to a lack of visibility to the test tool. That said, dynamic testing can uncover entire classes of vulnerabilities that are much more difficult to test for using static testing techniques, such as temporal issues, certain types of injection, and reflection techniques.

Peer Review

Peer review, or code review, is a manual process whereby another developer will conduct a systematic review of either the entire application or, more commonly, the area that has most recently been updated. The intention is to assess the code for mistakes of all types using an experienced eye.

This is not an automated process, so the number of false positives is often lower. The reviewer will typically validate her findings and so will naturally filter out false positives in the process. Of course this is a human process, and as with the initial creation of the code, is subject to human error. Additionally, the level of coverage will probably depend on the experience of the person conducting the testing. Someone who is not well versed in a particular type of issue or the specific nuances of the language being used could well miss classes of vulnerabilities.

System Development Lifecycle

As we have touched on in other chapters, consistency of process is a good way to ensure that you are in control of your environment and able to spot when things are not working quite as they should.

It is of note that in many systems (or software) development lifecycles (SDLC), security is not mentioned formally. If possible, being able to inject security directly into the SDLC could be very beneficial. Otherwise, security can be treated as an afterthought or optional extra, rather than a core component, which leads to it being lower priority than other criteria.

The SDLC is the normal way that processes around development are defined. There are a few variations on the SDLC from various organizations. However, most align to approximately the same structure with a few changes in nomenclature:

Training
> This is the building block upon which all other work is derived. Staff should not only be trained in the art of software development, but should also receive training in secure software development, threat modeling, security testing, and pri-

vacy principles. This will equip developers with the knowledge to not only write better code in the first place, but to understand the results and take appropriate action during testing and review.

Requirements

It is a common tendency to define functional requirements and security requirements as two separate lists. We would recommend that security requirements be included as functional requirements. This avoids ambiguity as to whether or not security requirements are mandatory. It also simplifies documentation and keeps security forefront of mind, as opposed to being an afterthought addressed after the all-important functional requirements.

Architecture and design

Determining an architectural model for a system prior to coding should lead to a more secure system overall. This is because the process of architecture and design should set high-level expectations such as where encryption will be used, where access controls are enforced, and where sensitive data will be located. Additionally, part of the architecture and design process should include threat modeling exercises to focus on high-level methods of attacking proposed solution designs. This will facilitate redesigns to reduce attack surface to an acceptable level and ensure that the appropriate controls are implemented in the right places.

Code and build

Coding takes place based on a combination on the architecture and design specifications, which in turn should meet the requirements laid out previously. Code should be built using the predetermined language, conform to any coding guidelines that have been set out by the organization, and align with any other agreed-upon best practices.

Test and results

The code should be tested, not just functionally, but using security testing methodologies—multiple if applicable—to determine any security defects. Defects should be assessed and entered back into the development process for the appropriate fix.

Release

Release the code as per the internal release process. This includes a final security review, ensuring that the system has been operationalized in terms of documentation, processes, and procedures such as incident response and business continuity, as well as handing over to operational support teams.

If you would like to learn more about SDLC, we would suggest reading the work that Microsoft (*https://www.microsoft.com/en-us/SDL*) has done in this field.

Conclusion

If your organization produces code either as a product or for internal use, there is always a risk that the code contains errors. Errors are what leads to vulnerabilities. By creating a software development lifecycle, testing your code, and making wide decisions about your code, these risks can be greatly reduced.

CHAPTER 18

Purple Teaming

Purple teaming can be described as the defensive professionals (blue team) learning and practicing offensive (red team) techniques. The more knowledge you have in regards to the attacks that others are performing on your environment, the better position you will be in to defend it. You can fill your shelves with the great red teaming books that are out there today, so we will be focusing on some general concepts, ideas, and exercises that would best benefit the blue team. Not only will implementing purple team practices and exercises in your organization give you a better overall security posture, but it can be that extra boost that shows upper-level management and key stakeholders why certain security measures need to be put in place without having to wait for an actual breach.

Open Source Intelligence

Open source intelligence, or OSINT, is defined as:

> "The discipline that pertains to intelligence produced from publicly available information that is collected, exploited, and disseminated in a timely manner to an appropriate audience for the purpose of addressing a specific intelligence requirement.
>
> Open-source intelligence (OSINT) is derived from the systematic collection, processing, and analysis of publicly available, relevant information in response to intelligence requirements."[1]

Many attackers or teams will use OSINT to gather information in a multitude of ways about your company or high-profile employees of your company. The information that is found will assist them in creating an attack strategy that is custom-tailored to

---

1 *https://fas.org/irp/doddir/army/fm2-0.pdf*

fit their needs based on the sector of business you are aligned with and even can include personal information about particular targets.

Types of Information and Access

The types of OSINT—physical assets, company assets, technology, and personal information—and the different ways to gather it provide a good idea of what information may be accessible in regard to your company. It is surprising to find the amount of information readily available about different companies. I suggest you take each one and have you or your team attempt to do your own gathering. By finding OSINT about your own company, you will gain insight on how to strategically change processes, policies, and defenses.

Physical assets

A large range of data, such as account numbers, names, services in use, and highly sensitive personal information could be located on physical assets. Throwing away old invoices, scrap papers, personnel records, or other potentially sensitive information enables attackers to use a technique known as "dumpster diving" to retrieve this sensitive data. Ensuring the proper processes and controls are in place to safeguard against the improper disposal of possibly sensitive information is a key step. It is best to keep boxes of paper waiting on being shredded under supervision or in a secure area.

Dumpster diving
> By removing trash and recyclables from the business the threat is introduced of any bystander being able to rifle through dumpsters or recycling containers. Throwing away old invoices, scrap papers, personnel records, or other potentially sensitive information allows the attacker to add to his overall profile. There is a possibility that a large range of data could be located on physical assets, such as account numbers, names, services in use, and highly sensitive personal information. Ensuring the proper processes and controls are in place to safeguard against the improper disposal of possibly sensitive information is a key step. It is best to keep boxes of paper waiting on being shredded under supervision or in a secure area.

Shoulder surfing
> Shoulder surfing is another technique attackers can use to steal sensitive information. Simply looking over the shoulders of someone sitting at a computer or using a smartphone enables an attacker to gain insight on software or services being used, the deployed operating systems and controls, or other sensitive information. It is best to protect against this by utilizing a monitor privacy screen, positioning computers away from areas where they can be easily viewed, and training users to be aware of their surroundings for this type of activity.

Company assets

Email addresses are one of the easier pieces of data to find on the internet. We will go over harvesting these in an automated way later on in this chapter. Lists of addresses can be used for larger phishing campaigns. While in this day and age it is close to impossible to prevent them from being on the internet in some shape or form, this can be used to your advantage. By creating "canary in a coal mine" email accounts, or honeypot accounts, suspicious activity can now be monitored and alerted on. They should be email addresses that look real and blend in with the real addresses of your organization. It is as simple as adding them somewhere on the organization's main website so it can easily be scraped by an email harvesting tool or you can use it to create an entire fake online persona. To ensure the fake email address is not used by a legitimate customer attempting to establish contact, it could be added as white text on a white background, or some other color that would blend in.

A business opens itself to a certain amount of risk when contracting with third-party services to save costs and allow itself to focus on its speciality as opposed to wasting time on other duties. Outsourcing takes place in a variety of situations. Roles such as housekeeping, food services, safety inspectors, and other professional services can be an avenue for a good social engineer to gain physical access to buildings. Educating against tailgating and keeping up-to-date on vendor access is a must.

Technology

There are many automated scanning tools, browser plug-ins, and scripts that will allow the gathering of external-facing server details such as operating system and software versions. More information can be added to a profile by utilizing the information gathered from public-facing devices and technolgy. This can uncover vulnerable applications or devices to anyone who is permitted to access them. For example, *builtwith.com* (Figure 18-1) can be used as a standalone website or as a part of tools such as recon-ng or Maltego, which we will cover later on.

Metadata, which is basically data about data, can contain a wealth of information about the person or company that it originated from. A common type of metadata is EXIF. Exchangeable image file format or EXIF are the properties of documents, images, and sound files. The list of properties that can be attached to these include the username of who created it, customized comments, created date, geographic location information, and sharing/permissions, just to give some examples.

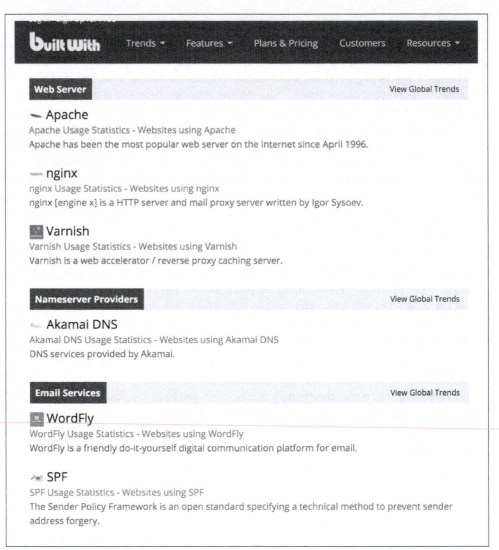

Figure 18-1. builtwith.com

Documents

Sensitive information included in documents can be obtained through several methods. One of the most popular, Google Dorking, has an entire section of the exploit-database website dedicated to new searches aimed at exfiltrating data (*https://www.exploit-db.com/google-hacking-database/*). For example, a Google search for inurl:wp-config -intext:wp-config "'DB_PASSWORD'" (*https://www.exploit-db.com/ghdb/4181/*) will provide a result with many different Wordpress database passwords.

Personal assets

The general population is not aware that personal social media posts can contain a great deal of information that an attacker can use for pretexting. Posts on various media, including geolocation to professional networking, give away what technologies may be being used internally. Without the proper security settings and knowledge, advanced targeting of specific employees becomes much easier for an attacker to paint a full picture of a person's habits and personality. This also falls back on user education and its effects transferring from the workplace to home. Having an all-encompassing program can assist in this becoming less of a problem.

Online forums, whether public or private, can present their own security concerns. Employees may reach out directly to vendors to ask specific questions on technology or to answer others' questions. This documentation could possibly list software build numbers, logfiles, error messages, or other sensitive data.

Ever since large companies have begun storing customer data, there have been criminals breaching their security infrastructure (if they had any to begin with) and publicly publishing the information for anyone to parse. In 2015 alone, CVS, Walgreens, Patreon, LassPass, Experien, UCLA, Ashley Madison, Anthem, IRS, and OPM were among the largest data breaches, releasing around 200 million customer records combined. Data mining can be performed against the released records, which would include information helpful to any OSINT campaign. Many times passwords are reused across multiple organizations and these can be leveraged for attacking other sites.

OSINT Tools

Many professional tools and websites are utilized for basic and advanced OSINT gathering. They range from free and open source to hosted and paid-for subscriptions. While we cannot cover each and every one in depth in a single chapter, we will go through some of the most popular options out there today and how to utilize a handful of their features.

Maltego

> "[Maltego provides] the aggregation of information posted all over the internet - whether it's the current configuration of a router poised on the edge of your network or the current whereabouts of your Vice President on his international visits, Maltego can locate, aggregate and visualize this information."[2]

Maltego is an incredibly powerful reconnaissance tool that many professional organizations use. Entire profiles can be built and visualized through this piece of software.

---

2 *http://tools.kali.org*

It has a smooth graphical user interface that allows you to drag and drop items, and perform many queries with several clicks. Depending on the size of the organization, it may not be worth the subscription prices for Maltego. It would depend on how often you believe this information changes, and how important it is to have it in a visually pleasing format.

You can find the free version of Maltego in both Kali and on their website Paterva.com. We are using the full version of the software in the following exercise to take you through the steps of setting up a single domain using Maltego:

1. To add the domain, just drag and drop the "Domain" object from the lefthand Palette menu under Infrastructure tab and give it the domain of your choosing, as shown in Figure 18-2.

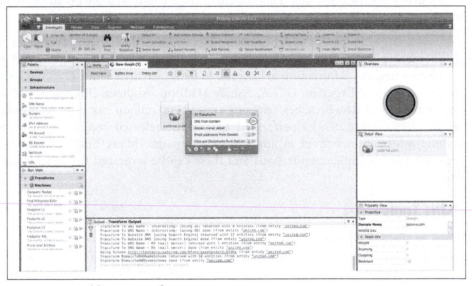

Figure 18-2. Adding a new domain

2. Select the "Run All Transforms" for "DNS for Domain" to populate all subdomains, as shown in Figure 18-3.

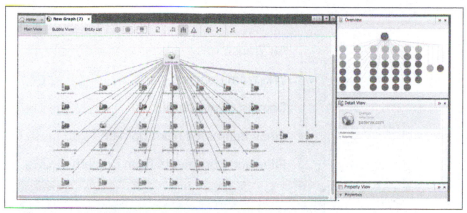

Figure 18-3. All subdomains for paterva.com

3. Choose "Select by Type" to choose all of the DNS names, as shown in Figure 18-4.

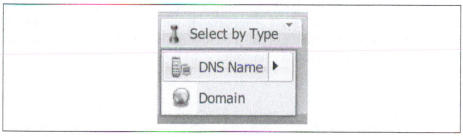

Figure 18-4. Type selection

And run other transforms such as resolving to IP address, discovering what websites are running on the servers, and GeoIP location.

 You can also select the domain to find interesting files and email addresses. This option will scrape the domain using different Google Dorks for different types of Microsoft Office files (see Figure 18-5).

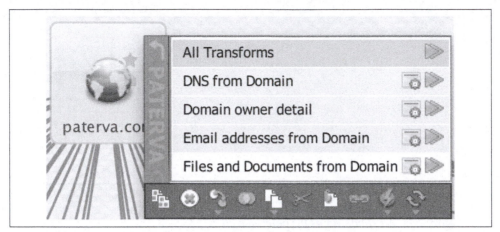

Figure 18-5. Selecting "All Transforms" can be an information overload, but it can be interesting to see the outcome

A comprehensive scan has the potential of giving too much information and being too noisy. Not only will it take a significant amount of time, but it will also fill the graph with an extreme amount of data that may not be beneficial. You can test this by running All Transforms against a domain.

recon-ng

"...is a full-featured Web Reconnaissance framework written in Python. Complete with independent modules, database interaction, built in convenience functions, interactive help, and command completion, Recon-ng provides a powerful environment in which open source web-based reconnaissance can be conducted quickly and thoroughly."[3]

Recon-ng is a tool written by Tim Tomes (@LaNMaSteR53). It is free and open source, written in the same style as the popular hacking tool Metasploit. We will set up and run a couple example exercises that will populate a database and give us the opportunity to create a report showing the findings:

---

3 *https://bitbucket.org/LaNMaSteR53/recon-ng*

1. Load recon-ng by navigating to the correct directory (on Kali it is */usr/share/ recon-ng*) and running ./recon-ng. As shown in Figure 18-6, you will add a workspace. Workspaces can be used for separate projects. In this example, we will be using the workspace for one domain.

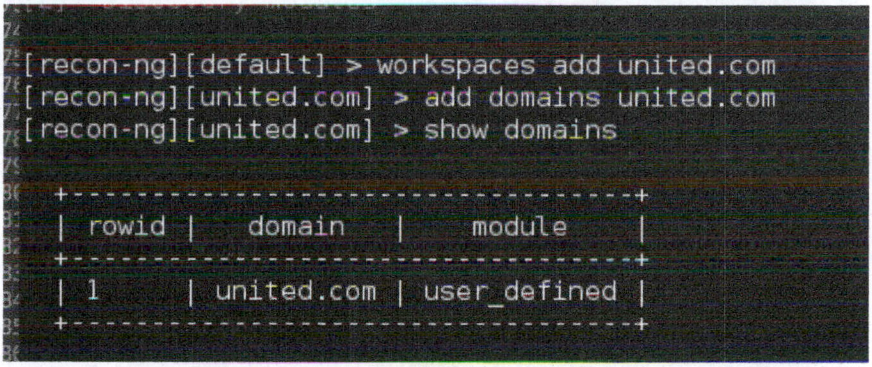

```
[recon-ng][default] > workspaces add united.com
[recon-ng][united.com] > add domains united.com
[recon-ng][united.com] > show domains


+-----------------------------------------------+
| rowid |     domain     |     module     |
+-----------------------------------------------+
| 1       | united.com | user_defined |
+-----------------------------------------------+
```

Figure 18-6. Creating a workspace

2. Use the netcraft module to search for subdomains in Figure 18-7. You can load a module by using the load or use command.

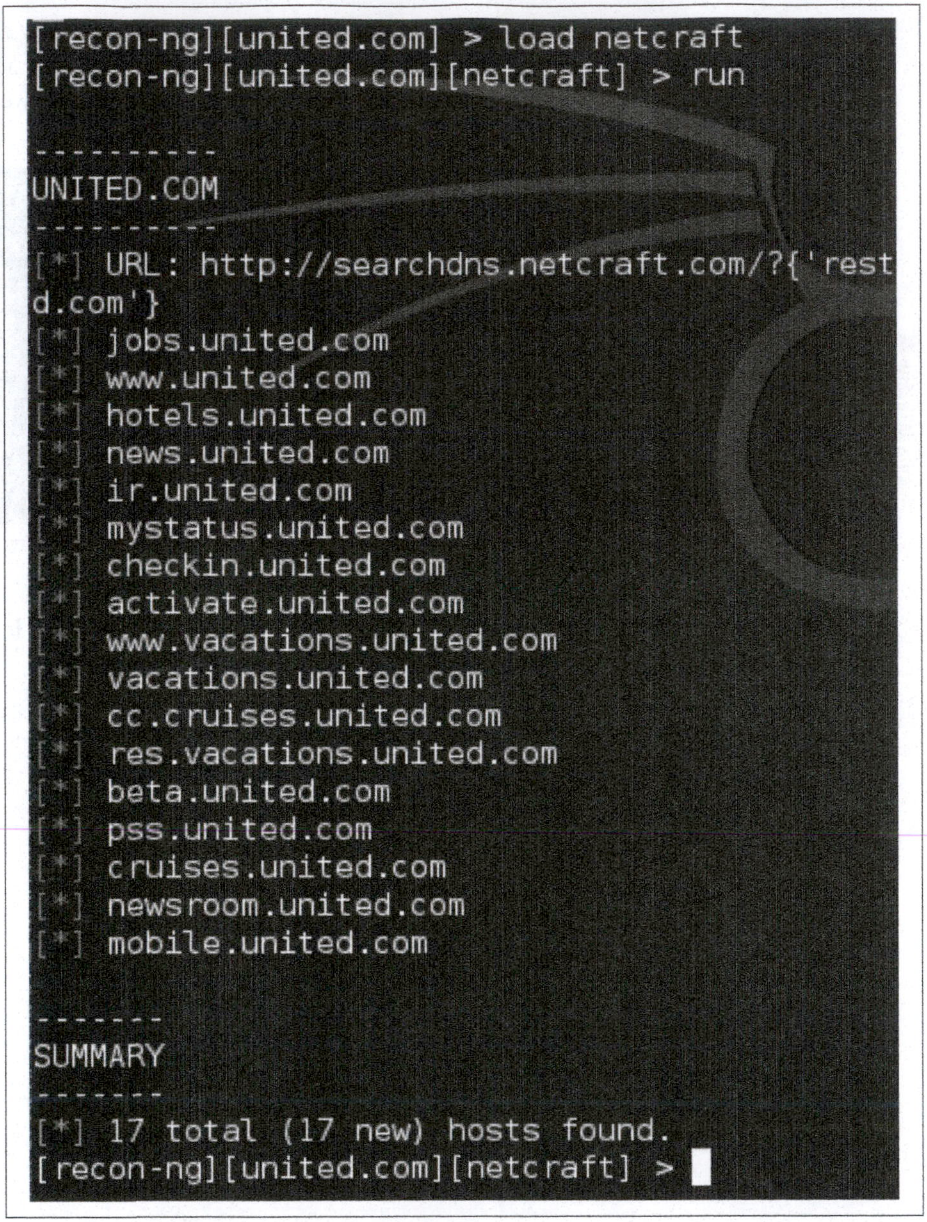

```
[recon-ng][united.com] > load netcraft
[recon-ng][united.com][netcraft] > run


---------
UNITED.COM
---------
[*] URL: http://searchdns.netcraft.com/?{'rest
d.com'}
[*] jobs.united.com
[*] www.united.com
[*] hotels.united.com
[*] news.united.com
[*] ir.united.com
[*] mystatus.united.com
[*] checkin.united.com
[*] activate.united.com
[*] www.vacations.united.com
[*] vacations.united.com
[*] cc.cruises.united.com
[*] res.vacations.united.com
[*] beta.united.com
[*] pss.united.com
[*] cruises.united.com
[*] newsroom.united.com
[*] mobile.united.com


-------
SUMMARY
-------
[*] 17 total (17 new) hosts found.
[recon-ng][united.com][netcraft] > █
```

Figure 18-7. Subdomains found by netcraft

3. Netcraft is one of many modules that can be run. Use the command show mod
ules to list everything available, as shown in Figure 18-8.

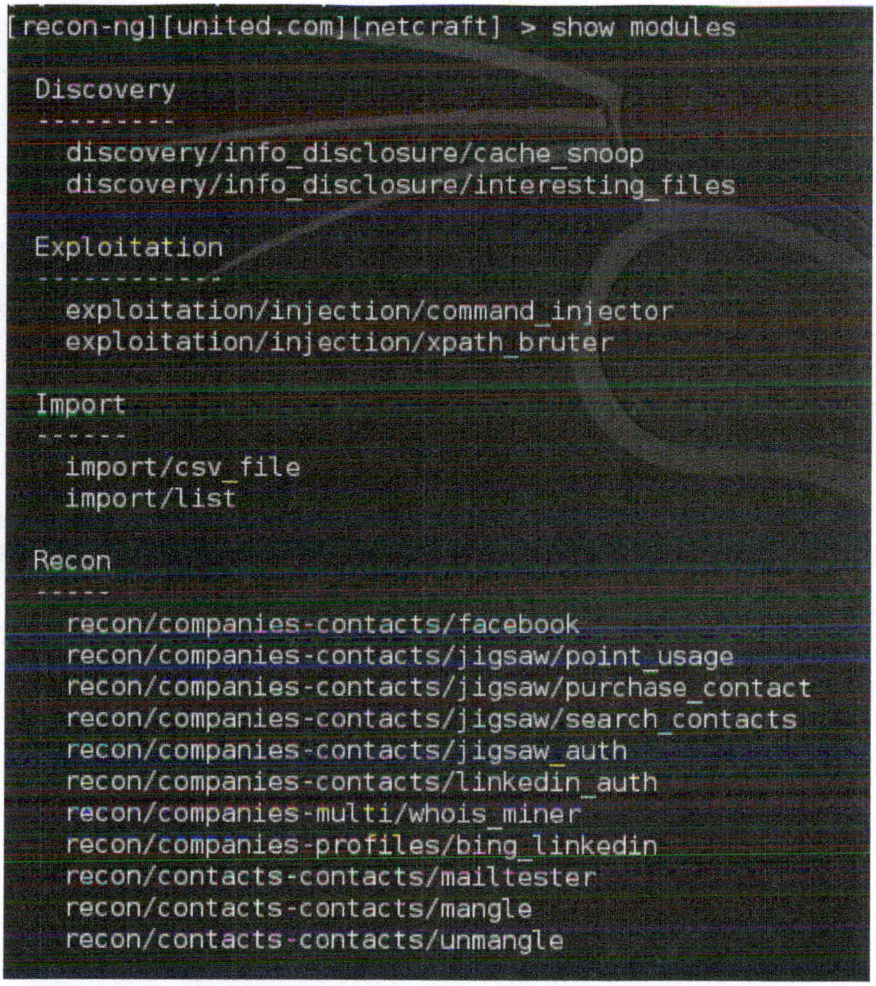

```
[recon-ng][united.com][netcraft] > show modules

Discovery
----------
   discovery/info_disclosure/cache_snoop
   discovery/info_disclosure/interesting_files

Exploitation
------------
   exploitation/injection/command_injector
   exploitation/injection/xpath_bruter

Import
------
   import/csv_file
   import/list

Recon
-----
   recon/companies-contacts/facebook
   recon/companies-contacts/jigsaw/point_usage
   recon/companies-contacts/jigsaw/purchase_contact
   recon/companies-contacts/jigsaw/search_contacts
   recon/companies-contacts/jigsaw_auth
   recon/companies-contacts/linkedin_auth
   recon/companies-multi/whois_miner
   recon/companies-profiles/bing_linkedin
   recon/contacts-contacts/mailtester
   recon/contacts-contacts/mangle
   recon/contacts-contacts/unmangle
```

Figure 18-8. Show modules

4. Many of the Recon-ng modules require you to have an API to use. To set these
   modules up to work, enter your API as shown in Figure 18-9. Many APIs are free
   for use and only require you to sign up for an account. The following example is
   shown with Builtwith (*http://www.builtwith.com*). This service will crawl a website and return all of the information it can about what technologies the site has
   been built with, as well as what type of servers and software that it runs on.

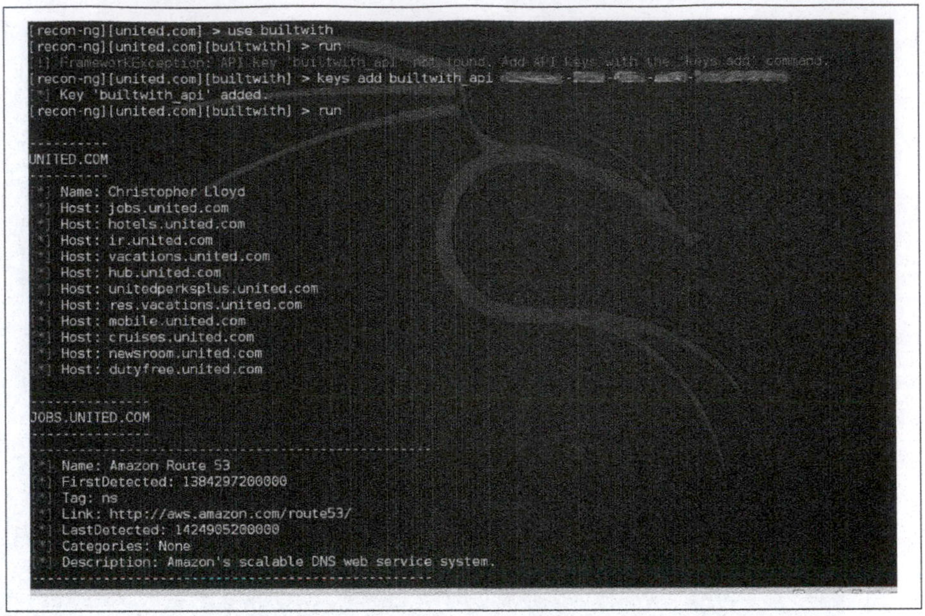

```
[recon-ng][united.com] > use builtwith
[recon-ng][united.com][builtwith] > run
[!] FrameworkException: API key 'builtwith_api' not found. Add API keys with the 'keys add' command.
[recon-ng][united.com][builtwith] > keys add builtwith_api ████████-████-████-████-████████
[*] Key 'builtwith_api' added.
[recon-ng][united.com][builtwith] > run

----------
UNITED.COM
----------

[*] Name: Christopher Lloyd
[*] Host: jobs.united.com
[*] Host: hotels.united.com
[*] Host: ir.united.com
[*] Host: vacations.united.com
[*] Host: hub.united.com
[*] Host: unitedperksplus.united.com
[*] Host: res.vacations.united.com
[*] Host: mobile.united.com
[*] Host: cruises.united.com
[*] Host: newsroom.united.com
[*] Host: dutyfree.united.com


--------------
JOBS.UNITED.COM
--------------

[*] Name: Amazon Route 53
[*] FirstDetected: 1384297200000
[*] Tag: ns
[*] Link: http://aws.amazon.com/route53/
[*] LastDetected: 1424905200000
[*] Categories: None
[*] Description: Amazon's scalable DNS web service system.
```

Figure 18-9. Adding an API key and running the builtwith module

5. It is also helpful to find the IP addresses that the domains and subdomains resolve to. You can do this by using the resolve module, as shown in Figure 18-10.

```
[recon-ng][united.com][builtwith] > load recon/hosts-hosts/resolve
[recon-ng][united.com][resolve] > run
[*] jobs.united.com => 50.19.241.165
[*] www.united.com => 23.64.113.213
[*] hotels.united.com => 216.251.126.253
[*] news.united.com => 12.130.158.199
[*] ir.united.com => 24.143.205.122
[*] ir.united.com => 24.143.205.194
[*] mystatus.united.com => 184.73.153.189
[*] mystatus.united.com => 54.225.185.153
[*] checkin.united.com => 216.136.1.157
[*] checkin.united.com => 12.169.195.157
[*] activate.united.com => 52.4.78.50
[*] activate.united.com => 54.165.93.21
[*] www.vacations.united.com => 199.66.249.105
[*] vacations.united.com => 199.66.249.104
[*] cc.cruises.united.com => 209.202.133.131
[*] res.vacations.united.com => 199.66.250.223
[*] beta.united.com => 23.64.113.213
[*] pss.united.com => 23.64.113.213
[*] cruises.united.com => 209.202.133.114
[*] newsroom.united.com => 199.230.28.57
[*] mobile.united.com => 23.64.253.86
[*] hub.united.com => 23.64.113.213
[*] unitedperksplus.united.com => 12.169.195.161
[*] unitedperksplus.united.com => 216.136.1.161
[*] dutyfree.united.com => 216.21.64.160

-------
SUMMARY
-------
[*] 5 total (5 new) hosts found.
```

Figure 18-10. Resolving hosts

6. The `interesting_files` module can be loaded (as seen in Figure 18-11) to scan potentially sensitive file locations to try and find a match. It downloads the files into a directory for later viewing. These files may give more insight into the company's server infrastructure.

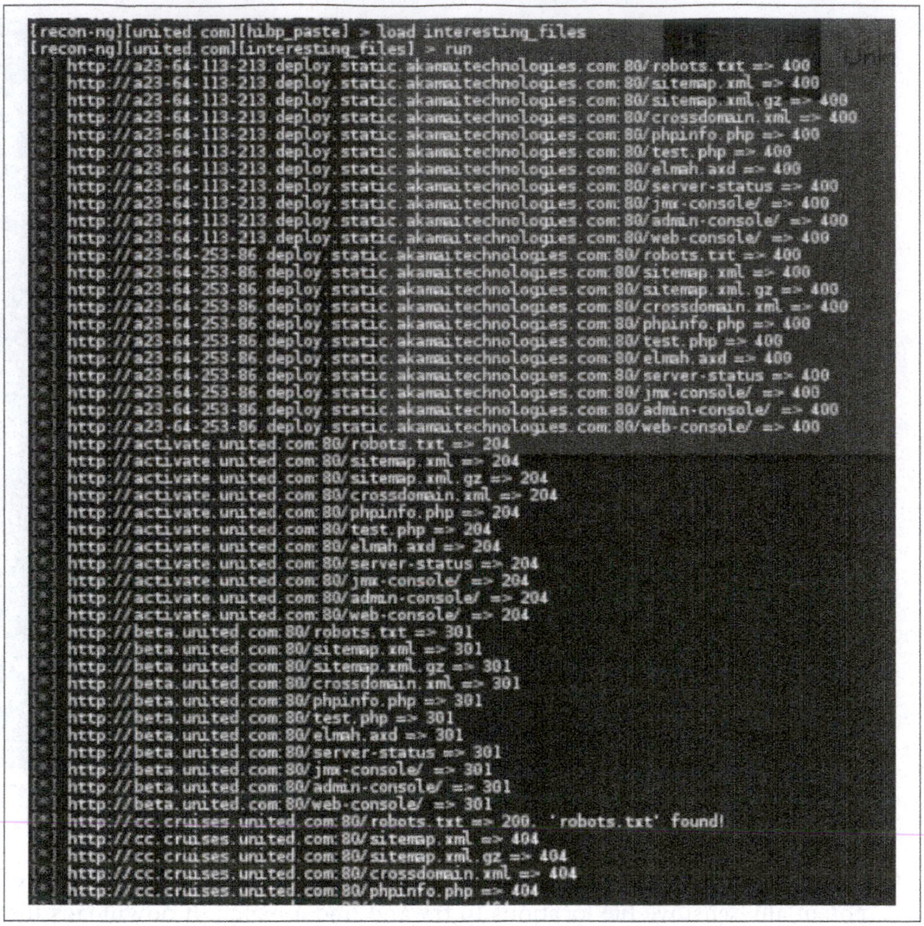

Figure 18-11. Finding potentially sensitive files

7. Now you can proceed to finding personal information, such as email addresses on individuals tied to the corporation. As shown in Figure 18-12, load the whois_poc module. This module finds the domain registrar Whois contacts and adds them to the database.

```
[recon-ng][united.com][ipinfodb] > load whois_pocs
[recon-ng][united.com][whois_pocs] > run

-----------------------
UNITED.COM
-----------------------
[*] URL: http://whois.arin.net/rest/pocs;domain=united.com
[*] URL: http://whois.arin.net/rest/poc/NAL6-ARIN
[*] Nelson Allen (nallen@westernunited.com) - Whois contact (Irvine, CA - United States)
[*] URL: http://whois.arin.net/rest/poc/BARRI31-ARIN
[*] ADAM BARRICK (adam.barrick@united.com) - Whois contact (Seatac, WA - United States)
[*] URL: http://whois.arin.net/rest/poc/CBI54-ARIN
[*] CANDICE BIGHAM (cbigham@careunited.com) - Whois contact (Laramie, WY - United States)
[*] URL: http://whois.arin.net/rest/poc/SBR228-ARIN
[*] Scott Brettin (SBRETTIN@cornerstoneunited.com) - Whois contact (Hickory, NC - United States)
[*] URL: http://whois.arin.net/rest/poc/MB136-ARIN
[*] Mark Brown (nbrown@westernunited.com) - Whois contact (Newport Beach, CA - United States)
[*] URL: http://whois.arin.net/rest/poc/CERVA3-ARIN
[*] JUAN CERVANTES (JUAN.CERVANTES@UNITED.COM) - Whois contact (San Diego, CA - United States)
[*] URL: http://whois.arin.net/rest/poc/CHIMO-ARIN
[*] HILDA CHIMON (hilda.chimon@united.com) - Whois contact (Chicago, IL - United States)
[*] URL: http://whois.arin.net/rest/poc/COWLE10-ARIN
[*] Cyndy Cowley (ccowley@cbunited.com) - Whois contact (Bellaire, TX - United States)
[*] URL: http://whois.arin.net/rest/poc/COWLE11-ARIN
[*] Cyndy Cowley (ccowley@cbunited.com) - Whois contact (Houston, TX - United States)
[*] URL: http://whois.arin.net/rest/poc/CROAS-ARIN
[*] Olga Croasdaile (olga@jrunited.com) - Whois contact (Miami, FL - United States)
[*] URL: http://whois.arin.net/rest/poc/OCR2-ARIN
[*] Olga Croasdaile (olga@jrunited.com) - Whois contact (Miami, FL - United States)
[*] URL: http://whois.arin.net/rest/poc/CUEVA1-ARIN
[*] Angie Cueva (angie.cueva@brownunited.com) - Whois contact (Duar, CA - United States)
[*] URL: http://whois.arin.net/rest/poc/CUEVA2-ARIN
[*] Angie Cueva (angie.cueva@brownunited.com) - Whois contact (Duar, CA - United States)
```

Figure 18-12. whois-pocs module

8. You can also run a search against public PGP servers, as shown in Figure 18-13, to capture names and email addresses. This search, however, will list every domain found with your domain it, and as you can see there are a few false positives.

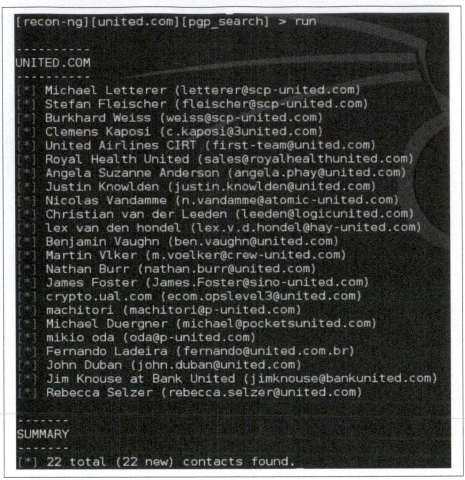

```
[recon-ng][united.com][pgp_search] > run

----------
UNITED.COM
----------
[*]  Michael Letterer (letterer@scp-united.com)
[*]  Stefan Fleischer (fleischer@scp-united.com)
[*]  Burkhard Weiss (weiss@scp-united.com)
[*]  Clemens Kaposi (c.kaposi@3united.com)
[*]  United Airlines CIRT (first-team@united.com)
[*]  Royal Health United (sales@royalhealthunited.com)
[*]  Angela Suzanne Anderson (angela.phay@united.com)
[*]  Justin Knowlden (justin.knowlden@united.com)
[*]  Nicolas Vandamme (n.vandamme@atomic-united.com)
[*]  Christian van der Leeden (leeden@logicunited.com)
[*]  lex van den hondel (lex.v.d.hondel@hay-united.com)
[*]  Benjamin Vaughn (ben.vaughn@united.com)
[*]  Martin Vlker (m.voelker@crew-united.com)
[*]  Nathan Burr (nathan.burr@united.com)
[*]  James Foster (James.Foster@sino-united.com)
[*]  crypto.ual.com (ecom.opslevel3@united.com)
[*]  machitori (machitori@p-united.com)
[*]  Michael Duergner (michael@pocketsunited.com)
[*]  mikio oda (oda@p-united.com)
[*]  Fernando Ladeira (fernando@united.com.br)
[*]  John Duban (john.duban@united.com)
[*]  Jim Knouse at Bank United (jimknouse@bankunited.com)
[*]  Rebecca Selzer (rebecca.selzer@united.com)

-------
SUMMARY
-------
[*] 22 total (22 new) contacts found.
```

Figure 18-13. PGP email address search

Other helpful commands for recon-ng are:

show info
> This command will return all information and settings on the particular module that is currently loaded.

show options
> This will show the different options that are available to set for the module that is currently loaded.

delete hosts "row id"

If there are hosts that have shown up that you don't wish to keep in any reports, they can be deleted per row, by comma delimitation, or if you have a range, a dash can be used.

Regon-ng also has several built-in reports that offer a variety of ways to display the information that has been gathered. The reports are also modules and can be *csv*, *html*, *list*, *pushpin*, and *xml* formats. Something to note is that the data from the database will need to be cleaned up if it is not required to be present in the report. Reports also have options that can be set to customize them further.

theharvester.py

"The objective of this program is to gather emails, subdomains, hosts, employee names, open ports and banners from different public sources like search engines, PGP key servers and SHODAN computer database."[4]

The Harvester (Figure 18-14) is a great simple way to scrape the internet for email addresses that match a certain domain name.

---

4 *www.edge-security.com/theharvester.php*

```
* TheHarvester Ver. 2.6
* Coded by Christian Martorella
* Edge-Security Research
* cmartorella@edge-security.com
****************************************************************

Usage: theharvester options

       -d: Domain to search or company name
       -b: data source: google, googleCSE, bing, bingapi, pgp
                        linkedin, google-profiles, people123, jigsaw,
                        twitter, googleplus, all

       -s: Start in result number X (default: 0)
       -v: Verify host name via dns resolution and search for virtual hosts
       -f: Save the results into an HTML and XML file
       -n: Perform a DNS reverse query on all ranges discovered
       -c: Perform a DNS brute force for the domain name
       -t: Perform a DNS TLD expansion discovery
       -e: Use this DNS server
       -l: Limit the number of results to work with(bing goes from 50 to 50 results,
       -h: use SHODAN database to query discovered hosts
           google 100 to 100, and pgp doesn't use this option)

Examples:
        theHarvester.py -d microsoft.com -l 500 -b google
        theHarvester.py -d microsoft.com -b pgp
        theHarvester.py -d microsoft -l 200 -b linkedin
        theHarvester.py -d apple.com -b googleCSE -l 500 -s 300
```

Figure 18-14. The Harvester command line

Here we will again be using united.com and running it against all data sources by using the command ./theHarvester.py -d united.com -l 500 -b all in Figure 18-15.

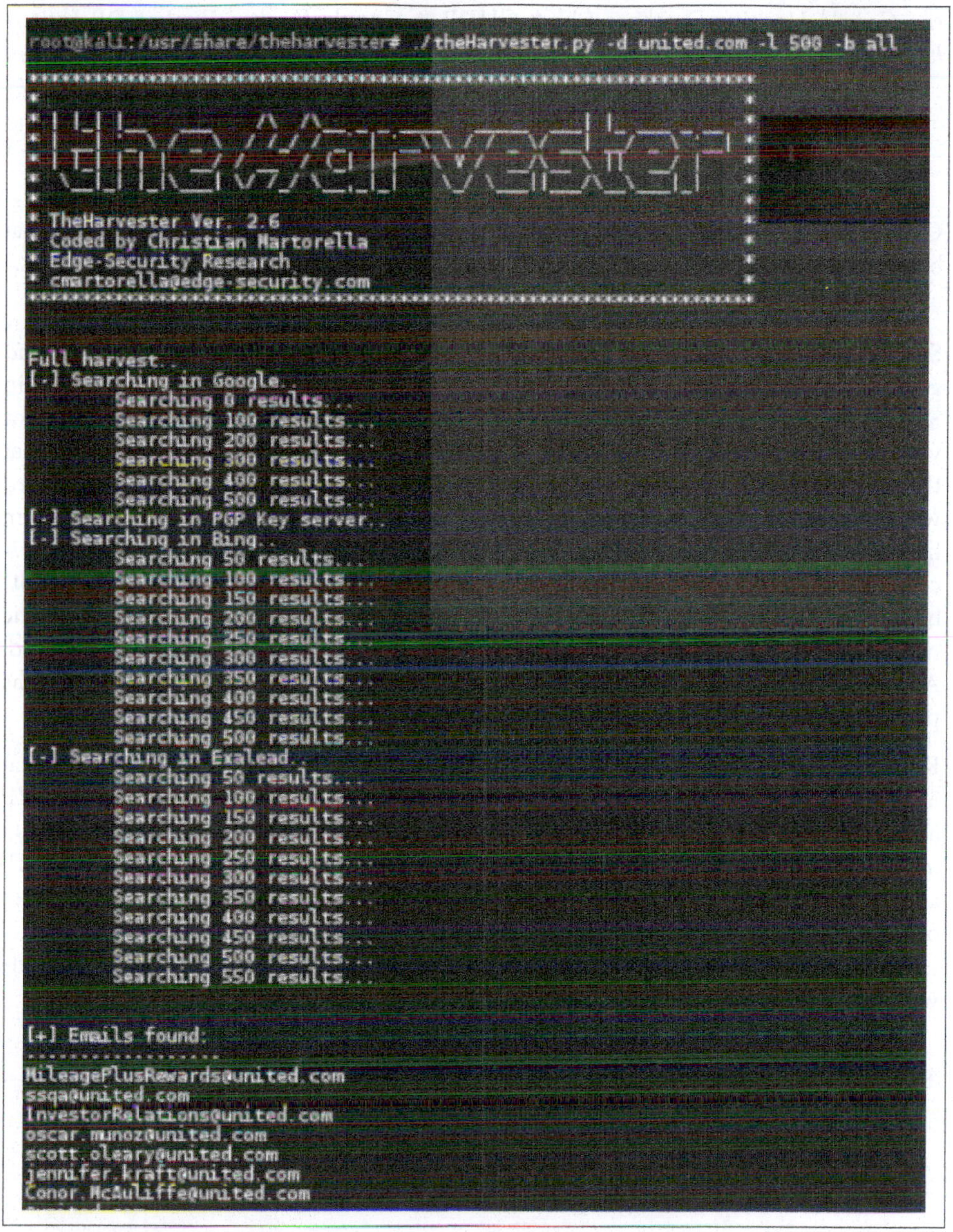

Figure 18-15. The beginning of the harvester results

Websites

There are many websites that we could list for OSINT gathering. Instead we will focus on the top two that will provide the most use in a purple team scenario. These two are the Google Hacking Database (AKA GHDB & Google Dorks—Exploit-DB (*http://bit.ly/2aNO16a*)) and Shodan.

> "Originally created by Johnny Long of Hackers for Charity, The Google Hacking Database (GHDB) is an authoritative source for querying the ever-widening reach of the Google search engine. In the GHDB, you will find search terms for files containing usernames, vulnerable servers, and even files containing passwords."[5]

GHDB is now maintained and hosted by Offensive Security, the same group that brings you Kali (a Linux hacking distro) and a range of ethical hacking certifications.

> "Shodan is the world's first search engine for Internet-connected devices."

Shodan was created by John Matherly (@achillean) in 2009 to crawl the web. The end goal for your environment should be to have the least amount of devices show up in Shodan (*http://www.shodan.io*) as humanly possible. If anything, when any amount of your IP address range is on Shodan, it should be something that you are aware that the entire internet has access to. For instance, a listing of a hardened and patched webserver, controlled mail relay, or DNS server would make perfect sense. However, having printers, database servers, out-of-date operating systems, or embedded devices directly connected to the internet is not only bad practice, but also a perfect foothold to the inside of a network. There are entire talks and research papers on the number of devices that are connected to the internet that Shodan has indexed. Accounts can be created for free and have a limited functionality option, as well as paid options that provide access to more results and reporting options.

Knowing the IP address(es) of your organization is the first step toward finding what is currently listed, but if you're not sure there are several options. You can use the IP addresses of the resolver that we utilized earlier in this chapter or you can look at *arin.net* (Figure 18-16). Using the resolver (or shodan) may return results of server IP addresses that are not owned by the company in question. They may be IP addresses of servers that are hosted somewhere like Amazon or another hosting provider. ARIN (American Registry for Internet Numbers) will display the resulting IP address network blocks that are owned by the organization.

---

5 *http://bit.ly/2lBaKZd*

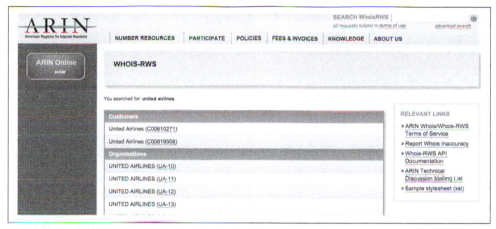

Figure 18-16. ARIN.net search for "united airlines"

Clicking one of the organizations listed (you may have to cycle through each one in a large company to see all netblocks) and then "Related Networks" presents a page that will list IP addresses associated with that specific organization. Searching for "united airlines" yields the results shown in Figure 18-17.

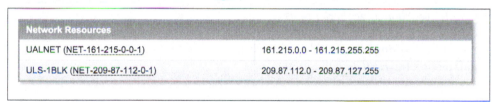

Figure 18-17. Specific network blocks

This now gives a specific list of what networks to search for on Shodan. By using the search string "net:209.87.112.0/24" we find 23 results of differing services all in the United States. Figure 18-18 shows all HTTP, HTTPS, and DNS servers located in the US. From here, Shodan will link to the website itself or show more information about what is housed on that particular IP address. While Shodan doesn't have all 65535 ports of every IP address indexed, it does have the most popular ones, and it is adding more consistently.

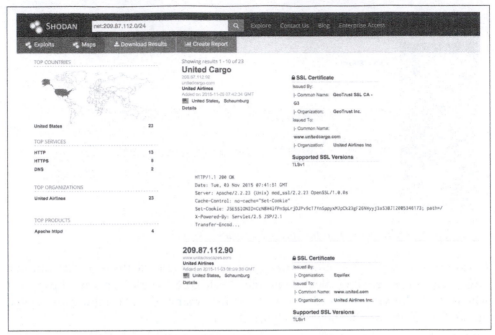

Figure 18-18. Shodan netblock results

You can find a comprehensive list of searches and guides using the API in the official Shodan book (*https://leanpub.com/shodan*).

Red Teaming

Once there is a solid security posture for your environment, it is essential that your measures and defenses are tested on a regular basis. The process of testing defensive controls by using offensive measures is commonly referred to as *red teaming* or *offensive security*. It is common practice to outsource offensive testing to penetration testers and other consultants as opposed to hiring a dedicated position, especially for small to midsize corporations. There are several offensive-based drills and skills that any blue team would be able to benefit from above and beyond OSINT gathering. Two of the more popular pentesting distros include Kali Linux and Pentoo, which come prebuilt with many of the tools that are needed to perform these tests and exploits. This section will focus on a few to get you started, as well as the concept and practice of disaster drills.

Responder

> "Responder is a multi threaded tool that answers to IPv4 LLMNR (Link-local Multicast Name Resolution) and Netbios Name Service (NBT-NS) queries."[6]

One of the first methods of attack that can be performed is using Responder by SpiderLabs. This tool allows the spoofing of LLMNR and NBT-NS responses to queries that Windows workstations broadcast by default on a network. By default, when a Windows workstation requests a name lookup, it performs the following three queries: Local Hosts File, Configured DNS Servers, and NetBIOS Broadcasts. If the first two queries return no results, the machine broadcasts an NBT-NS request, which any device on the network would be able to respond to. LLMNR queries are made after a DNS query fails to see if the device in question is on the local network. By using Responder you can answer these requests and possibly gain usernames and password hashes.

Here are some Responder command examples:

- `-I` is for the ethernet interface traffic is being redirected to
- `-w` starts the wpad proxy
- `-r` will allow the device to respond to netbios wredir queries and should be used with caution as it can cause problems if used in a production environment
- `-f` will fingerprint the host to return operating system it is running
- Just typing `./Responder.py` will display full output of available commands
- `./Responder.py -I eth0 -wrf` yields the results shown in Figure 18-19 on the test network

---

6 *http://bit.ly/2lB47pT*

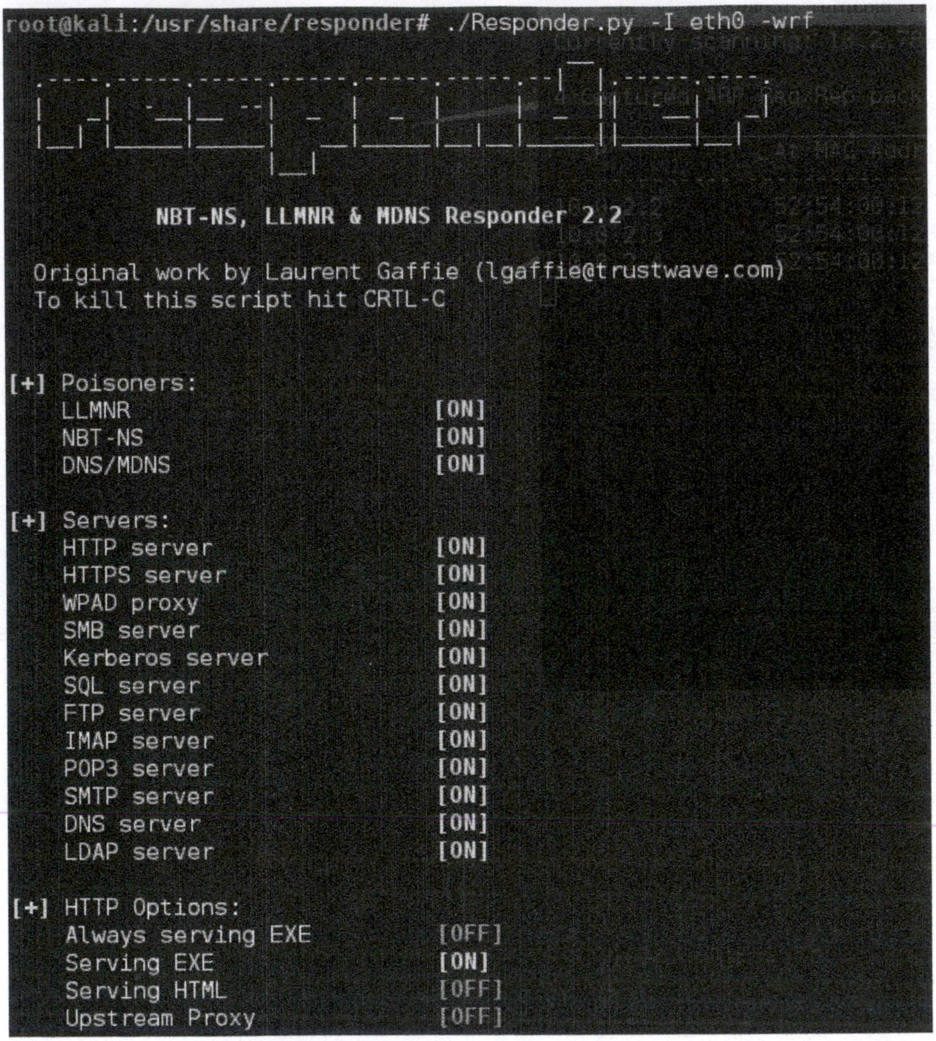

```
root@kali:/usr/share/responder# ./Responder.py -I eth0 -wrf


       ___       _        _       _     _      _
      |  _|     | |      | |     | |   | |    | |
      |  _|     | |      | |     | |   | |    | |


              NBT-NS, LLMNR & MDNS Responder 2.2

      Original work by Laurent Gaffie (lgaffie@trustwave.com)
      To kill this script hit CRTL-C


   [+] Poisoners:
       LLMNR                         [ON]
       NBT-NS                        [ON]
       DNS/MDNS                      [ON]

   [+] Servers:
       HTTP server                   [ON]
       HTTPS server                  [ON]
       WPAD proxy                    [ON]
       SMB server                    [ON]
       Kerberos server               [ON]
       SQL server                    [ON]
       FTP server                    [ON]
       IMAP server                   [ON]
       POP3 server                   [ON]
       SMTP server                   [ON]
       DNS server                    [ON]
       LDAP server                   [ON]

   [+] HTTP Options:
       Always serving EXE            [OFF]
       Serving EXE                   [ON]
       Serving HTML                  [OFF]
       Upstream Proxy                [OFF]
```

Figure 18-19. Starting up Responder

In Figure 18-20, we've successfully captured a username and password hash for a Microsoft local account. This information can be used in a Pass the Hash attack without having to crack/decrypt the password. If it is a poor password, it can be cracked giving the user's full username and password.

Figure 18-20. Successful capture of credentials using Responder

Rawr

The Rapid Assessment of Web Resources (Rawr) will allow the scanning of a network, which will report on and pull screen grabs of all listening web pages. Created by Adam Byers (@al14s), it is a useful tool to combine a quick view of pages all in one place, among a variety of other useful information.

To use Rawr, follow these steps:

1. To download Rawr, type `git pull link-to-git-repo`.

2. To install rawr with any dependencies that you may need, type `./rawr.py -install`.

3. To run with common netblocks or by following other possible inputs dictated by the documentation, type `./rawr.py 192.168.11.0/24`, as shown in Figures 18-21 and 18-22.

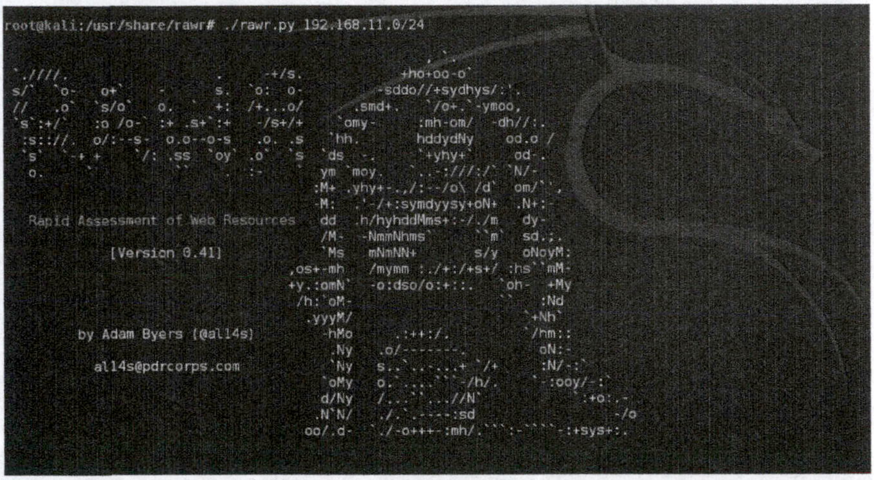

Figure 18-21. Running rawr.py

Figure 18-22. Rawr raw output

4. The end result is an *.html* report page offering up screen captures of any responding websites, a report on security headers, and much more, as shown in Figures 18-23 and 18-24.

Figure 18-23. Rawr site output

Figure 18-24. Rawr report output

Conclusion

Working in the defensive security field can be extremely difficult. While an attacker only has to get it right once to succeed, you have to get it right every time. While we'll spare you the Sun Tzu quotes that every other piece of defensive material uses, it is true that knowing how your enemy thinks will greatly benefit your overall strategy. Filling in between professional penetration testing with something other than vulnerability scans will improve the overall security of the organization every time.

CHAPTER 19

IDS and IPS

Intrusion detection systems (IDS) and intrusion prevention systems (IPS) provide insight into potential security events by observing activity on a network, as opposed to examining activity locally on a host as an antivirus would, for example.

By not relying on end devices and monitoring network traffic, you are able to remove the problem that a potentially compromised host is the one performing the checks, removing confidence in the integrity of the detection and alerting mechanisms.

The use of IDS and IPS also overcomes the issue that alerts may be something that is not deemed a security issue by endpoint security tools. For example, the use of legitimate file sharing technologies would most likely not be flagged by antivirus as unusual; however, if this was your financial database server, this sort of connection would certainly be worthy of investigation.

IDS and IPS are very similar technologies, with one key difference: an IDS will detect, log, and alert on traffic it deems worthy of attention, whereas an IPS will, in addition, attempt to block this traffic.

Types of IDS and IPS

IDS and IPS are terms that are sometimes used interchangeably. NIDS is often missed entirely and misclassified as some kind of antivirus, or grouped under the more general banner of IDS. Before we do anything else, let's define what IDS, IPS, and NIDS actually are.

Network-Based IDS

Network-based IDS systems, or NIDS, typically use a network card in promiscuous mode to sniff traffic from a network and perform analysis on that traffic to determine if it is malicious or otherwise worthy of further investigation. Typically, a NIDS will sit on a span port of a switch, sometimes referred to as a *mirror port*, which outputs duplicate traffic to that which is passing through the switch. This allows for passive interception of all traffic without having to be inline or otherwise tamper with traffic in order to make it visible. This also allows the simultaneous monitoring of multiple ports via a single port.

Alternatively, an Ethernet Tap (also called an Ethertap) can be used. An Ethertap is a device placed inline on an Ethernet cable and provides "tap" ports. The device typically has four ports, two of which are used to place the device inline on the cable that is being tapped, and two of which are used for passive tapping, one for inbound traffic and one for outbound traffic.

Typically, a NIDS will have some form of signature or fingerprint that it uses to detect potentially malicious traffic. In many cases this will not be too dissimilar to a regular expression for network traffic. The bulk of most signatures are based on the contents of the packet payload, although other parameters such as IP and TCP header information are often used as well. For example, some IDS signatures may trigger based on a known bad IP address, such as a malware command and control node appearing in network traffic.

Commercial NIDS platforms can be expensive and are often based on open source NIDS solutions with the added benefit of commercial support, hardware warranties, and service-level agreements. However, if you are working on a tight budget, the open source versions can be made to serve your needs quite nicely. The three most popular open source NIDS tools are Snort (*https://www.snort.org*), Suricata (*https://suricata-ids.org*), and Bro (*https://www.bro.org*), all of which run on standard hardware with open source operating systems such as Linux. Additionally, the Security Onion (*https://securityonion.net*) is a Linux distribution that contains all of these tools and more, in one convenient location.

Snort is probably the most widely known, most mature, and most well documented platform, and it has many signatures available for free online. However, Snort is also lacking some features of the other available options. Suricata supports Snort fingerprints and so can benefit from the wealth of data available for it, but also has better support for multithreaded operation. Multithreaded operation provides performance improvements for hardware platforms with multiple cores or processors, which in modern computing is most of them. Bro does not use a signature language; rather, it takes the approach of general network analysis with pluggable scripts. In many ways it is a more general-use network analysis tool than a strict NIDS; however, a network-based IDS is still the most popular use for Bro.

Host-Based IDS

A Host-Based IDS (HIDS) is a software-only solution that is deployed directly to the host it is monitoring. Typically, a HIDS will be deployed to many hosts rather than a few key monitoring points like a NIDS. This brings both advantages and disadvantages over NIDS. A compromised host can mask its activities from software running on that host, and so it is technically possible to blind a HIDS after compromise. However, a HIDS has an advantage over NIDS insofar as it has access to additional data, such as locally held logfiles and process information, which can be used to make determinations about activity and does not have to rely solely upon observed network traffic.

Two of the most popular open source HIDS systems are OSSEC (*https://ossec.github.io*) and Samhain (*http://www.la-samhna.de/samhain/*).

Both focus on data from local artifacts such as logfiles and file integrity monitoring, as well as various techniques for rootkit detection and other indicators of malicious activity locally. Neither attempt to monitor network traffic—that task is assumed to be handled by a NIDS or IPS.

IPS

An intrusion prevention system (IPS) typically works very much like a NIDS, except that instead of passively monitoring traffic it is itself a routing device with multiple interfaces. It is placed inline to allow the blocking of connections it deems malicious or against policy. It can be considered very much like a firewall, except that the decision to block or not is based upon matching signatures, as opposed to the IP addresses and ports commonly used by a firewall. There are some IPS solutions that are not inline and function like an IDS, except they inject reset packets into TCP streams in order to attempt to reset and close the connection. This avoids having to insert an inline device; however, it is not a hard block and can be circumvented in certain circumstances by someone who knows of this technique.

The most popular open source IPS system is probably Snort with "active response" mode enabled, which sends TCP RST packets to connections that trigger on a signature and thus attempt to cause the connection to reset and drop.

A number of commercial IPSs are also available.

Cutting Out the Noise

Running an IDS or IPS with its default configuration typically generates an excess of alerts, far more than anyone would want to manage. Unless you are already used to dealing with telemetry data with any kind of volume, it is entirely likely that you will soon suffer from alert fatigue and cease to act on, or even notice, alerts. This is far from ideal.

The essence of being able to keep the number of alerts low enough to manage is to determine your purpose in deploying an IDS or IPS to start with. Is it to catch exploits coming from the internet toward your web server, to catch members of staff using unauthorized messaging clients, or to discover malware activity? By keeping your goals in mind you can quickly make decisions about which alerts you can remove until you have a manageable set.

The source of the volume comes from two main sources: false positives, and alerts on events that naturally occur frequently. By cutting down on these two groups of alerts, you will be able to keep the number of incidents that require investigation to a minimum and make better use of the data.

What to Log

Logs and alerts with no one looking at them may as well not exist for any reason other than historic record. It is better to alert on a few key items and actually act on them, than to alert on everything and ignore most of them.

False positives can be dealt with using a few different approaches. The simplest one is to simply remove the signature in question. This brings the obvious benefit of instantly stopping all those false positives. This approach should be tempered with losing visibility of whatever the alert was meant to highlight in the first place. This may be unacceptable to you, or it could be merely collateral damage.

If your IDS/IPS permits you to create your own rules or edit existing rules, it may be possible to refine the rule to remove the false positive without stopping the original event from being missed. Of course, this is very specific to the rule in question. Prime examples of where a rule can be improved are setting a specific offset for the pattern-matching portion of the rule (see the following writing signatures example), setting specific ports or IP addresses for the signature, and adding additional "not"-type parameters to filter the false positives.

Finally, if there is ample time to write some scripts, it may be possible to filter false positive–prone alerts into a separate log, as opposed to the main log. They can then be retained for historic use and to create an aggregated and summarized daily report. This way those tasked with responding to alerts will not be swamped, but the alerts will not be completely removed. Of course we should remember that the summary report will not be real time and so there could be several hours between a signature being triggered and someone investigating it.

Frequently occurring alerts that are not false positives can also clutter up logfiles and contribute to alert fatigue. It is worth remembering that just because a signature is being correctly triggered, you do not necessarily need to know about it. For example, alerting that someone is attempting a Solaris-specific exploit against your entirely FreeBSD estate may be triggering correctly, but in reality, do you care? It's not going to do anything. Determining the answer to "do I care?" will allow you to simply trim a certain number of signatures from your configuration.

As mentioned before, if there is time to write some scripts, it may be possible to filter frequently occurring alerts into a separate log, which can be retained for historic use and be used to create an aggregated and summarized daily report. Again, those tasked with responding to alerts will not be swamped and the alerts will not be removed.

Writing Your Own Signatures

Many people opt to use the readily available repositories of signatures alone, and that is a perfectly valid strategy to use. However, the more in-depth knowledge that is gained over time about the network may lend awareness to the need of writing customized rulesets, or simply require rules that do not exist.

Let's use an example that we encountered in real life.

Upon discovering Superfish installed on devices on our network, we wanted to ensure that there were no other devices present on the network running the application. The environment included user-owned devices—not just corporate devices—so endpoint management tools did not offer adequate coverage. After taking multiple packet dumps of communication from Superfish to the internet, we noticed that although the connection was encrypted, the TLS handshake was unique to this application and remained constant. These two criteria are the hallmarks of a good signature.

Let's start with a very minimal signature.

We will use the Snort signature language in this section, as it is supported by both Snort and Suricata and is therefore the most likely format that you will encounter:

```
alert tcp any any -> any 443 (msg:"SuperFish Test Rule";
    sid:1000004; rev:1;)
```

This rule will match packets that are TCP with a destination port of 443, with any source or destination IP address. The msg parameter is what will be logged in the logfiles, the sid is the unique ID of the rule, and the rev is the revision, which is used to track changes to the rule in subsequent versions of the signature files.

The first order of business is to capture the unique portion of the data—the larger, the better—to reduce the risk of accidentally triggering on other partially matching traffic. To illustrate, when searching a dictionary for the word "thesaurus," we could find matches with the search "t", "the", or "thesaurus". However, "thesaurus" is the better search as it is less subject to finding false positive results than the other two search options. In this situation, the list of ciphersuites is the object of the search. In hex, this list is:

```
c0 14 c0 0a c0 22 c0 21 00 39 00 38 00 88 00 87 c0 0f c0 05 00 35
00 84 c0 12 c0 08 c0 1c c0 1b 00 16 00 13 c0 0d c0 03 00 0a c0 13
c0 09 c0 1f c0 1e 00 33 00 32 00 9a 00 99 00 45 00 44 c0 0e c0 04
00 2f 00 96 00 41 00 07 c0 11 c0 07 c0 0c c0 02 00 05 00 04 00 15
00 12 00 09 00 14 00 11 00 08 00 06 00 03 00 ff
```

Luckily the Snort rules format supports being able to search for both hex and ASCII in documents, and to do this we use the `content` argument. To search in hex, as opposed to ASCII, we merely wrap the hex representation in pipes. So "00" would match an ASCII 00, whereas "|00|" would match a hex 00. And so the rule becomes:

```
alert tcp any any -> any 443 (msg:"SuperFish Test Rule";
content:"|c0 14 c0 0a c0 22 c0 21 00 39 00 38 00 88 00 87 c0 0f
c0 05 00 35 00 84 c0 12 c0 08 c0 1c c0 1b 00 16 00 13 c0 0d c0
03 00 0a c0 13 c0 09 c0 1f c0 1e 00 33 00 32 00 9a 00 99 00 45
00 44 c0 0e c0 04 00 2f 00 96 00 41 00 07 c0 11 c0 07 c0 0c c0
02 00 05 00 04 00 15 00 12 00 09 00 14 00 11 00 08 00 06 00 03
00 ff|"; sid:1000004; rev:2;)
```

In many cases this could be enough. Indeed, many rules that you find online will be complete at this point. However, IDS and IPS systems can generate false positives, and being able to reduce these as much as possible will make the system more effective. Other features in the language can be leveraged to improve upon this rule. First of all, we know that the list of ciphersuites occurs at a set offset from the start of the packet, in this case 44 bytes. By specifying this we can match this data only at the specified offset and so if it coincidentally appears elsewhere in a packet, a false positive will not be created. To set the offset, we use the `offset` parameter:

```
alert tcp any any -> any 443 (msg:"SuperFish Test Rule";
content:"|c0 14 c0 0a c0 22 c0 21 00 39 00 38 00 88 00 87
c0 0f c0 05 00 35 00 84 c0 12 c0 08 c0 1c c0 1b 00 16 00
13 c0 0d c0 03 00 0a c0 13 c0 09 c0 1f c0 1e 00 33 00 32
00 9a 00 99 00 45 00 44 c0 0e c0 04 00 2f 00 96 00 41 00
07 c0 11 c0 07 c0 0c c0 02 00 05 00 04 00 15 00 12 00 09
00 14 00 11 00 08 00 06 00 03 00 ff|"; offset: 44;
sid:1000004; rev:3;)
```

Both Snort and Suricata maintain state in that they are aware of the direction that data is flowing, and so we can use the `flow` parameter to analyze only packets flowing from client to server. Finally, we can use `reference` to add a URL to be logged with further information, such as an internal wiki. We have completed our rule:

```
alert tcp any any -> any 443 (msg:"SuperFish Test Rule";
flow:to_server; reference:url,https://MyReferenceUrlGoesHere;
content:"|c0 14 c0 0a c0 22 c0 21 00 39 00 38 00 88 00 87 c0
```

```
0f c0 05 00 35 00 84 c0 12 c0 08 c0 1c c0 1b 00 16 00 13 c0
0d c0 03 00 0a c0 13 c0 09 c0 1f c0 1e 00 33 00 32 00 9a 00
99 00 45 00 44 c0 0e c0 04 00 2f 00 96 00 41 00 07 c0 11 c0
07 c0 0c c0 02 00 05 00 04 00 15 00 12 00 09 00 14 00 11 00
08 00 06 00 03 00 ff|"; offset: 44; sid:1000004; rev:4;)
```

This example is not comprehensive with regards to options within the signature language. It is worth consulting the online documentation (*http://bit.ly/2lBqWK7*) to obtain more details. The preceding process can be repeated with other options in order to create very specific rulesets for many types of traffic you may encounter on your network.

NIDS and IPS Locations

For devices that are network based, placement of the device will alter which traffic it is able to inspect and the types of attack it will block.

The typical approach to this is to place devices at key choke points in a network, typically the internet connection along with any other WAN links, such as those that may connect offices and datacenters. This way traffic that traverses those links will be analyzed and will capture the events that the majority of people are concerned about. It is worth noting that this will miss traffic that does not flow over these links. How relevant this is to you will depend on the context of your network topology and the sort of traffic that you would like to receive alerts on.

In the example shown in Figure 19-1, Tap Position 1 will capture all traffic between a corporate network and the internet, in theory capturing attacks that are incoming from the internet and unwanted connections leaving the environment. However, it will be blind to any traffic within the networks. In Tap Position 2, all traffic between the internal LAN and the internet, and the internal LAN and the DMZ will be analyzed, providing some insight to internal traffic as well as some internet traffic; but it is blind to traffic between the DMZ and the internet. Tap 3 is completely blind to traffic other than that which starts or ends on the internal LAN, but will have visibility of all internal traffic between workstations and internal servers, for example.

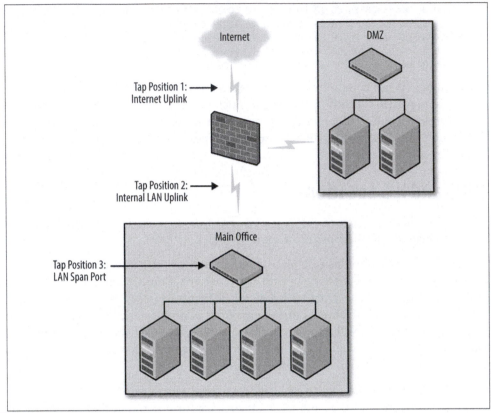

Figure 19-1. Proper IDS/IPS network positioning

Of course, which is most relevant to any environment will depend on the specific configuration, the areas considered to be most valuable, and the areas that are more likely to be attacked. In a perfect IDS/IPS world, network taps would be deployed throughout; however, in reality cost is likely to mean that a decision should be made as to which are the most useful links to monitor.

Encrypted Protocols

Network-based IDS and IPS technologies analyze data as it is transmitted across the network and do not have access to the data on either endpoint. This means that unless provided with the keying material to decrypt an encrypted session, they are effectively blinded to the payload content of encrypted communications.

Many classes of attack will be missed due to this lack of visibility. An exploit against a vulnerable script in some widely available blogging software, for example, would be missed as the exploit is hidden within an encrypted connection. The IDS and IPS are only able to detect attacks that can be found based on the unencrypted portions of the communications—for example, HeartBleed (*http://heartbleed.com*).

This vulnerability was present in the unencrypted handshake of TLS connections, not the encrypted payload. Additionally, signatures that are based on other data, such as IP addresses and port numbers, will continue to work. There are some emerging tools and techniques that can be used to lessen this effect, but they are not in as widespread use as standard IDS and IPS technologies.

FingerprinTLS (*https://squarelemon.com/tls-fingerprinting/*), for example, can be used to determine which client has initiated an encrypted connection. This can provide an additional level of understanding of encrypted traffic by offering the indicator of knowing if traffic originated from a browser, script, or penetration testing tool.

Conclusion

Both IDS and IPS solutions are a useful part of the information security arsenal. Vendor selection, device placement, and configuration are all important technology decisions, but ensuring that logs are collected and a process is in place to handle any alerts is critical. Collecting data that no one looks at achieves very little.

IDS and IPS are not a panacea. Detection is limited to traffic with a defined signature and they are blind to encrypted protocols, for the most part. They should be used as part of your larger security strategy.

CHAPTER 20

Logging and Monitoring

Most operating systems and applications produce some kind of log. Many people consider logs to be a historical record that can be used to retrospectively debug issues such as why an email wasn't delivered, why a web server isn't running, or how long a server had been complaining about a failing disk before it exploded and somebody actually looked at the logs. Logs can, however, be used much more proactively from a security perspective, and they can be used to provide not only retrospective insights, but much more proactive views into the environment.

The same can be said of other types of monitoring, too. Companies generally have a better handle on monitoring than logging. Telemetry data such as disk, memory, CPU, and network interface usage can be used for capacity planning and to provide pre-emptive information regarding potential issues. This sort of data can be used to provide additional insight into potential events that are happening within the environment.

In this chapter, you will learn what to log, where to log it, and what to do with those logs to gain the best advantage you can from the information that you already have.

What to Log

What to log can be a contentious issue. There are often perceived to be two schools of thought on this:

Everything

> This generally stems from the point of view that what is required is not known until it is needed, thus storing everything and searching and filtering later is adopted. This does indeed provide access to all the possible data that may be required, but also provides more of a challenge when it comes to storage, index-

ing, and in some cases transmitting the data. If a commercial solution is used, licensing may also depend on volume.

Only what you need

Rather unsurprisingly this is the polar opposite to everything. Technology resources are way less utilized in this scenario, but there is a risk that something will be missed. When beginning with a new system of log collection and correlation, it is best to start slowly with what is needed and then build upon it.

In reality the answer to what to log is probably driven mostly by costs. If this is the case, it is best to consume logs more aggressively from high-value systems, high-risk systems, and those facing external networks, and make savings in areas that are of lesser importance from a security perspective.

Where to Log

Operating systems tend to have some kind of log repository. On Windows this is the Event Viewer and on Unix platforms this is typically the *var/log/* directory arriving either via the filesystem directly or via *syslog*. The common feature between these methods is that the logs are stored on the host from which they originated. In the case of a compromise this leaves the logs exposed, as the evidence that you wish to examine is being protected by the very host that you can no longer trust.

The solution to this problem is to collect and aggregate logs at a central location. This provides two key benefits:

- Logs are no longer stored on the host that created them. In the event of a compromise, hardware failure, or rogue member of staff, the logs are still intact, and if properly configured, in a state whereby they cannot be tampered with.
- Aggregated logs provide better data for analysis than looking at discrete logfiles individually. But we'll come back to this.

In the past, centralized log aggregation may have simply been a Unix host with a large amount of storage running *syslogd* and collecting the logs for the environment to its own *var/log/* directory. However, now we have Security Information & Event Management (SIEM) platforms that perform this role and much more.

Security Information and Event Management

A SIEM not only collects logs, it takes those logs and other security-related documentation and correlates them for analysis. This correlation activity allows more intelligent security-related alerts, trends, and reports to be created. Correlation logic should be the backbone of every SIEM solution and is much more effective when used over a range of log sources. For example, an organization can correlate various security events like unusual port activities on routers and firewalls, suspicious DNS activity, signature matches from a web application firewall and IDS/IPS, and threats recognized from antivirus or endpoint solutions to detect a potential threat.

SIEMs can be set up in one of several different configurations; software installed on a local server, a hardware appliance, a virtual appliance, or a cloud-based service. Many times a SIEM is put in place and expected to just automatically work to detect all possible malicious activity in an enterprise. While many do come preconfigured with a certain amount of alerts, dashboards, and reports, they still need to be customized. When a SIEM is added to any environment, it must be trained on what exactly to look for. Every environment is completely unique and as such, to have a properly configured and tuned SIEM it must be tailor-fit to the environment. Additionally, not only will this be one of the most customized pieces of a security architecture, it will also require a significant amount of time. As the network changes, new software is added, new threats are realized, or new behavior is seen, the SIEM must continue to be updated and tuned.

Designing the SIEM

Before a SIEM is implemented it is best to not only have an overall knowledge of what should and should not happen on the network, but also what the major pain points of the organization are that it will attempt to address. Steps prior to implementation include:

1. Define the coverage scope. Many organizations put a SIEM in place to cover a compliance requirement. This compliance may drive which sections of the network are initially focused on. Other areas maybe be left out of the scope altogether, such as a segmented guest network.

2. Establish threat scenarios/use cases. Use cases are when risk and threat scenarios are played out step by step and tied to different levels of an overall attack. It is possible to tie these levels of attack to the Intrusion Kill Chain, as mentioned in Chapter 1. When this approach is used, individual detection and alerting configuration can be used to counteract an attack at each level of the kill chain.

3. Define the priority of threats. During design and as a possible step in the creation of an overall risk profile, different threats should be prioritized. A match on a PCI data alert won't be something to be categorized as critical if there is no PCI data present on the network. Walk through the threats that have been identified and alerts that come standard with the SIEM to prioritize what makes sense for the specific network it will be placed on.

4. Perform a proof of concept. Just because there are active rules and alerts on a SIEM doesn't necessarily mean they will capture what you think they will. These proofs of concept will not only help strengthen internal security, but it will also build the purple team skillset. If there is an alert created for detecting port scans,

don't only attempt to trigger it but also attempt to get around it triggering to assist in finding potential gaps in the alert.

Log Analysis

Once logs are stored in some sort of central repository, it is time to start performing analysis. The ideal situation is one whereby logs are monitored and analyzed in near real time and raise alerts for events, or combinations of events, that are worthy of further investigation.

Depending on the software or service that is selected, it may be difficult to jump directly to this stage. Many higher-end SIEMs come preconfigured with at least a default set of alert rules, some of which are integrated with threat intelligence feeds; other times there may be a period of running ad-hoc queries in order to see what works and what doesn't. Once the rules are tuned to an acceptable level of false positives and false negatives, they can be moved to real-time alerting.

The aim of log analysis is not to produce an exhaustive list of all events. If that were the case, people would be employed to just tail logs all day.

If too many alerts are generated they will be lost in the noise or simply ignored by analysts due to alert fatigue. Keep alerts to only those that should be acted upon, and keep the alerts useful and actionable.

Logging and Alerting Examples

Creating alerts based on logs can be a very useful way of discovering unusual activity within your environment. Of course, context is key and tailoring alerts to your specific environment will yield the best results. This section details some generic examples to illustrate the sorts of alerts that can be easily generated via log analysis.

Authentication Systems

Authentication systems are an obvious starting point for analysis as usage of user credentials is typically well understood. By analyzing the contents of authentication logs within the context of the environment, there are several tests that can yield immediate results:

Users logging into systems at unusual hours
    If users typically only connect during office hours, alerts on activity between 7pm and 7am, for example, are likely to be suitably few and suitably relevant for investigation.

Repeated login failures

Repeated login failures above a set threshold could be a sign of a brute force attack, misconfigured clients, or simply a user who cannot remember his password.

Users logging in from unusual or multiple locations

Most users have a predictable number of IP addresses that they may connect from. Most users also log in from one geographic location at a time. If a user is seen logging in from her normal office IP address, and five minutes later logging in from somewhere that is five time zones away, something might be wrong.

Insecure authentication

Certain types of authentication are inherently insecure, such as logins over HTTP or telnet that are transmitted in cleartext over the network. Alerting on cleartext authentication can assist in removing it completely from your environment.

Default accounts

As mentioned in previous chapters, default accounts should be only used when necessary, as they are considered shared accounts. Alerting on the use of these accounts when not approved can point to activity of an unknown origin.

Domain admin group changes

Changes to the domain admin group in AD should be a rare occasion. While a malicious addition is normally well into the later stages of an attack, it is still vital information to alert on.

Application Logs

Most server applications generate logs of one type or another. This includes services such as email servers, web servers, and other (probably) internet-facing services. These logs can provide useful insight into adversaries performing attacks against these hosts or performing reconnaissance. For example:

- Too many 4XX responses from a web server can indicate failed attempts at exploitation. 4XX codes are failed responses such as "not found," "access denied," and as such are a common byproduct of people attempting, and failing, to call vulnerable scripts. Searching for a high frequency of 4XX errors may indicate an attack or scan in progress.
- Too many hits on one specific URL on a web server could indicate that something is being brute forced or enumerated. Of course, repeated calls to the same URL could be normal depending on the website setup, and so applying the context of the environment is required in order to determine if this is applicable.
- Connects and disconnects with no transaction on multiple types of servers can be an indication that someone is probing the network. This can be caused by simple

port scanning, scraping protocol banners, probing TLS stacks, and other types of reconnaissance.

- New services, processes, and ports should not be an unplanned configuration change, especially on servers. Identifying a baseline per host as well as unwanted or unapproved services, processes, and ports can be useful for detecting malicious program installations or activity.

Proxy and Firewall Logs

Firewalls, proxies, and other systems that provide per-connection logging can be very useful indeed, particularly in discovering unexpected outbound traffic and other anomalies that could indicate a threat from an insider or an intrusion that is already in progress:

- Outbound connections to unexpected services can be an indicator of data exfiltration, lateral movement, or a member of staff who hasn't read the acceptable use guide properly. Again, context is necessary, but connections to cloud-based file storage, instant messaging platforms, email services, and other systems can often be identified by hostnames and IP addresses. If these connections are not expected, they are probably worthy of further investigation.
- Matching IP addresses or hostnames on blacklists is a little contentious, because blacklists are generally not complete, or up-to-date. However, seeing connections to know command and control (C&C) infrastructure is used as the server side of malware and ransomware. There are publicly available lists for known C&C servers that can be used for blocking at the firewall for both egress and ingress as well as SIEM alerting.
- Connections of unexpected length or bandwidth can be an indicator that something unusual is happening. For example, running an sshd on port 443 can fool many proxies and firewalls; however, an average HTTPS session does not last for six hours, and even a site that is left open for long periods typically uses multiple smaller connections. The ssh connection to a nonstandard port would quite possibly appear to be long in duration, and low bandwidth.

Log Aggregation

Log aggregation is useful for purposes other than centralized management of logs. Logs that span multiple hosts, even if only one type of log, provide a much richer context from which it is possible to derive security events.

If, for example, an analyst reviews the failed logins for a single host in isolation and sees a single failed login for a user, it will most likely not raise any alarms. This can easily be written off as a mistyped password or a user accidentally connecting to the wrong host. Consider, however, if this query were run against the authentication logs for an entire server estate and it is then observed that the same single user made a single failed login to each of 350 hosts in 2 minutes. Given this broader context it becomes apparent that this is not merely a typo, but part of something that should be investigated. There are similar examples that can be drawn for almost every log type.

Use Case Analysis

With multiple log types across the entire enterprise collected into a single repository, new areas for analysis become possible. Use cases, otherwise known as threat models, should be built around the major risks previously identified using this analysis. Some of the more common areas to focus on are access control, perimeter defenses, intrusion detection, malware, application defenses, and resource integrity. Creating and tuning use cases will never be a finished project because the threat landscape is ever changing. There are always new threats to model, and new indicators to monitor for. For example:

Brute-force attack

It is incredibly trivial to install and run password brute-forcing and cracking software. Correlating logs for detection of this requires both success and failure audits to be captured. As users may legitimately enter wrong passwords, it is important to test both methods to see the difference of the logging.

Data exfiltration

Data exfiltration by an inside threat can be one of the more difficult and highly advanced attacks to detect. Start by logging which resource is being accessed by whom and when, identifying critical resources and users, develop a baseline to identify threshold limits, and monitor user activity during and after business hours. It is next to impossible to alert on all data exfiltration; the key is identifying what constitutes the highest risk. More than likely the recipe to Coca-Cola isn't sitting in a text file on a shared drive.

Impossible or unlikely user movements

These can be detected. For example, if the log repository contains logs from proximity card readers for doors or elevators, this can be correlated against authentication data to highlight users who have logged in remotely, within a short period of time of having swiped a card within a physical office location.

Ransomware

Ransomware is not only one of the more common struggles in enterprises today, but is extremely fast moving, making worthwhile detection that much more difficult. Advanced file auditing is a necessary component if the behavior of ransomware is to be detected. Figure 20-1 shows an example of a spike of file audit activity before a ransomware attack and during the encryption of files.

217 events at 3:06 PM Thursday, January 16, 2014

2:00 PM   3:00 PM

Figure 20-1. Spike in advanced file audits could point to a possible ransomware infection (Source (http://bit.ly/2m1SKDG))

Conclusion

Logs can be one of the most powerful detection tools in an environment. However, as powerful as they can be, they also can take a substantial amount of time and capital to make significant use of. With a solid, steady design planned around relevant risks, log correlation and a SIEM can greatly decrease the time it takes to detect and mitigate security issues in an environment.

CHAPTER 21

The Extra Mile

Congratulations! You've made it to the last chapter! Here's a cookie:

```
document.cookie = "username=LastChapter; expires=OnReceipt 12:00:00 UTC";
```

After reading this book, you should be ready to provide the sound building blocks of an information security program. You should also be fully equipped to handle the common insecure practices that we've seen in so many environments. But the learning doesn't stop here! Here in the extra mile we'll give you some additional tidbits of information and some great resources for you to go check out that will make your defenses that much stronger.

Email Servers

Running and installing an email server is a large time and technology commitment. Modern spam filters block 99.99% of email, while more than 80% of daily email traffic is junk mail. Bulk spam and phishing issues will be concerns, as well as other commonly misconfigured server settings.

Many email servers currently on the internet are misconfigured, which contributes in part to the amount of spam being sent. These configurations not only contribute to spam, but they may delay or prevent the organization's mail from being delivered. Certain configurations will land the IP or domain of the mail server on a blacklist, which organizations can subscribe to for enhancing filtering efforts. There are some common configuration checks should be performed on mail servers being hosted in your environment. MXToolbox (*http://www.mxtoolbox.com*) provides a large list of different tests that can be performed to test these configurations.

There are several configurations that should be made to a mail server on the internet:

Open mail relay

Having a mail server set up as an open relay allows anyone who can access it on port 25 to send mail through it as anyone she wants. Mail servers should be configured to only relay messages for the domains that they are associated with.

Server hello

A mail server hello (aka HELO/EHLO) is the command an SMTP server sends to identify itself during a message exchange. While having an incorrect hello does not impact the server's ability to send or receive mail, it should identify the sending server in such a way that it can be used to identify servers with problems, such as leaking spam or incorrectly formatted emails. An example of a correct mail server hello is `HELO mx.batsareawesome.com`, while other settings such as localhost or 74.122.238.160 (the public mail server IP address) are against the RFC and best practice.

Mail reverse DNS

Another property that spam filtering uses is looking at reverse DNS (rDNS) or PTR (pointer) records on an IP address attempting to deliver mail. A generic reverse DNS record is common when the device sending mail has no control over changing it to a correct setting. For example, a residential IP address through a local DSL provider will have a record of something like "dsl-nor-65-88-244-120.ambtel.net" for the IP address 65.88.244.120. This is a generic rDNS that is autogenerated for the majority of public IP addresses dynamically given from internet service providers (ISPs). When operating a mail server, more than likely the IP address will be a static address that will need to be configured to have an rDNS record to match that of the server. Unless your organization owns and controls its own public IP addressing space, the ISP or other upstream provider will need to be contacted to make the change on their nameserver to match the hostname and corresponding A record of the sending server (instead of using an individual's account, an alias of mail.batsareawesome.com).

Email aliases and group nesting

While not necessarily a direct security issue, making use of email aliases and group nesting (groups within groups) is a good habit to get into. For example: Aaron is the lead security engineer. He has all licensing information and alerting sent to his mailbox and uses rules to disperse them throughout the different teams. When Aaron leaves, his account becomes corrupted somehow, or something else happens to it, and it becomes a large task to reset everything to go to a new person. Instead, an alias of *high-ids-alerts@lintile.com* could contain both the SOC group and SecEngineer group, which would automatically disperse the alerts to where they need to go regardless of whether Aaron stays with the company. Another example would be for licensing information. Many times management and engineers need to have working knowledge of license expiration and renewals. For example, the BHAFSEC company could use a specific alias account such as *licensing@bhafsec.com*. This could be used for SSL and software licensing, and contain the Exec and SecEngineer groups. These examples greatly reduce the amount of possible miscommunication.

Outsourcing your email server is not a crime

> Given all the effort involved to keep an email server running, filtering spam, not acting as an open relay, and any number of other issues, it may well suit your organization to simply outsource the day-to-day management of your email. Google Apps and Office 365, for example, both offer managed services whereby user administration is the only task left. Both organizations have large, capable security teams, which could free you up to pursue other more important tasks.

DNS Servers

Domain Name Servers/Service (DNS) is a main building block of the internet and technology in general. There are several main attacks (*http://bit.ly/2m1Jvn6*) to design a DNS infrastructure around preventing DNS spoofing, DNS ID hacking, and DNS cache poisoning. DNS spoofing is a term referring to the action of a malicious server answering a DNS request that was intended for another server. Spoofing can only be completed with the addition of ID hacking. DNS queries contain a specific ID that the attacker must have to successfully spoof the server. DNS cache poisoning is an attack consisting of making a DNS server cache false information. Usually this consists of a wrong record that will map a domain name to a "wrong" IP address. All of these are in an attempt to force connections to a malicious service or server.

Steps can be taken to prevent and safeguard against attacks on DNS servers and infrastructures:

Restrict recursive queries

> Recursion is the process a DNS server uses to resolve names for which it is not authoritative. If the DNS server doesn't contain a zone file that is authoritative for the domain in the query, the DNS server will forward the connection to other DNS servers using the process of recursion. The problem is that DNS servers that perform recursion are more vulnerable to denial of service (DoS) attacks. Because of this, you should disable recursion on the DNS servers in your organization that will only answer queries for which they are authoritative—typically, this means queries for your internal resources.

Segregate internal and external DNS servers

> Restrict the possible queries and the possible hosts who are allowed to query to the minimum. Not every network device needs to be able to resolve addresses on the internet. In most cases, the only machines that need to be able to resolve external addresses are gateway devices, such as a web proxy server. The majority

of devices will be configured to use internal DNS servers that do not perform recursion for public names.

Restrict DNS zone transfers to only trusted name servers

By issuing a specific request (AXFR), the entirety of the DNS server database can be obtained. While this isn't a significant security threat, it does give an attacker an upper hand by having internal information and a list of subdomains and settings.

Implement passive DNS

A passive DNS server (shown in Figure 21-1) will cache DNS information, queries, and errors from the server-to-server communication between your main DNS server and other DNS servers on the internet. The passive DNS server can take this information, and compress it into a centralized database for analysis. This database can be used for security measures such as new domain alerting. A good percentage of brand new domains are spun up solely for the purpose of distributing malware.

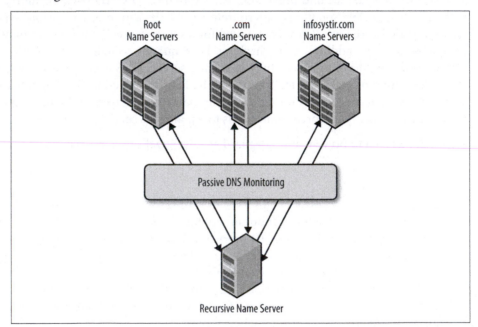

Figure 21-1. Passive DNS

Implement a DNS sinkhole or BlackholeDNS (http://bit.ly/2m2hiwb)

A DNS sinkhole server works by spoofing the authoritative DNS server for known bad domains to combat malware and viruses, as shown in Figure 21-2. It then returns a false address that is nonroutable, ensuring the client is not able to connect to the malicious site. Malicious domains can be gathered from already known C&C servers through the malware analysis process, open source sites that are providing malicious IP details, and phishing emails. They make use of Response Policy Zone (RPZ) DNS records.

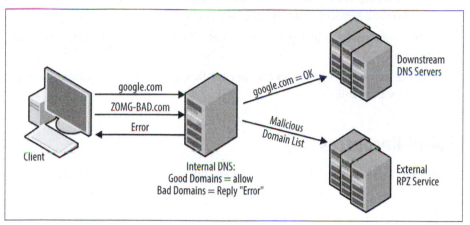

Figure 21-2. Sinkhole DNS

DNSSEC

DNS Security Extensions is a set of extensions to DNS that provide the resolvers origin authentication of DNS data. We recommend that you do not implement this. It has extremely high risks for the small amount that may be gained. Not only is there risk of taking down all of the DNS infrastructure, but it can provide attackers with a reliable source of dDoS amplification using the large secure DNS packets.

Security through Obscurity

Security through obscurity is the term used for "hiding" assets, services, or procedures in nonstandard ways. When used as the basis of a security program it is useless, but there are some methods than can be used just as an added measure.

Do:

- Set up services on nonstandard ports. Instead of a web administrative logon listening on port 443, change it to 4043 or set the ftp server to listen on port 2222.
- Rename the local Administrator account to something else that makes sense for your organization.
- Reconfigure service banners not to report the server OS type and version.

Don't:

- Block Shodan's scanners/crawlers or other internet scanners from accessing public IP addresses. Just because a single service won't be indexing the data doesn't mean malicious people aren't going to find it. As we've demonstrated, you can use Shodan's services to assist in finding security gaps.

- Label datacenters and equipment closets "Network Data Center" or something super obvious.

- Put any device or service on an internet-facing connection without having it tested for vulnerabilities.

Useful Resources

Finally, we finish with a list of books, blogs, podcasts, and websites that we find useful.

Books

- *Blueteam Handbook: Incident Response Edition* (*http://www.blueteamhandbook.com*) by Don Murdoch
- *Building an Information Security Awareness Program: Defending Against Social Engineering and Technical Threats* by Bill Gardner and Valerie Thomas
- *Complete Guide to Shodan* (*https://leanpub.com/shodan*) by John Matherly
- *Designing and Building Security Operations Center* by David Nathans
- *Hacking Exposed Industrial Control Systems: ICS and SCADA Security Secrets & Solutions* by Clint Bodungen, Bryan Singer, Aaron Shbeeb, Kyle Wilhoit, and Stephen Hilt
- *How to Develop and Implement a Security Master Plan* by Timothy Giles

Blogs

- Hurricane Labs (*https://hurricanelabs.com/blog*)
- Internet Storm Center (*https://isc.sans.edu*)
- Milton Security (*https://www.miltonsecurity.com/company/blog*)
- Room362 (*https://room362.com*)
- Schneier on Security (*https://www.schneier.com*)
- SpiderLabs Blog (*https://www.trustwave.com/Resources/SpiderLabs-Blog/*)

Podcasts

- Brakeing Down Security (*http://www.brakeingsecurity.com*)
- Down the Security Rabbit Hole (*http://podcast.wh1t3rabbit.net*)
- Defensive sec (*http://www.defensivesecurity.org*)
- PVC sec (*http://www.pvcsec.com*)
- Risky Business (*http://risky.biz*)
- Southern Fried Security (*http://www.southernfriedsecurity.com*)
- TrustedSec, LLC podcast (*https://www.trustedsec.com/podcast/*)

Tools

- Lynis (*https://cisofy.com/documentation/lynis/*): Linux/Unix/MacOS security auditing tool
- Microsoft Sysinternals: Suite of helpful Microsoft troubleshooting tools
- Netdisco: Network mapping tool

Websites

- Motherload security link dump (*http://bit.ly/2m237HC*)
- A list of upcoming CTFs (*http://ctftime.org*)
- Overall Information Security (*http://www.darkreading.com*)
- Multi-Blacklist Mail Server check (*http://multirbl.valli.org*)
- The National Vulnerability Database from NIST (*https://nvd.nist.gov*)
- List of OSINT tools & sites (*http://osintframework.com*)
- Helps learn/validate Regular Expressions (*http://www.regexr.com*)
- Non-flash, Non-Java, Internet Speed Test (*http://speedof.me*)
- Reverse Image Search (*http://www.tineye.com*)
- US government Configuration Baseline (*https://usgcb.nist.gov*)
- Windows Security (*https://www.ultimatewindowssecurity.com*)
- Analyze suspicious files/URLs (*https://www.virustotal.com*)

User Education Templates

Live Phishing Education Slides

This template (or one like it created by you and your team!) can be used when auto-directing users after a live phishing campaign, as well as for normal instruction.

You've Been Hacked!

But it's OK...and it was only a quiz (the real test is from an attacker). (Click the arrows for more info!)

What Just Happened, and Why?

- Did you know: real attackers are making these same attempts all the time against our network?

- We'd rather help ourselves become stronger before the attackers can help themselves to our patients' data.

- No matter how many advanced technical hurdles internet security puts in place, the best defense is always an alert member of the team (you!).

- Classroom is theory—treating that first patient wasn't. It's better to practice when it's safe.

Social Engineering 101(0101)

Computers are black and white, on or off; humans aren't, so unfortunately we present a better target to attackers:

- RSA (security company) hacked in 2011 via email (*http://bit.ly/2lEpV4b*)

- HBGary (security company) hacked 2011 via reused passwords, email (*http://bit.ly/2lEj7Dn*)
- Google/Adobe—hacked, operation Aurora 2010 (*http://bit.ly/2lEkFxa*)

So It's OK That You Were Exploited (This Time)

- If people who work for computer technology companies—some of which specialize in security—fall for attacks, it's to be expected that you would fall for similar attacks as well.
- We get better with practice; this is an opportunity for that practice.

No Blame, No Shames, Just...

- You work for a healthcare organization where listening and trusting people is a priority! That's good!
- ...but social engineering plays on your good nature and trust by building rapport ("I love our patients, too!"), making a request ("Password, please!"), and often faking urgency ("The CEO/CIO/CNO all want this done now!").

A Few Strategies for Next Time

- If you aren't expecting an email from someone (even if you know them), don't click the links or open the attachment.
- If you think it might be work-related, reply to the person and ask for more specifics.
- If a website is asking for personal information (like your password), and you don't recognize the site, call the IT helpdesk.

Because There Will Be a Next Time

- If the site looks correct, make sure that it is a secure site (*https://* in the URL bar, look for the lock).

If Something Feels Funny

- You just logged in, and you went immediately back to the login page.
- The site doesn't use HTTPS but requests a password.

- You received an email from someone you don't know or about a package you didn't send.
- A document that claims to have payroll information in it.
- A greeting card as an attachment.

If Something Looks Funny

- You open an attachment and you get a weird error, or the document doesn't contain what it said it would.
- You are prompted to turn on macros or install a driver update, or a new version of Flash player.
- The website looks like ours, but the website address (URL) in the address bar looks different.
- You find a USB thumb drive or a CD/DVD lying around.

If Something Sounds Funny

- You get a call from "IT" and they ask for your username and password, or say they are working on a problem you have *not* reported.
- A call from a new vendor who wants to know who our current vendor for *xyz* is (so they can call back and pose as being from that company).
- A request from the "fire marshal" to look at the extension cords under your computer desk (should be with facilities).
- You find a USB thumb drive or a CD/DVD lying around.

Feels, Looks, or Sounds Funny—Call the IS Helpdesk

- If it is something normal, they can help you.
- If it is not, they'll escalate the issue so we can take swift, appropriate action and warn other users.

What If I Already Clicked the Link, or Opened the Attachment?

- No blame, no shame, but please—CALL NOW!

- The sooner your IT team knows, the sooner they can help you and prevent the issue from going farther.

What If I Didn't Click the Link or Attachment?

- If you think it looks suspicious, better safe than sorry.
- Your IT team still needs to know about the possible threat to our patients' protected health information (PHI).
- Other users might not be as discerning.
- The attacker might come back with something better next time.

Your IT Team Is Here for You!

- Would you like a one-on-one session to talk about any of this information?
- Do you lead a team who could benefit from this material?
- If so, please contact the helpdesk at x1111 and let us know!

Phishing Program Rules

Some explanation and rules of the phishing program will help your users get excited and involved in the rewards program.

Phishing is the act of attempting to acquire information such as usernames, passwords, and credit card details (and sometimes, indirectly, money) by masquerading as a trustworthy entity in an electronic communication.

The IT team would like to present a new contest called "Something Smells Phishy!"

We'll be putting on our hacker hats and trying to get you to fall for our security tests. While we won't be trying to gather your credit card details, there are currently real hackers out in the world trying to get every bit of information they can.

They are the real bad guys and the whole point behind this campaign. Expect to see more training and key points to remember:

1. Don't click links in emails.
2. Don't open attachments that you aren't expecting.
3. Never give your username/password to anyone.
4. If it smells phishy REPORT IT!

All of this is a training exercise and the more you learn, the safer we all are and the more chances you have to win some awesome prizes! Each time you report a legitimate phishing attempt (either from us or a real attacker) your name gets entered into the phish bowl for the following prizes!

Things that should be reported:

1. Suspicious emails trying to get your information (usernames, passwords, what software we use, banking info, etc).
2. Suspicious emails with attachments that you didn't expect.
3. People attempting to access your computer that you haven't authorized.

Index

V

W

setting proper authentication settings in Group Policy, 131

Windows Server 2008 Native Mode, 133

Windows Server Update Services (WSUS), 82

Windows systems
    built-in firewall, 119
    disabling services, 117
    Event Viewer, 226
    full-drive encryption, using BitLocker, 120
    keeping endpoints up to date, 114
    PowerShell, 17
    security vulnerability, mapping anonymous session to hidden share IPC$, 132
    Windows Management Interface (WMI), 17

Windows Update for Business, 114

Windows Update service, 114

wiping data from drives, 15

wireless protocols, transmission of PCI DSS data over, 62

Wireshark
    PCAP analysis with, 51
    user permissions for Windows infrastructure, 87

WMI (Windows Management Interface), 17

workspaces (recon-ng), 195

X

xinetd utility (Unix), 106, 118

Y

yubikeys, 140

Z

zone transfers (DNS), restricting, 236

About the Authors

Lee Brotherston is a senior security advisor, providing information security consulting services to a range of clients. Having spent nearly two decades in information security, Lee has worked as an internal security resource across many verticals, including finance, telecommunications, hospitality, entertainment, and government, in roles ranging from engineer to IT security manager.

Amanda Berlin is an Information Security Architect, co-hosts the "Brakeing Down Security" podcast, and writes for several blogs.

Colophon

The animal on the cover of *Defensive Security Handbook* is a Malayan porcupine (*Hystrix brachyura*), which is a species of rodent native to South and Southeast Asia. This porcupine can be found from Nepal through northeast India, central and southern China, Myanmar, Thailand, Vietnam, peninsular Malaysia and throughout Borneo. It's also found on the island of Penang, Malaysia.

The Malayan porcupine's body is large, stout, and covered with sharp, rigid quills, which are modified hair. Quills on the upper body are rough and black with white or yellow stripes. Their short, stocky legs are covered in brown hairs; they have four claws on the front legs and five on the hind legs. Young porcupines have soft quills that become hard as they enter adulthood.

This porcupine often lives in forest habitats or open areas near forests. It inhabits dens near rocky areas by digging into the ground where it lives in small groups. They can also live in burrows connected by a network of trails or in a hole in tree bark or roots. The Malayan porcupine can give birth to two litters of two to three young annually; its gestation period is 110 days. They forage at night and typically feed on roots, tubers, bark, and fallen fruit, and sometimes on carrior and insects. During the day, they rest singly or in pairs. They can live up to 27 years.

Many of the animals on O'Reilly covers are endangered; all of them are important to the world. To learn more about how you can help, go to *animals.oreilly.com*.

The cover image is from *Beeton's Dictionary*. The cover fonts are URW Typewriter and Guardian Sans. The text font is Adobe Minion Pro; the heading font is Adobe Myriad Condensed; and the code font is Dalton Maag's Ubuntu Mono.

Learn from experts.
Find the answers you need.

Sign up for a **10-day free trial** to get **unlimited access** to all of the content on Safari, including Learning Paths, interactive tutorials, and curated playlists that draw from thousands of ebooks and training videos on a wide range of topics, including data, design, DevOps, management, business—and much more.

Start your free trial at:
oreilly.com/safari

(No credit card required.)

CPSIA information can be obtained
at www.ICGtesting.com
Printed in the USA
LVOW05s2152230517
535558LV00020BA/308/P